American Idle

Inequality at Work: Perspectives on Race,
Gender, Class, and Labor

*Series Editors: Enobong Hannah Branch
and Adia Harvey Wingfield*

Inequality at Work: Perspectives on Race, Gender, Class, and Labor provides a platform for cultivating and disseminating scholarship that deepens our knowledge of the social understandings and implications of work, particularly scholarship that joins empirical investigations with social analysis, cultural critique, and historical perspectives. We are especially interested in books that center on the experiences of marginalized workers; that explore the mechanisms (e.g., state or organizational policy) that cause occupational inequality to grow and become entrenched over time; that show us how workers make sense of and articulate their constraints as well as resist them; and that have particular timeliness and/or social significance. Prospective topics might include books about migrant labor, rising economic insecurity, enduring gender inequality, public and private sector divisions, glass ceilings (gender limitations at work) and concrete walls (racial limitations at work), or racial/gender identity at work in the Black Lives Matter era.

Celeste Vaughan Curington, *Laboring in the Shadow of Empire: Race, Gender, and Care Work in Portugal*

Julie C. Keller, *Milking in the Shadows: Migrants and Mobility in America's Dairyland*

David C. Lane, *The Other End of the Needle: Continuity and Change among Tattoo Workers*

Annette Nierobisz and Dana Sawchuk, *American Idle: Late-Career Job Loss in a Neoliberal Era*

American Idle

Late-Career Job Loss in a Neoliberal Era

ANNETTE NIEROBISZ AND DANA SAWCHUK

Rutgers University Press
New Brunswick, Camden, and Newark, New Jersey
London and Oxford

Rutgers University Press is a department of Rutgers, The State University of New Jersey, one of the leading public research universities in the nation. By publishing worldwide, it furthers the University's mission of dedication to excellence in teaching, scholarship, research, and clinical care.

 Support for this book has been generously provided by Carleton College.

Library of Congress Cataloging-in-Publication Data

Names: Nierobisz, Annette Marie, 1968– author. | Sawchuk, Dana, 1968– author.
Title: American idle : late career job loss in a neoliberal era / Annette Nierobisz, Dana Sawchuk.
Description: New Brunswick, New Jersey : Rutgers University Press, [2025] | Series: Inequality at work: perspectives on race, gender, class, and labor | Includes bibliographical references and index.
Identifiers: LCCN 2024046778 | ISBN 9781978835863 (paperback) | ISBN 9781978835870 (hardcover) | ISBN 9781978835887 (epub) | ISBN 9781978835894 (pdf)
Subjects: LCSH: Older unemployed—United States—Social conditions. | Unemployment—Social aspects—United States. | Older people—Employment—United States. | United States—Economic conditions—21st century.
Classification: LCC HD6280 .N54 2025 | DDC 331.3/980973—dc23/eng/20250130
LC record available at https://lccn.loc.gov/2024046778

A British Cataloging-in-Publication record for this book is available from the British Library.

Copyright © 2025 by Annette Nierobisz and Dana Sawchuk

All rights reserved

No part of this book may be reproduced or utilized in any form or by any means, electronic or mechanical, or by any information storage and retrieval system, without written permission from the publisher. Please contact Rutgers University Press, 106 Somerset Street, New Brunswick, NJ 08901. The only exception to this prohibition is "fair use" as defined by U.S. copyright law.

References to internet websites (URLs) were accurate at the time of writing. Neither the authors nor Rutgers University Press is responsible for URLs that may have expired or changed since the manuscript was prepared.

♾ The paper used in this publication meets the requirements of the American National Standard for Information Sciences—Permanence of Paper for Printed Library Materials, ANSI Z39.48-1992.

rutgersuniversitypress.org

To our interviewees and, with love, to Robert, David, Michael, and Benji

In loving memory of Waldemar Nierobisz

Contents

1	"Broke, Unemployed, Downsized Again"	1
2	Hard Falls and Soft Landings	13
3	Generations at Work	28
4	In God We Trust	46
5	"Here's Where I Am, Here's Where I'll Stay"	64
6	Silver Linings and Positive Thinking	82
7	Where Are They Now? And What Can We Do?	98
	Appendix A: Studying Late-Career Job Loss in the Land of 10,000 Lakes	117
	Appendix B: Tables	127
	Acknowledgments	133
	Notes	137
	Bibliography	165
	Index	185

American Idle

1
"Broke, Unemployed, Downsized Again"

Wendy arrived early to her research interview at a suburban Minnesota library. The sixty-three-year-old seemed to have it all pulled together. She was organized, articulate, confident, and highly perceptive—the embodiment of white-collar success. Yet within the privacy of the library's conference room, Wendy calmly shared her heart-wrenching story with us. It was not the first time appearances would be misleading; Wendy was the forty-seventh person interviewed for the *American Idle* research project, and her experiences were far from unique.

With a rewarding sales career in consumer goods, an analytical mind, and a keen desire to keep learning, Wendy planned to work beyond a conventional retirement age for, as she put it, "as long as I'm able." Instead, by the time we met, Wendy had weathered six tumultuous years buffeted by the U.S. economy and was ill-equipped to maintain her standard of living, let alone entertain notions of retirement. A pair of major job losses left her reeling. The first came in 2008, the calendar year economists peg as the heart of the Great Recession, when she was laid off from a high-end sales position. Unemployed for fifteen months, Wendy was relieved when her former employer reached out, this time offering an account manager position. She accepted the job, only to be downsized again in 2013. "They just went through every department and cut people," Wendy recalled, deftly shorthanding many corporations' now-standard strategic response to market fluctuations and the desperate desire to maintain profitability. A year later, she was still jobless.

Between December 2007 and June 2009, the Great Recession pummeled the U.S. economy. In this combined housing and financial crisis, nearly four million home mortgages were foreclosed and almost nine million individuals lost their jobs. Official unemployment statistics nearly doubled in these eighteen months, but the big surprise was that these figures continued climbing even after economic recovery was supposedly underway. It took seven months for the national rates to plateau, peaking near 10 percent by January 2010. This was a number unseen in the United States since a stock market crash in 1929 ignited the Great Depression.[1] Amid record-high long-term unemployment, a period of joblessness stretching longer than six months, national survey data began to confirm that labor market conditions had become particularly unforgiving to older workers.[2] Not that Wendy needed anyone to tell her that.

At her September 2014 interview, Wendy had just a week of unemployment benefits remaining. Her personal savings were nearly exhausted, and she feared soon she would have to tap into her retirement account, eroding her long-term stability even more than her divorce had done some years earlier. The middle-class life she knew was on the verge of collapse, and, without familial assistance to cushion the blow, Wendy had concluded her only possible option was to sell the house, her last asset, and move in with her significant other. "Thank God we love each other," she remarked dryly.

This book is based on sixty-two interviews with older, white-collar workers. Our interviewees are baby boomers who lost their jobs, through no fault of their own, sometime during the Great Recession and its languishing recovery. The interviews were conducted from July 2013 to October 2014, a period in which rising rates of social inequality were fomenting political unrest.[3] While some of our interviewees had experienced job loss when they were younger, none had encountered this particular mix of prolonged unemployment accompanied by employers' pervasive disinterest. Many described finding themselves in an unfamiliar occupational mode: idle. Yet the participants in our sample, all of whom identified as White, were born into a position of privilege in this country's racial hierarchy and into its Golden Age postwar economy. They were raised accustomed to the bounty of middle-class comforts and, prior to job loss, felt themselves securely in possession of the American dream. After job loss, a rare few remained well positioned. Most, however, even those who had safeguards and resources that cushioned their fall, shared stories about anxieties and financial hardships they never imagined would tarnish their golden years. Their experiences simply bore no resemblance to their identity-based expectations for this stage in the life course, a disjuncture that amplified their sense of vulnerability.

We are living in a moment of great societal upheaval, our current headlines a dynamic swirl of dire stories on climate change, the aftereffects of a global pandemic, racial inequality, and political instability. Whether or not you personally know someone like Wendy, millions of older Americans are living a version of her story—and we believe this, too, is a troubling, newsworthy phenomenon. Demographically, our interviewees are considered baby boomers, a large population group that until recently was the largest generation recorded in U.S. history.[4] Combined with the trend toward living longer, healthier lives, this means there is an enormous cohort of people hitting traditional retirement ages (with sixty-five as an oft-cited benchmark) and finding they are ill-equipped to self-fund a retirement that may stretch several decades. Now, adding the upsurge in late-career job loss and long-term unemployment, we begin to get a picture of an economic, social, and political problem with the potential to intensify over subsequent generations.

The stories in this book can, and should, be read as cautionary tales that urge major economic overhauls as well as careful personal planning, but they are just as interesting sociologically for the way they are told. *American Idle* examines how a highly select group of boomers negotiated and interpreted late-career unemployment, and how and why they narrated their very real distress in the neoliberal language of blessings, opportunities, and individual effort. Neoliberalism provided our interviewees with a cognitive framework for interpreting the job loss experience, though they recognized its one-size-fits-all solutions as incompatible with their circumstances—the odd coupling of their current life stage with their rather undeniably advanced ages. In the pages that follow, we explore such contradictions, probing a new perspective on one of the most disruptive economic recessions in recent memory. And, by engaging with the well-documented financial vulnerability of older workers, we hope that the insights we present prove instructive for the graying workers who meet roadblocks in the path ahead.[5]

A Shifting Employment Contract

When sociologists interpret human social behavior, we refrain from explanations that center the individual and their psychological state. Instead, we situate people in social and historical contexts, recognizing that major macro-level external events, like a global financial meltdown, will also impact people's lives. This analytical foundation stems from an idea proposed by C. Wright Mills in his influential book, *The Sociological Imagination*. To quote Mills, "Neither the life of an individual nor the history of a society can be understood without understanding both."[6] Thus, it is our scholarly obligation to note, had our interviewees been born a decade or two earlier, they would have had a different set of work experiences, likely including job stability, a comfortable salary, and what would now be considered an outrageously generous retirement package or pension plan. More crucially, it is all but certain they would not be scrambling to locate new employment at ages that so recently called for retirement parties replete with sheet cakes and gold watches. So, what happened? Why are the employment fortunes of white-collar workers so radically different today?

When our interviewees first began working, an unspoken social contract existed between employers and employees that might strike younger readers as peculiar. Specifically, loyal white-collar employees who performed their jobs well could expect career stability (often with a single employer) and financial security. These employment conditions, certainly unusual from today's perspective, were a legacy of unprecedented growth and expansion in the U.S. economy, as its productive post–World War II economy stretched beyond the mid-1940s, all the way through 1973. The upswing was ignited by demographic trends, fueled by middle-class consumerism enabled through postwar government entitlements, and stoked by the fact that the infrastructure of many global competitor countries lay in ruins. Under these anomalously prosperous conditions,[7] an employment contract that first took shape in the 1930s solidified. This implied agreement built on the New Deal legislation that responded to the Great Depression with wage and working-hour regulations, regarded labor unions as necessary checks on company malfeasance, and mandated health insurance, unemployment insurance, and monthly Social Security disbursements to retired workers. Together, these established a social safety net meant to enhance public well-being.

Worker-friendly policies and practices continued expanding in the postwar years, largely because strong economic demand necessitated a stable workforce of committed employees and strong profits and policies solidified the status quo (though scholars are careful to note that the primary beneficiaries of these favorable conditions were White men[8]). Today, concepts like employment stability and financial security are foreign to most workers. The prosperity and mutual obligation of the "age of security" shattered in the mid-1970s, when many older baby boomers were already well established in the labor force. Accelerating inflation, the OPEC oil crisis, and other economic forces plunged the United States into recession, just as the domestic markets were flooded by high-quality, low-cost, foreign-made consumer goods.[9] U.S. corporations, convincing legislators to favor deregulation over fledgling ideas about tying wages to inflation, responded by adopting cost-cutting measures focused on reducing labor costs. It was the birth of downsizing. By the late 1980s, a wide array of organizations (including financially strong ones) across industries routinely eliminated workers, cutting costs, raising shareholder returns, reducing future obligations, and generally chasing profit in ways that were somewhat familiar to blue-collar workers but entirely new to their white-collar, middle-class counterparts. Over the course of our interviewees' careers, a new playbook emerged.

Older workers experienced this transition *in situ*. Much like the proverbial frog in a slowly heating pot, they failed to realize the ultimate outcome of these incremental changes.[10] It was as though they had formulated their expectations under the postwar employment contract, and though they saw changes on the horizon, these workers never anticipated the outcomes that seemed inevitable in hindsight: their own job losses. Interestingly, however, when our interviewees talked through their experiences, from minor indignities to economic devastation, their reactions fit into a collective pattern, revealing that somehow, they had implicitly bought into what social scientists call the neoliberal turn.

British writer George Monbiot once called neoliberalism "the ideology at the root of all our problems."[11] That may be hyperbole, but it is an exaggeration based firmly in fact. Many trace the introduction of neoliberal economic policies to American society to President Ronald Reagan, elected in 1980 and serving in office until 1989; but the stage was initially set in the late 1970s when the Carter Administration responded to the combination of a stagnating economy and rising inflation (a phenomenon known as stagflation) by deregulating several U.S. industries, including airlines, trucking, and telecommunications.[12] A few years earlier in Latin America, militarized governments in countries including Argentina and Chile had introduced privatization and deregulation schemes that shrank the state and greatly reduced government spending on public services.[13] With this real-world ideological inspiration, the Reagan Administration undertook its own sweeping free-market reforms to undo the robust welfare state created under the Roosevelt Administration.[14] This calculated move strongly favored corporate and financial interests over public needs. At this point in history, our oldest interviewees were full-time workers. The youngest were preparing to enter the labor force.

As public policy embraced market fundamentalism, the idea that free markets rather than government can best solve social and economic problems, individuals became less secure and social safety nets less able to catch them. This neoliberal turn exploited a vocabulary familiar in American culture: competition, privatization, and government deregulation at the macro level; personal responsibility, self-reliance, and the importance of material success at the micro level.[15] Scholars argue that these ideas seeped into our collective conscience, radically reconfiguring our interactions with, reactions to, and interpretations of the world around us. Indeed, today neoliberal logic informs a wide variety of social institutions. It is evident in common exhortations to run our families like business firms;[16] in Evangelicals' embrace of "antigovernment individualism";[17] in individualist educational philosophies aimed at the future, which demand children accumulate human capital to become competitive and financially successful;[18] and in the myriad legal decisions that insulate corporations from redressing collective harms.[19] Neoliberalism has become the currency of bootstraps and common sense.

One hundred years ago, in an era colloquially referred to as the Roaring Twenties, workers' rights and labor's demands were routinely crushed by employers and the courts. New Deal reforms rebuilt the economic arrangement on more favorable terms for workers, and the frothy post–World War II economy enshrined an employer-employee relationship based in loyalty, mutual respect, and reciprocity. Today's workers, by contrast, are encouraged to "think they own themselves as though they are businesses—bundles of skills, assets, qualities, experiences, and relationships, bundles that must be consciously managed and constantly enhanced."[20] Anthropologist Ilana Gershon employs the metaphor "self as business" to describe these neoliberal impacts on the employment relationship.[21] Employees are expected to be responsible for themselves and take ownership over their circumstances while at the same time, jobs have become more insecure and workers themselves have less control over workplace conditions.[22] In less than a half century, the employment contract has transformed from the collective "we're all in this together" to the individualistic "you're on your own."[23] Little wonder, then, that one of our respondents mournfully characterized his current employment status as "broke, unemployed, downsized again."

To return to our slowly stewing frog, we can think of the American populace as having been systematically reprogrammed over the past four decades by neoliberalism, without any formal awareness it was happening.[24] And despite the term *neoliberalism* being used by intellectuals long before it informed public policy,[25] this ideology has nevertheless remained well hidden from public discourse. A recent media analysis by sociologist Michèle Lamont shows scant few mentions of the term *neoliberalism* in U.S. news from 1980 to 2015, when it was so dramatically reshaping society and social relations.[26] Our interviewees never used the word at all. Yet when we asked about the effects of job loss, fruitless job searches, and their overall reflections about the experience of unemployment, they repeatedly cited specific aspects of the economic environment created by neoliberalism. They spoke about the necessity of corporate bottom lines, diminished job security, taking initiative, and the importance of maintaining a positive mindset in the face of structural obstacles. Neoliberalism crept in at the margins, a pervasive force in the interpretive frameworks these individuals drew upon to make sense of their experiences.

Another key study, recounted in anthropologist Carrie Lane's 2011 book, *A Company of One*, found something similar.[27] The IT workers she interviewed lost their jobs in the dot-com bubble crash of the early 2000s. Though they did not mention neoliberalism, they frequently recited its core tenets as a sort of mantra in their efforts to move on. For example, Lane's respondents accepted the necessity of job insecurity and embraced the idea that they were free-market agents. Although this new landscape had diminished their financial and personal standing, they were notably optimistic and retained unwavering faith in the market-oriented economic system.

In some respects, our study picks up where Lane left off. We study similarly life-disrupting job loss, but with crucial differences in our approach. Our focus is on older workers from a wide range of mostly white-collar occupations. They experienced job loss at a later stage in life, making financial recovery difficult (perhaps impossible) and ageism a distinct disadvantage when it came to even getting a foot in the door with new employers. At a key moment, our interviewees experienced enormous disruption, many finding themselves precariously situated late in life, with little time to make up lost ground. Finally, their job losses were due to a global economic recession rather than an industry crash, with older workers uniquely disadvantaged.

The Great Recession and Older Workers

From the standpoint of older workers, three factors set the Great Recession and its recovery apart from other downturns they had experienced. First, they disproportionately experienced long-term unemployment. Second, the downturn came with a concurrent housing crisis. Finally, the financial crisis on Wall Street swept away retirement savings and left interest rates on deposits near zero.

In the glacial recovery period that followed, long-term unemployment plagued the entire labor market. By January 2010, the average length of unemployment reached twenty-one weeks, versus the nine-week averages recorded for other recent recessions.[28] Two years later, in the first quarter of 2012, almost 30 percent of unemployed U.S. workers had been jobless for at least a year. And still, it was worse for some: unemployed workers aged fifty-five years and older had the highest rates of joblessness for one year or longer, followed by workers aged forty-five to fifty-four.[29] For reference, our respondents' modal age was fifty-eight in late 2014.

The second distinguishing characteristic is the dramatic decline in housing prices that both triggered and sustained the Great Recession. Home prices had risen steadily for nearly a decade until their peak in 2006.[30] When prices began to tumble in 2007, a wave of homeowners found themselves underwater. The collapsing values meant they suddenly owed more on their properties than the market could return. With negative equity, homeowners struggling to make their mortgage payments in a historic recession could not rely on their largest asset as a safety net, and foreclosures quickly followed. And given that long-term unemployment was concentrated among older adults, this group that had long been shielded from housing market instabilities became immensely vulnerable: between 2007 and 2011, individuals aged fifty and up had the highest risk of mortgage delinquency.[31] In this book you will hear from a few people who lost their homes to loan foreclosure.

Finally, the financial crisis of 2008 reduced household financial wealth, both through a dramatic decline in stock prices and a reduction in interest rates on savings accounts and other deposits.[32] Between 2007 and 2010, individuals nearing retirement were estimated to have lost, on average, one-third of the value of their retirement portfolio. By 2011, the value of the average retirement account remained "about 15 percent below its peak."[33] Losses like these affected workers from every generation, but especially older adults who had fewer remaining years in the labor force to recover financially. According to survey data collected in early 2009, this group was forced to recalculate their retirement expectations rapidly amid the Great Recession: slightly more than half of working adults between ages fifty and sixty-four reported that they intended to delay their retirement, and another 16 percent reported that they no longer expected they could ever stop working.[34] More recent statistics show that, regardless of age, many American workers now view retirement as entirely out of reach.[35]

Anecdotal stories of how older unemployed adults experienced the turbulent economic conditions have already been offered in many popular accounts of the Great Recession and its languishing recovery. While compelling, these stories lack scientific credibility. For instance, we often do not know whether the individual in any gripping account is representative of a larger group or if pertinent information may have been omitted in order to craft a better tale. We observed that these accounts are missing a sociological framework that might help us understand how the wider population of older, unemployed adults collectively understands their predicaments and imagines possible avenues forward. This book aims to address these gaps.

Our Research Method

Our study is based in Minnesota. This Midwestern state is celebrated for its natural resources, economic opportunities, and overall infrastructure, three of many factors to which Minnesotans' high quality of life are attributed.[36] With more than a dozen Fortune 500 companies headquartered in and around the Twin Cities, it certainly is a good place to be a white-collar worker. It is also a good place to lose your job, given Minnesota's relatively generous social safety net; the length of its benefits and its average weekly payments put the state in the top ten when it comes to unemployment support.[37] Unfortunately, these factors were insufficient to shield many of the people who participated in this study from the deleterious effects of late-career unemployment in a neoliberal economy.

The in-depth, conversational interviews on which we draw throughout this book were conducted from July 2013 to October 2014, a period in which Minnesota's economy was rebounding but job opportunities remained limited for the long-term unemployed.[38] Those able to find new employment were increasingly likely to take jobs with lower pay, with fewer benefits, and in fields unrelated to their work histories and expertise. No wonder growing numbers of aging Americans report that economic necessity is driving their decision to work past age sixty-five.[39]

Though the Age Discrimination in Employment Act treats employees over the age of forty as older workers, our respondents were required to be age fifty, at minimum, to ensure they were born no later than 1964, the last year of the post–World War II growth and the commonly designated final birth year of the baby boom generation. Sixty percent of the interviewees were between the ages of fifty and fifty-nine; the remainder were between sixty and sixty-eight years old. The most common year of their job dismissal was 2011, two years after the official end of the Great Recession. However, the recession was still present in the terminology they used to describe their job loss: "downsizing," "reorganization," and "business closing" were frequently cited as the reason for dismissal.

In many respects, the individuals who were attracted to this study were a privileged group. In addition to their upper-middle and middle-class status, the participants benefited from societal-level advantages historically denied to BIPOC (Black, Indigenous, and People of Color) groups in the United States. Interviewees resided in Minnesota, which experienced moderate unemployment rates during the Great Recession and its recovery compared with other states. Because most interviewees had been employed in "good jobs," they were equipped with resources many other unemployed workers lack.[40] For example, some had institutional support in the form of generous severance packages, pension plans, and extended health insurance. More than a few had financial security derived from personal savings and mortgage-free homes. Some individuals had domestic partners who held professional or managerial occupations or other family members who were able to provide financial support. Even so, a substantial portion of our interviewees were unemployed or underemployed, left psychologically and economically distressed by later-life job loss.

In appendix A, we provide additional detail about the recruitment and selection of respondents; the semi-structured, in-depth interviews conducted with sixty-two respondents, most of whom lost white-collar jobs; and our data analysis strategy. However, we must emphasize the degree to which our interviewees were a racially homogeneous group. While social research confirms that racialized workers tend to experience greater disadvantage in the hiring process,[41] only White people responded to our recruitment. While this study strived to attract all voices, in appendix A we speculate about the reasons why our respondents, and not other individuals, contacted us. What stood out during the data collection phase, however, was the interviewees' shared perception that in their job dismissals and reemployment search disappointments, they were victims of age discrimination. They felt that it was important that their stories be shared, perhaps because they were confronting diminished privilege for the first time on multiple levels: their economic privilege had been reduced by the unexpected dismissal, and their social privilege had been reduced by their advanced age.[42]

Our sample included individuals who were financially well positioned to begin early retirement, however involuntary, when they were dismissed, as well as people who were old enough to access Social Security benefits and Medicare. Of those still searching for reemployment, there were those who had safeguards and resources tempering their financial hardship, while others experienced food insecurity, low wages, and other difficulties that eventually stripped them of their middle-class standing. After digesting the endless media accounts painting a uniformly dire picture of job loss among aging baby boomers, we did not expect to find so much variability in the unemployment experience; that we did leaves us with a paramount disciplinary lesson. Conventional wisdom is not always backed up by the patterns revealed through sociological research. The span between perception and reality is frequently where the most fascinating science occurs.

The Organization of This Book

In chapter 2, "Hard Falls and Soft Landings," we introduce life course theory, the theoretical perspective that provides the context for several discussions to come; we also expand our case for studying the job loss experiences of older workers. This chapter provides more detail about the sixty-two older workers who sat across from us as interview participants, demonstrating how late-career job loss experiences vary even within a relatively homogenous sample.[43] We differentiate, broadly, between what we call "hard falls" and "soft landings," while acknowledging those somewhere in between. Individuals experiencing hard falls found their lives intensely disrupted and reported a variety of negative outcomes, including evaporating retirement accounts, neglected medical needs, and the resulting depression and anxiety. Other respondents found the experience trying, yet familial assistance and the vestiges of institutional support emblematic of the post–World War II economy cushioned their dismissals. Notably, while men were most likely to have a soft landing and women were more likely to report a hard fall, experiences of ageism were common across gender, and so we also discuss how our interviewees acted in the face of such discrimination.

Chapter 3, "Generations at Work," is organized around generational understandings of employment in the neoliberal economy. While we problematize popular understandings of generations and generational difference, we also recognize that such categories and concepts are meaningful, to both our participants and readers. We specifically highlight the ways interviewees construct a picture of contrasts across three particular generations: their own, baby boomers; that of their parents'; and that of their younger colleagues and labor market gatekeepers. Through their accounts, we learn about our interviewees' nostalgia for their parents' age of security as well as their disdain for the lack of employer-employee commitment in the present-day workplaces they associate with the perceived shortcomings of "kids today." While we discuss how some of our interviewees avoided narratives of intergenerational conflict, we also explore how the more common understanding of generational difference ultimately reinforces the divide-and-isolate strategy for which neoliberalism is known.

Another facet of the neoliberal economy, more prominently under George W. Bush and through the White House Office of Faith-Based and Community Initiatives, is its shifting of responsibility for social services provision from the government to faith-based organizations. Chapter 4, "In God We Trust," looks specifically at the faith-based job clubs in Minnesota and explores the positions of the nearly three-quarters of our interviewees who referenced God, faith, and church in narrating and describing how they coped with their job losses. Here, there are participants who speak of the comfort and solace their faith provides, the strength congregations offer, and a willingness to surrender to God and the deeper meaning of their job losses. Conversely, there are also lengthy quotes in which people express anger and resentment toward God and, specifically, the unsatisfactory religious rhetoric espoused in the faith-based job clubs many had joined. Again, neoliberalism threads through the chapter, but in reverse: we explore how religious institutions and interpretative frameworks, no matter how comforting, reflect and reinforce the neoliberal emphasis on personal responsibility and as such may also obscure or counter critical understandings of the structural context of participants' distress.

In chapter 5, "'Here's Where I Am, Here's Where I'll Stay,'" we consider the approaches these older workers took toward gaining new employment in an economy that demands individuals, not employers, manage careers by becoming "flexible workers." Significantly, we found even the most eager job seekers tended to resist one tactic: relocation. Despite limited local opportunities, the overwhelming majority restricted their job searches to a limited radius. What explains this relative inflexibility? Here, we return to life course theory, as respondents experience the friction between neoliberalism's flexible worker ideal and the reality of their life stages. Participants detail how their relationships with immediate family and friends included age-specific challenges such as the need to care for elderly parents, assist aging siblings, and nurture children entering adulthood; these responsibilities, as well as deep attachments to homes, neighborhoods, communities, and/or the state influenced their decisions to stay in place. In this chapter, we acknowledge that some of our participants' financial privilege and middle-class social standing allowed them to manage unemployment without relocating. For others, however, it was the opposite: the recession had restricted their finances and thus their options. And there were many who were keenly aware that their relocation could not safeguard them from precarity; as they had painfully learned, they could always be terminated, no matter where they lived.

Chapter 6, "Silver Linings and Positive Thinking," reveals a curious paradox we discovered in many of the stories: alongside the difficulties of late-career job loss, our interviewees also took care to extol its silver linings. These optimistic perceptions coalesced around improvements to quality of life, often in terms of the physical or mental health boosts that came with escaping "toxic" or stifling workplaces, and around opportunities for personal growth, in which job loss was presented as an invaluable chance for personal reinvention, the reevaluation of priorities, and relationship growth. These comments demonstrate how our interviewees embraced and exemplified neoliberalism's happiness imperative. For our interviewees, it appeared neoliberalism both fueled their job loss woes and guided them toward more optimistic interpretations of their unemployment trials.

In our final chapter, "Where Are They Now? And What Can We Do?," we provide an update on our participants' lives approximately ten years after their first interviews. We present the findings from our 2023 survey of the original interviewees and in-depth follow-up interviews with six of the survey respondents. We update these latter workers' stories in light of the book's themes and their present economic context, and we convey their advice to those who may be facing their own job loss struggles. Finally, we close by looking ahead to the ways interviewees' insights, our analysis, and other recent social scientific research and theory can provide guidance and hope for workers, job clubs, and the rest of us.

Though the Great Recession seems firmly in America's rearview mirror, we cannot forget the words of warning: *Objects in (the) mirror are closer than they appear.* Life for workers, who in past eras enjoyed a great deal of stability, has been made precarious by the neoliberal turn. Such insecurity is devastating to older workers but is undeniably affecting us all, showing no signs of abating and persisting through pandemic-related and subsequent economic turmoil as neoliberalism and unemployment solidify into American institutions.[44] If we are to hope and work for an alternative to the neoliberal era, we cannot afford to overlook the cautionary words and wisdom of older workers.

2
Hard Falls and Soft Landings

In most other chapters of this book, we open with one of our interviewees' stories. But for these stories to help contextualize our arguments throughout, it is important that you get to know about some overarching differences across our interviews. Broadly speaking, the job loss experiences of our sixty-two research participants (table B2 in appendix B briefly summarizes all interviewees, thirty-three men and twenty-nine women) fell on a continuum bounded by two extremes: hard falls and soft landings. In this chapter, we highlight the structural and organizational factors that helped determine which end of the spectrum individual interviewees experienced.

The analysis here and elsewhere in this book is informed by a life course perspective, specifically the approach developed by sociologist Glen Elder.[1] Elder established the framework in his highly acclaimed book, *Children of the Great Depression*. This work examines the life course impacts of the Great Depression on the adolescents who participated in the 1931 Oakland Growth Study and three decades of subsequent follow-ups.[2] We find that Elder's scheme is just as powerful when we focus on the life course impacts of the Great Recession on older workers. Certainly, these economic crises have several similarities,[3] and, as the mainstream media notes, they are considered "the two greatest economic catastrophes in the U.S. of the last one hundred years."[4] So let's look more closely at life course theory.

Life course theory broadly examines macro-level patterns in individual life pathways, and Elder specifies four main tenets. The interplay of human lives and historical times, a first life course tenet, draws attention to the role of historical forces in shaping individual life pathways. Our respondents lost their jobs between 2007 and 2014, and their dismissals were situated in the Great Recession's onset, expansion, and/or protracted recovery. While no one was immune from the impact of this recession, older adults were uniquely affected. They endured the highest and longest rates of unemployment, the greatest risk of mortgage delinquency, and the largest losses to their retirement savings. This chapter considers how this macroeconomic context shaped our interviewees' job loss experiences.

Elder's second tenet, the timing of lives, recognizes a person's age will determine the impact and meaning of their life events. As members of the baby boom generation,[5] our respondents experienced job loss during the later years of midlife or middle adulthood, a stage scholars define as spanning ages forty to sixty-four.[6] Previous research, which we will review next, shows just how detrimental job loss at this life course stage can be for individuals like our respondents, who were nonetheless privileged by their race (White), social class (middle and upper-middle), and former job (predominantly white collar).

A third tenet of the life course perspective, linked or interdependent lives, specifies that social relationships link people together. As our findings show, familial responsibilities, relationships, and the resources these offered were among the many factors determining postdismissal experiences. Individuals who lacked these relational connections tended to encounter more difficulties after job loss.

Elder's final tenet, human agency in choice making, recognizes that individuals actively respond to the situations in which they find themselves. This agency, however, is contingent on available opportunities as well as existing sociocultural constraints.[7] One constraint our interviewees encountered was ageism in their labor market interactions. We will conclude this chapter by examining how they responded to this bias.

A few additional life course concepts are central to our analysis. The term *age structuring* refers to the idea that life transitions are typically paired with age norms. These norms are reflected in demographic patterns and understandably influence societal expectations. For example, given contemporary educational and occupational trends, middle-class parents might expect a neurotypical child to complete high school in their late teens, graduate college in their early twenties, and spend that remaining decade establishing a chosen career path. We become aware of these taken-for-granted age and life stage norms when individuals do not reach particular milestones at the socially prescribed age. The popular idiom "failure to launch," for instance, describes a young adult who is delayed in transitioning to self-sufficiency and financial independence.

In contemporary society, many life events and transitions are less likely to follow the standardized, linear trajectory earlier cohorts encountered. Careers, for example, once slotted neatly into a "first school, then work, then retirement and with it old age" series as life course scholar Phyllis Moen notes in her study of boomers' late-career employment shifts.[8] Today's workers can no longer anticipate staying with a single employer for their entire careers and retiring at age sixty-five. In fact, such a career path is now statistically rare. But the older workers we interviewed were well down this career path when it dissolved.

Some transitions in the life course may be ill-timed and difficult to navigate, including late-career job loss. Older workers who are laid off are often too young to retire from the labor force and may be financially underprepared to afford today's longer life expectancies.[9] At the same time, they may also be considered too old by hiring managers who, as statistics show, tend to favor younger workers.[10] In a life course perspective, these disparities represent a mismatch between organizational practices and contemporary social expectations and realities.[11]

A Case for Studying Job Loss among Older Workers

Research shows that losing one's job can be challenging, regardless of age. Yet the physical and mental health impacts of involuntary job loss on older workers can be devastating. When workers over the age of fifty lose their jobs, they face increased risk of heart attack and stroke, weight gain, tobacco use or a return to smoking after cessation, and depression and mental health struggles more broadly.[12] In one study, a full 94 percent of older workers described experiencing at least one negative social-psychological consequence of job loss, whether it was isolation, depression, or, tellingly, a "loss of trust in the traditional social contract of employment, which they were socialized under."[13] Evidence also reveals an ominous uptick in suicide, one type of "death by despair,"[14] among adults between ages forty and sixty-four affected by job or financial distress during the Great Recession.[15]

As you might expect, the negative physiological and psychological effects of job loss and ensuing unemployment are particularly acute for those who are economically vulnerable or have financial problems.[16] This finding might suggest the middle- and upper-middle-class respondents in our study are relatively buffered from post-layoff problems. Instead, researchers document what management scholar Janina Latack and her collaborators term the "harder-they-fall" effect, whereby relatively affluent workers, because they may derive more of their identity from work, experience greater emotional and psychological problems than blue-collar workers when it comes to coping postdisplacement.[17] Management expert Stephen Fineman, for instance, documents white-collar workers' struggles with post-unemployment feelings of rejection and failure.[18]

Other research chronicles unemployed managers' self-doubt and self-recrimination, and jobless professionals' struggles with stigma management.[19]

Sociologist Ofer Sharone finds U.S. white-collar workers engaging in self-blame, while fellow sociologist Dawn Norris underscores emotional pain and identity threat as especially salient aspects of the modern job loss experience.[20] In another analysis of the job loss narratives of managers and professionals in their fifties, organizational studies scholar Yiannis Gabriel and his colleagues characterized many of their respondents as "wounded," "fragmented," and even "broken" as a result of their unemployment ordeals.[21]

Statistics show that the financial impact of job loss persists much longer for older adults. For example, the employment rate of older displaced workers remains 20 percent lower than nondisplaced workers' for several years after job loss.[22] This employment gap may explain why the earnings of displaced workers are also far below expected levels for up to a decade after termination.[23] Older displaced workers are also more likely to retire prematurely, possibly because of this inability to locate new employment.[24] But this is not a happy retirement that comes with a party and a cake: the decision to retire after job loss challenges wealth accumulation, putting older workers at risk of diminished economic security, sometimes to the point of "near poverty," at a critical juncture in the life course.[25]

Our study builds on these extant findings. When we spoke with our respondents, we used a semistructured interview design. This conversational style allows the interviewer to follow up on comments or pursue fruitful tangents. There were six categories of questions, beginning with interviewees' sociodemographic background, occupational identity, and dismissal experiences. Next, we moved into people's perceptions of how job loss affected their sense of self, relationships, and finances; descriptions of their experiences of searching for new employment; and overall reflections on late-career job loss. In the course of answering these questions, many of our respondents conveyed their struggles with a similar set of mental health outcomes noted in previous research. Depression, anxiety, and distress were frequently expressed, as were feelings of fear, shock, shame, anger, self-doubt, and self-blame. Such psychological reactions were relatively consistent across the sample. The financial impacts of job loss, on the other hand, were far more varied. Together, these factors—which a sociological lens helps clarify—seemed to sort out those individuals who experienced hard falls from those with soft landings.

Hard Falls

Long-term unemployment, multiple job losses, evaporating personal wealth, and difficulty paying for basic necessities were among the troubles reported by the thirteen respondents we classify as having hard falls when they experienced later-life job loss. The stories we heard from this group are indicative of a larger phenomenon called *intragenerational downward mobility*. As opposed to intergenerational downward mobility, which occurs within families across generations, this type of downward mobility occurs for individuals within their own lifetime. Late-career job loss is understandably a powerful catalyst for intragenerational downward mobility.[26]

Our data reveal a striking gender difference: women were five times more likely than men to report hard falls. This finding is consistent with sociologist Sarah Damaske's research, which also finds that job loss within the context of the Great Recession was more financially detrimental for women.[27] Consider the experience reported by Cassandra; the transcript from her interview reads like a prophecy for late-career job loss in a neoliberal era.

Sixty-one years old when we met her, Cassandra had been self-employed as a human resources recruiter.[28] She was specializing in construction-related jobs when this industry faltered. With the onset of the subprime mortgage crisis that triggered the Great Recession, the construction industry recorded the largest sector decline of employment from December 2007 to June 2009 according to the U.S. Bureau of Labor Statistics.[29] Cassandra's contracts dried up, and the industry did not recover for many years. But where other respondents were able to avoid financial insolvency by leveraging job-related programs, including federal and state extended relief programs for unemployed workers who had exhausted their benefits yet still remained unemployed,[30] a self-employed contractor like Cassandra was ineligible for such support. She was left to fend for herself.

At first Cassandra tapped into her personal savings. She was cautious, almost fearful of spending money unnecessarily. With a lifestyle she described as "frugal" and her debt limited to a mortgage and an auto loan, Cassandra was able to fund her unemployment for about a year and a half while feverishly applying for jobs. When she ran out of money and still had not found work, Cassandra resorted to a set of survival means her younger self would have never imagined. She got by on a combination of monthly welfare checks, groceries from a community food shelf, and meals selected from McDonald's $1 menu on those days she was too weary to cook.[31]

The financial hit of job loss upended Cassandra's life in other unexpected ways. Socially, she suffered. "The guy" she was dating "dumped me because I could not afford to pay for stuff." Cassandra's two sisters, her only living family members, "shunned" her for fear that she would become "burdensome to them." Even coffee with friends became unfeasible because "I couldn't afford coffee." Without the vital financial or emotional support of a life partner, adult children, parents, or siblings, Cassandra's mental health declined.

Even as she spiraled into a fog of depression and anxiety, Cassandra's determination to find a job never wavered. And when the job search failed to produce a favorable outcome, she dumbed down her résumé, eliminating all signs of her professional accomplishments and extensive educational background, including two advanced degrees: "I took off all my education. I even took off my bachelor's degree . . . and I just put down my last job . . . instead of 'business owner [and] independent contractor.' . . . I took everything [in the] past off. Took all my volunteer work [and] everything else that I do off, and just did a little short one-page resume." This strategic approach eventually landed Cassandra a sales position. The job came with employer-sponsored health insurance, but the salary was substantially less than what she used to earn. Cassandra was just getting by when we met one year later, and she was fearful for her future self: "I have thirty more years to live. . . . I'm going to be on welfare. There is no way around it. . . . I have no idea what I'm going to do [laughs]. I even, my new car that I bought, I jokingly said to a friend of mine, 'Yeah, you know I figured out I could live in the back if I had to.' I mean—and I'm joking but I'm not. And [pause] you know, and it's just scary to think that I might live to be ninety. Oh my God, what am I gonna do?"

Of the female respondents who reported a hard fall, there were those like Cassandra: single women without children who had once had good jobs and then a spate of bad luck. They included Dawn, a mechanical drafter who was downsized at age fifty-three, then, when she entered a new line of more physically challenging work, was injured on the job, and Meg, a lawyer whose contract with her law firm ended in November 2007 at age sixty-one. With the onset of the Great Recession just one month later, reemployment eluded Meg. Both women responded to their downward descent with drastic lifestyle adjustments. For example, after Dawn's severance payment ran out, she employed several desperate strategies to cover her living expenses: withdrawing money from her 401(k) retirement account, managing her apartment building in exchange for reduced rent, and boarding cats in her apartment for owners who were traveling. Meg applied for her Social Security benefits at age sixty-two, a calculated move that knowingly reduced her payout to 70 percent of the full benefit but at least gave her "something to live on."[32] She also sold the biggest asset she had, a house in the Twin Cities, and moved in with a friend. This living arrangement worked out well until the friend's new romantic partner wanted to move in, too. Sadly, Dawn's and Meg's stories are representative of a larger phenomenon documented among unmarried baby boomers: they are more likely to live in poverty than their married counterparts.[33] Here, too, another gender difference is apparent: the largest proportion of unmarried boomers are female.[34]

The financial vulnerabilities Cassandra, Meg, and Dawn noted were also reported by some married respondents. They included Nadine, whom you'll meet in chapter 4, and Charles, whom you'll meet in chapter 5. Nadine and Charles were the primary income providers in their respective families, and their households suffered critical income losses when they were laid off. And there is Heather. She specialized in title insurance, another industry negatively impacted by the housing market collapse that ignited the Great

Recession. Her husband was employed, but he had never financially recovered from losing a well-paying job in 2000. Thus, when Heather was laid off in 2007, again in 2008, and then fired from a third full-time job shortly thereafter, the couple lost their home to a bank foreclosure. Unable to secure permanent employment, Heather accepted a temp job outside her field of expertise. This job came with low pay, no benefits, and a set of tasks and responsibilities Heather found "beneath" her.

As the sixth person we interviewed, and the first to report a hard fall, Heather alerted us to the cascading financial toll of multiple job losses. Several of the respondents with hard falls shared this type of job loss experience.[35] Recent research summarized by the Brookings Institution shows that the earnings losses from a single layoff can persist for a decade or longer.[36] Now consider the aggregate effects of repeat job loss.[37] Equipped with this understanding, it was not surprising to hear another interviewee, Helen, exclaim she lost "everything!" from four job losses between 2007 and 2009. We'll find out more about Helen's story in the next chapter.

Late-career job loss can be complicated by health conditions more common in midlife. When Sara experienced two back-to-back layoffs followed by long-term unemployment, she dug into her retirement savings. When this money was gone, Sara accepted a temp job that paid less than half of her previous earnings and lacked the health insurance she needed so desperately. There was no money for essential medications to treat her diabetes, glaucoma, cataracts, or depression, so she resorted to self-medicating with marijuana and alcohol. She was haunted by the entirely valid fear that "one medical emergency" would "destroy" her financially.

Teresa was receiving cancer treatments when she lost her clerical job in 2011. Her medical circumstances stood in the way of actively searching for jobs, as Minnesota's unemployment insurance program requires of its recipients. She explained, "I mean you're dealing with the chemo—I was bald-headed.... I didn't feel like I could go apply for a job because I can't sit across from you and say, 'Well, I need every third Friday off [for chemotherapy treatments].'" During her fifteen months of unemployment, Teresa received food stamps and relinquished her house in a short sale. This type of profitless transaction occurs when homeowners are financially distressed and most likely behind on their mortgage payments. It is considered a voluntary action by a homeowner rather than the involuntary home foreclosures both Heather and Helen experienced.[38]

Soft Landings

Equivalent hardships were glaringly absent from the job loss narratives we classify as soft landings. Respondents with this dismissal experience were left more or less financially unscathed by their late-career job losses. Here, too, there was a gender gap: fifteen of the eighteen respondents we classify as having had a soft landing were men.

One group of respondents with soft landings were downsized by the same Fortune 500 employer,[39] a multinational conglomerate based in the Twin Cities. These respondents began their unemployment experience from a uniquely privileged position: a severance payout of two weeks' salary for every year of service,[40] access to outplacement services, employer-sponsored health care during the severance period, and—for those long-term employees fifty-five years and older—the ability to begin withdrawing from the company pension plan. Presented with this package, two of our respondents decided to retire impromptu. Felix, for example, had worked for this employer his entire career, close to thirty-four years. He survived several previous restructurings until his luck ran out in 2012. "Looks like I'm retired," Felix giggled when describing the text message he sent his wife immediately after receiving news of his pending layoff.

While Felix was disappointed he could not control his official retirement date, he was nonetheless chuffed that "things just fell into place." Because he was fifty-six years old at dismissal, Felix was eligible to draw from and receive the peace of mind associated with a defined-benefit pension plan.[41] Additionally, Felix's employer offered him a fifteen-month consulting gig shortly after his termination. This unexpected financial windfall allowed Felix and his wife, a stay-at-home mom, to purchase a second home on the Gulf Coast. They subsequently became snowbirds, escaping Minnesota's coldest months to bask in the sunshine and warmth with extended family. Felix's delight over his new circumstances was obvious throughout our interview, even when he noted, "Now, for the first time in twenty-plus years, we have a budget." His only major concern was, "Am I going to get bored?"

Of course, not all the respondents with soft landings were as content. Tad, laid off in the same downsizing as Felix and similarly retired in his fifties, summarized his emotional state in the weeks following the dismissal: "It's like a divorce. You just—emotionally, you're tanked." Clearly, respondents with soft landings were not always immune from the emotional distress of late-career job loss. What set these respondents apart from the others is that they avoided falling down the rungs of the socioeconomic ladder as those with hard landings did.

In summary, what factors contributed to a soft landing among our respondents? It certainly helped to have been employed by a large corporation paying lucrative salaries (which also, incidentally, translates into higher unemployment insurance benefits[42]) as well as providing optimal severance packages when downsizings were deemed necessary. These perks are reminiscent of the "we're all in this together" mentality characterizing the post–World War II employment contract. During this period, many of the professional employees staffing these organizations were men; in part, this may help explain why more of our soft landing respondents were also men.

The financial support of parents and spouses likewise ensured a soft landing. Isaac, for example, "did pretty darn well" after his 2008 downsizing from his senior marketing position. The combination of six months' severance, personal savings, and a consulting contract helped him maintain his financial standing. Then, when the contract expired and he was unable to locate new employment, Isaac's parents stepped in with a generous financial gift, enough that he could retire comfortably at age sixty-one. Other respondents in the sample also credited parental financial assistance, though no one described having parents as wealthy as Isaac's.

When we met Beth, one of three female respondents who experienced a soft landing, she had been unemployed for a full year after her 2012 downsizing. While negotiating this situation, several factors worked in her favor, including a severance package yielding forty-two weeks' salary, substantially lower mortgage payments through refinancing,[43] a "fabulous support system" consisting of family and friends, and—perhaps most importantly—a common-law partner who provided financial assistance, emotional support, and access to health insurance. Many other respondents benefited from having spouses employed in well-paying jobs. Lars, who found new employment relatively quickly after his 2012 downsizing, drew attention to the supportive role played by his own spouse: "Being in a . . . couple, married or living with somebody—the upside is you've got backup. You've got somebody who's bringing in an income."

Finally, three respondents experienced soft landings simply because they located new employment with relative ease. Five months after his 2008 downsizing, Colin switched career paths and became an unemployment counselor at a Minnesota WorkForce (now CareerForce) center. The WorkForce wages were considerably less than those he earned as a media manager at a large multinational corporation. Colin's tenure before his 2008 downsizing, however, gave him access to a defined-benefit pension plan that closed the earnings gap. Six and a half months after Kai's dismissal, a new employer matched his previous salary. Frank found new employment within four months but at a reduced salary. Eleven months later, his former employer rehired him with a salary nearly equal to his previous earnings. These examples bring to the fore another factor worth mentioning: Frank, Kai, and Colin worked in fields relatively unscathed by the Great Recession—systems engineering, information technology, and unemployment counseling, respectively.[44] Field of employment, then, appears to be another factor determining a hard fall or soft landing after job loss.

Falling in Between

Thus far we have examined the defining parameters of the hard falls/soft landings continuum. Yet the job loss experiences of the largest number of our respondents ($N = 27$) fell somewhere in between. One example is fifty-nine-year-old Sally, a former financial services professional. She was one of the casualties when her industry shed almost 4 percent of its jobs during the Great Recession.[45]

Consistent with some respondents experiencing hard falls, Sally suffered two sequential job losses. Yet, similar to some respondents with soft landings, she acquired a consulting gig within six months of her second job loss. While she escaped severe financial distress and corresponding downward mobility, her new job lacked the benefits she once enjoyed as a senior executive: "There is no vacation, there [are] no holidays, you always have to work a little bit more to cover . . . the eight hours if you want to take a day off." Though the job was less than ideal, Sally was the sole income provider for her family. With her personal savings depleted and facing health care expenses related to her husband's cancer diagnosis and treatment, she felt compelled to accept this demotion. As life course theorists would say, Sally's choice was constrained by circumstances beyond her control.

Other respondents we classify as falling in between had a bumpier ride after job loss. Lyle, whom you will meet in chapter 6, had a total of three job losses: a first in 2006, a second in 2009, and a third in 2013. The latter two were followed by bouts of long-term unemployment—eighteen months and two years, respectively. To make ends meet, Lyle and his wife reduced their expenses but racked up credit card debt and withdrew nearly all the funds from their retirement savings. Lyle also took on low-wage temp positions, which brought some welcome income into the household. Still, while his experience appears comparable to the stories narrated by Heather, Sara, and other respondents with hard falls, there was one crucial difference. "My wife," Lyle said, "has a good job, and she has good benefits." Spouses with well-paying jobs reduced the risk of downward mobility for respondents we classify as in between just as spouses did for those who experienced soft landings. While this situation demonstrates the importance of linked lives for negotiating the job loss experience, five male respondents, including Lyle, felt emasculated. "[I] have a diminished sense of being a provider in the family," noted Victor, a former director in financial services who was having difficulty locating permanent employment after his 2012 downsizing. Such remarks expose the tenacity of traditional gender norms, which frame breadwinning as a male activity and, much to the chagrin of heterosexual working wives, domestic labor as a female activity.

Four respondents had experienced late-career job loss so recently before our interviews that it was unclear where they would land on the hard falls/soft landings continuum. Sean in his early fifties, was two months into his downsizing, as were Benjamin, Martin, and Cat, who were in their sixties. All were receiving unemployment benefits when they were interviewed; when these benefits expired, Benjamin, Martin, and Cat's ages gave them the option of beginning their Social Security benefits. Sean and other younger respondents lacked this choice.[46] Perhaps this additional resource informed Cat's assurance that her late-career job loss would not result in financial ruin: "Unlike 80 percent of the world, I will not go to bed hungry. I will not go to bed without electricity. I will not go to bed without food. I will not go to bed without a warm blanket. . . . And I will never experience that in my lifetime."

"Keep Young and Beautiful, If You Want to Be Loved"

Americans tend to stigmatize people who experience job loss, unfairly assuming they are somehow at fault. Perceived shortcomings of the unemployed include not working hard enough to find a job and failing to save enough money to survive job loss financially intact.[47] Such accusations, however, do not consider the wider historical context in which a termination occurs or the social structural factors that lead to variations in dismissal and rehiring experiences.

Our interviewees were laid off during a global economic crisis that lasted well beyond the official end of the Great Recession. Their abilities to manage this experience without succumbing to downward mobility depended on several factors, with gender being paramount. Whether a person was male or female structured their employment path and later shaped how well they were positioned at dismissal. Just as in the larger labor market, the men in our sample tended to be better positioned and therefore more likely to experience soft landings.[48] Linked lives mattered, too. Individuals with spouses employed full-time in well-paying jobs were better equipped to avoid downward mobility, as were respondents whose parents could provide generous financial assistance. Employer type was another critical factor. Respondents who were dismissed from large corporations with employee pensions and unemployment assistance were simply better off. Industry type was important to the extent that respondents working in high-demand fields tended to find new jobs more quickly. Finally, age mattered. Respondents who were old enough to apply for Social Security benefits and Medicare had a broader social safety net than younger respondents.

Despite this breadth of postdismissal experiences, there was one pervasive thing nagging most of our respondents: ageism in the labor market. Age discrimination increased markedly during and after the Great Recession, resulting in older workers being the first fired and the last hired.[49] No study of unemployment among older workers would be complete without considering how this form of discrimination can compound the problems of job loss. When psychiatrist, activist, and Pulitzer Prize–winning author Robert Butler coined the term *ageism* in the late 1960s, he argued that it is both similar to and often related to other forms of discrimination.[50] In contrast to most other social biases, however, none of us can escape ageism.

Butler acknowledged that both the young and old can be victims of age bias, though he spent most of his career exploring ageism against older adults. He concluded that ageism for this group involves the "systematic stereotyping" of older people as "senile, rigid in thought and manner, [and] old-fashioned in morality and skills."[51] Ageism also encompasses individual attitudes and behaviors, such as younger people's expressions of disdain for, dislike of, and desire to avoid older people. As you will learn in our next chapter, this contempt was highly visible early in the COVID-19 pandemic when memes such as #Boomer-Remover populated social media. As a recent headline from the American Psychological Association states, "Ageism is one of the last socially acceptable prejudices."[52]

Discriminatory practices are born from the myths, attitudes, and biases we have about older adults. These practices lead to poorer outcomes for older adults in many realms, including health care, housing, employment, and unemployment, as many of our respondents note.[53] Ageism also shapes how older individuals view themselves. Research confirms that the internalization of ageist stereotypes can negatively impact a person's physical, cognitive, and mental health.[54] Given the ageist labor market experiences our interviewees reported, it is little wonder so many described mental health struggles.

In the United States employment discrimination on the basis of age is prohibited by law. The 1967 Age Discrimination in Employment Act (ADEA) makes it illegal to hire, fire, pay, promote, or otherwise treat an employee on the basis of their age as opposed to their ability.[55] But plenty of illegal things are commonplace, including some of the ways employers skirt anti-ageism laws in the hiring process. It is illegal to ask directly about age on a job application, but all you need is an applicant's high school graduation date to estimate their birth year.[56] As one of our respondents, Teresa, sarcastically quipped, "It doesn't take ... Einstein to do the math there." Legal prohibitions also dictate how employee terminations can be conducted. Minnesota employers, for instance, can eliminate an employee for any reason except those deemed discriminatory, with age being one of eleven grounds.[57] In spite of this legislation, our respondents noticed the disproportionate number of older colleagues who were laid off with them and the preponderance of older adults attending Minnesota's numerous job clubs (we will explore these job clubs in chapter 4). Many also discovered they had been replaced by "younger people [with] lower salaries."

Management scholar Stephen Fineman observes that "our CVs and biographies are saturated with age signposts, embedded in our education and work history."[58] In an ideal world, age and experience would be seen as objective testaments to a job candidate's strength. Years of experience in successively more senior positions in a given industry indeed convey both broad and deep industry-specific knowledge but, when viewed through an ageist lens, look like signs of a potential poor fit when hiring panels assume an applicant is too old for a given position. Our interviewees confirmed that older workers are imagined to be poorer performers, resistant to change and learning new skills, prone to sickness and absenteeism, or too expensive to hire and retain because their amassed experience merits higher salaries than younger employees, or their insurance costs will be too high and their benefit payouts too near in the future. Fineman enumerates these stereotypes and more, citing research that dispels each, no matter how tenaciously the falsehoods persist in many workplace practices.[59]

Mechanisms such as the ADEA and state-level legislation are not sufficient safeguards against age discrimination, especially when ageism can be as subtle as what our respondents experienced in job interviews: "a pregnant pause," "a feeling," or an irrelevant question like "How long have you been married?" or "When did you graduate from this college or high school?" Legal policies may even be associated with increased adverse effects on older workers, possibly because age discrimination laws create higher termination costs, which in turn dissuade employers from hiring older workers in the first place.[60] Recognizing that age was hindering their own job searches and regarding legal protections as too cumbersome to pursue, our interviewees took matters into their own hands. They engaged in several strategies to combat age bias in their labor market interactions.

For example, conceding that they were no longer "spring chickens," a popular idiom within our sample, respondents believed it was vitally important to appear younger than they actually were. Cassandra told us that she advised a friend who was also unemployed: "One of the things that you're going to have to do, like we all do, is become a chameleon. You have to look younger. You have to act younger. You have to speak younger. You really do. You have to stay hip." Cassandra practiced what she preached but regretted not being able to afford "Botox or anything for my face, you know." At that point in the interview, Cassandra spontaneously broke into song: "Keep young and beautiful, if you want to be loved."[61]

Several respondents embraced Cassandra's advice. Beth showed up to job interviews dressed "younger" and "overtly . . . energetic and enthusiastic and willing to learn." Dylan also tried to appear "energized" and "enthusiastic" as well as "technologically in the know" and "savvy." Sara, on the other hand, was pleased that her use of current "buzzwords," "memes," and particular "concepts" meant that her younger colleagues were not aware of how old she was. Kai discussed not acting his age, which meant that "people don't usually expect that I'm over fifty."

Interviewees also engaged in various forms of body and beauty work. Losing weight was a common strategy for masking one's age. Charles lost thirty pounds, Victor lost twenty, and Kirk lost ten "cuz I was fat," though Kirk made this comment in relation to a recruiter telling him to dye his gray hair, which he refused to do. Olivia understood she was "competing against other younger people" so she "went to Medifast and ... lost some weight." This decision, as Olivia continued explaining, was also prompted by being denied medical coverage "based on my body mass index." Comments like these convey that our respondents had internalized a combination of age and weight biases, much in line with a societal context that associates being young and slim with being attractive and desirable, among other qualities.[62] Physical exercise was another strategy our respondents used to appear younger than they were. Sean had a vigorous full-body workout schedule that included meeting "with a personal trainer a couple times a week." As a former creative director in an industry dominated by young people, he believed "if I am fifty-two years old, I better not look like I'm an old man." Victor worked out in order to strengthen his "aerobic capacity." He felt it was important "if I'm meeting with somebody and we're walking somewhere, I'm not out of breath. I can carry out a conversation while we're walking." To him, this signaled vitality and youth.

Finally, some respondents employed cosmetic strategies to disguise their age. Charles shaved off his beard "because I wanted to look younger" and wore his hair in a buzz cut "just to remove some of the gray." Victor colored his hair and, due to blocked vision, had an eyelid lift that helped him feel and look younger. Kaaryn went so far as to have "a neck lift" so that prospective employers "can't tell my age." A 2018 study published in the *Aesthetic Surgery Journal* reports that almost one-third of the fifty patients surveyed were undergoing antiaging cosmetic surgery (e.g., Botox, fillers, breast implants, laser resurfacing) because of age discrimination in a variety of realms including the workplace.[63]

Undergoing the trials of job loss and with so much seemingly out of their control, many of our respondents attempted to assert agency in the search for new employment. They could not, for example, change their gender or suddenly gain access to well-resourced friends and family, but aware of the many ways their age might hinder their ability to move forward, some tried to turn back the clock through body and beauty work. It is unclear whether these efforts truly changed their trajectories or pushed them further toward the soft landings end of the spectrum of job loss experiences, but it may have been enough to help them regain a crucial sense of self-efficacy.

Isolated Problems and Individual Responses

In this chapter, we have introduced you to many of our interviewees and several of the individual and structural factors shaping their job loss experiences and subsequent searches for new employment. It is key to remember that they lost their jobs in a specific historical context—the Great Recession and its recovery—and during a life stage that employers typically do not favor. What happened next, whether a hard fall or a soft landing, had a great deal to do with linked lives and the availability of familial assistance. Though structural conditions largely dictated the job loss and unemployment experience, individual conditions and individual responses—the currency of neoliberalism—suffused the stories we were told. Think, for instance, of those who encountered ageism and responded by choosing to conceal their age. You will continue to meet these and other respondents throughout this book. In this chapter, we have also presented the four tenets of life course theory, tying them to the job loss experience and its immediate aftermath in these older Americans' lives. We will come back to life course theory most explicitly in chapter 5, where we see how these four tenets inform interviewees' job searches.

Notably, when we began writing this chapter, waves of protest were just beginning to roil France. In the face of pension reforms shifting the age of retirement from sixty-two to sixty-four, millions of protestors stormed into the streets, disrupting key services such as waste removal and public transportation for months. We are struck by the collective nature of this response and how it sharply contrasts with the ways our American respondents framed their late-career employment experiences. Rather than protesting their dismissals, their financial hardships, or widespread age discrimination on an institutional level, our respondents framed these as isolated problems and developed individual responses that lacked the political power of a unified voice. Absent structural responses to structural problems, they largely accepted their hard falls and soft landings and worked to navigate them to the best of their individual abilities. Neoliberalism, however, suffers no impediment when individuals choose to respond to structural problems in this way. In the pages that follow, we will explore several further related themes bound up in the neoliberal framework of our interviewees' lives: generationalism, religious coping, geographic (in)flexibility, and positive thinking.

3
Generations at Work

This chapter is about generational differences and how they manifest in our interviewees' interpretations of the workplace and job loss. We, your authors, were both born in 1968, right between the so-called Summer of Love and Woodstock's Three Days of Peace and Music. Social unrest, urban riots, and the assassinations of Robert F. Kennedy Sr. and Martin Luther King Jr. are among the key events that distinguished the year that "shattered America."[1] While we of course have no recollection of these events, we do share fond memories of listening to cassette tapes (with our Sony Walkmans!), talking to friends for hours on end (on our landline telephones!), and using computers for the first time to write essays (in college!). There are also not-so-fond memories of fearing nuclear war, acid rain, and a newly emerged disease called AIDS. We, in the words of novelist Douglas Coupland (who coined the term in 1991),[2] are members of Generation X. And, as you will see in this chapter, such generational identifiers are both significant and potentially problematic.

Our birth year marked the tail end of the post–World War II economy. As young children, we had no sense of the economic twists and turns that lay ahead: recessions, downsizings, outsourcings, and the emergence of a global, neoliberal economy that privileges deregulation, privatization, austerity measures, and individual responsibility. Instead, we were fed a steady diet of *Happy Days*, a popular 1970s sitcom that presented a nostalgic view of life in the American Midwest during the "golden decades" of the 1950s and '60s. This was a time when the economy was dominated by secure employment contracts, higher wages (once adjusted) than most workers earn today, and benefit schemes that catapulted many Americans into the middle class. When we graduated from high school in the mid-1980s, however, a new era had dawned: that of the neoliberal, flexible economy.

Like all the participants in our study, Helen's employment was affected by this new era. A dynamic and fiercely intelligent sixty-year-old, Helen needed two interview sittings to tell her whole story. Little about the most recent decade of her life had been particularly easy. Her lingering grief was evident as she recounted the much-too-soon passings of her sister and brother, the death of her father after years of decline following a catastrophic stroke, and a heartbreaking divorce due to the infidelity of a husband with whom she "was deeply in love." In her words, "there was loss everywhere." When we met Helen in August 2013, she was working part-time as a human resources consultant; her full-time hours had just been reduced because her employer had lost a lucrative contract.

This was not the only employment predicament Helen had encountered. Despite two advanced degrees, she was among our interviewees who experienced a hard fall. From 2007 to 2009, she weathered four job losses, the first of which she described as an unexpected "capstone" to the losses of the previous years, a harsh betrayal (coming at the hand of someone whom she considered a close friend), and a devastating blow to her identity. That first dismissal was, she confided, "Unbearable. *Un-freakin-bearable.*" By the time she had endured the fourth, Helen's job losses had overturned her middle-class life and pushed her over the edge emotionally and financially: "I lost everything during that . . . two and a half years of unemployment. Everything! . . . My townhome was foreclosed on. My credit was destroyed . . . I had nothing. I was living on money from friends and a little bit of money my mother would give me—she was making my car payments. I had nothing. I was getting food stamps . . . [and] I was getting welfare."

Even at just part-time, the consulting job had come as a lifeline; with it, she had begun to bounce back from the years of losses. And, while our conversation with Helen did not focus much on the nature of her consulting, she mentioned teaching organizations how to "manage and motivate" different generations at work. Helen referenced the baby boomers, Generation X, and Generation Y—otherwise known as "the millennials"—and commented that each group had different characteristics, values, and ambitions. That meant, to Helen, that each needed different types of employment "incentives" to thrive in the workplace.

All the interviewees in this book are baby boomers, and many of them referenced generations in the workplace during their conversations with us. As we discussed in chapter 1, throughout their working lives, each interviewee had experienced what could be called a generational shift in the employment contract and its accompanying values and expectations. In this chapter, you will hear how they understood themselves in generational terms and interpreted the shift they experienced using some of the same concepts and assumptions that

Helen employed in her consulting. They spoke with nostalgia about the employment security they saw buoy their parents' generation and, often, with disdain for what they saw as the younger generations' lack of commitment and responsibility. But before we can look more closely at such comments and at some of the intergenerational tensions to which they give rise, we must first take a step back to review what sociologists and others mean when they invoke "generations." We hope you will keep this section in mind as you read about generations in this book and talk about them in your lives.

How Sociologists and Others Think about Generations

The modern study of generations is attributed to Hungarian-born sociologist Karl Mannheim. In his influential essay, "The Problem of Generations,"[3] Mannheim postulated that when young people[4] born at the same moment in historical time experience a momentous social, political, or economic event—examples for readers of this book might be the Great Depression, the Vietnam War, the Black Lives Matter movement, or a global pandemic—they organically develop a unified consciousness that informs their attitudes and behaviors and instills a shared sense of belonging. Mannheim's idea that defining historical moments can produce within a cohort of young people a collective mindset and greater unity lives on in more current scholarship.[5]

Today generations are popularly distinguished by a span of birth years associated with a demographic trend. Perhaps the most widely acknowledged generational label is the one that is most relevant to our study: that of the baby boomers. The Pew Research Center, a prominent nonpartisan organization that conducts a wide variety of public opinion, polling, and demographic research routinely based on generations as an independent variable, defines the baby boomers as a generation born in the United States from 1946, the end of World War II, to 1964.[6] In this period, the United States experienced a sharp increase in fertility rates (a baby boom). The baby boom generation is further associated with the rebounding postwar economy (an economic boom) and with considerable social upheaval within U.S. society and beyond.[7] That said, the precise years defining this generation differ from account to account. Management consultants Lynne Lancaster and David Stillman employ a slightly expanded time span of 1945 to 1964,[8] while generational theorists William Strauss and Neil Howe use an earlier range, 1943 to 1960,[9] to bookend the baby boom generation. The Pew Research Center has also demographically delineated the Silent Generation (born 1928 to 1945), Generation X (born 1965 to 1980), and the millennial generation (born 1981 to 1996),[10] with the dates ascribed to each varying widely in other sources.[11]

As anyone familiar with the once-ubiquitous "OK boomer" meme can attest, what political scientist Jonathan White has called "generationalism"[12] or "generation-talk" has seeped more broadly into the public sphere where "often, and increasingly, social and political life is narrated using the concept of generation."[13] The phrase "OK boomer" began to circulate widely on the video sharing platform TikTok in 2019. It captured broader media attention in November of that year when Chlöe Swarbrick, a twenty-five-year-old New Zealand parliamentarian, used it as a retort to an older colleague who heckled her while she spoke on a climate change bill.[14] Generally speaking, "OK boomer" is used to dismiss and critique a generation seen to be ignorant of important sociocultural trends and out of touch with, if not directly culpable for, the dire environmental and economic realities of the current age. Social media discourse about generations took a more vicious turn early in the COVID-19 pandemic as content deeming the virus a #BoomerRemover made the rounds.[15] Memes and social media aside, politicians and journalists have used generationalism as an ideational framework that has stoked intergenerational conflict for decades. Today, the baby boom generation is no longer only a convenient shorthand to describe a demographic phenomenon. As cultural critic Margaret Morganroth Gullette notes, the popular label is now akin to libel,[16] positioning selfish and aging boomers as denying economic stability to future generations.[17]

Helen's story points to yet another realm in which generational categorizations are common: that of the contemporary workplace. According to a wide variety of popular management books, the multigenerational workplace can be a tricky-to-navigate arena wherein different generations coexist uneasily, experience "friction,"[18] and even "collide"[19] or "clash"[20] given their purported differences in attitudes, abilities, values, and work styles.[21] Some scholars have tried to disentangle fact from stereotype, showing workplace generational differences in some cases but significant similarities in others.[22] Of course, management gurus have less motivation to parse generational stereotypes. As management expert Stephen Fineman observes, it can be beneficial for these practitioners to promote descriptions of generational differences and conflicts when they are also selling the solution to them.[23]

Along with the potential to stoke or overexaggerate intergenerational conflict, generational labels can be problematic in other ways. Some of these problems were summarized by sociology professor Philip N. Cohen in his 2021 *Washington Post* op-ed, "Generation Labels Mean Nothing. It's Time to Retire Them."[24] In the piece, Cohen argues that generation labels are imprecise and unscientific and that they do more harm than good. Characterizing these labels as "either embarrassing stereotypes or caricatures with astrology-level vagueness,"[25] he asserts that broad generational categories fail to capture the diversity of experiences within generations based on race, socioeconomic status, gender, and other personal characteristics (indeed, Cohen notes that Michelle Obama and Donald Trump, two diametrically opposed political figures, are both baby boomers). Intragenerational diversity is frequently noted by other scholars,[26] and this phenomenon is illustrated in the previous chapter to the extent that some of the boomers we interviewed had hard falls, while others had soft landings. The argument in Cohen's op-ed corresponds to his more collegial and academic open letter to the Pew Research Center itself, urging the think tank to stop using generation labels in their research.[27] To its credit, in May 2023 Pew released a statement describing similar downsides to their existing generational labels[28] and another one announcing that, moving forward, they would refrain from using these labels when not appropriate.[29]

We agree that generational labels and generationalism overall can be problematic. But what should we do? Sociological critique aside, Helen and so many other people in our study frequently drew on, unprompted, broad generational differences and stereotypes when discussing conflicts and frustrations in their neoliberal workplace. Whether these interviewees used Pew-style generational labels or simply referred to the older/younger generation,[30] generation-talk was common and clearly meaningful to them. As such, and to paraphrase what is known in sociology as the Thomas theorem,[31] generational distinctions, perceived to be real, are real in their consequences. Accordingly, we follow the lead of scholars who concentrate not on verifying the validity of generational categories per se but rather on exploring how they function in practice to help people make sense of the social world[32] and particularly how they function to organize understandings of age at work.[33] Of course, this inclination of ours also responds to the life course perspective we use throughout this book.

Two tenets of life course sociology are particularly salient to this chapter. Echoing Mannheim's assertion, the first tenet is that generations, like individuals, are situated in historical time and context.[34] Life course scholars have found that large-scale events transpiring in individuals' earlier years leave an imprint on their later behaviors, attitudes, and paths chosen.[35] The idea of a complex interplay between historical time and human lives resonates with a central claim of this chapter: two specific socioeconomic and cultural contexts, the age of security and the neoliberal age of flexibility, shaped the career trajectories of our boomer interviewees, and later informed their comments about different generations in relation to the workplace.

A second relevant tenet of the life course perspective, which builds on the first, is that historical change impacts different generations of people differently.[36] As we will discuss, with the emergence and entrenchment of neoliberalism, our interviewees experienced—in vivo—a major historical, organizational, and ideological transformation. They began their careers in and had their expectations shaped by a historical moment that offered job stability and secure retirements for valued employees, then they experienced the Great Recession and late-career job loss in an era that privileges individual autonomy over corporate responsibility. One can imagine the cognitive dissonance of negotiating two contrary sets of employment expectations in a single career.

Our interviewees' younger colleagues, on the other hand, came to the workplace already socialized in the ideas of the neoliberal flexible economy. In this regard, they lack lived experience with an earlier set of conditions more favorable to the physical, mental, and financial health of employees and so they understandably negotiate the postrecession era in a different manner. Whether our interviewees recognized this or not, they were right, in some sense, that the younger generations in their workplaces had a different relationship with employment.

Next, we will explore how our interviewees' impressions of generational differences give them an important interpretive framework for addressing the frustrations and conflicts of the neoliberal workplace. We will also dig into the ways their beliefs about generation-based characteristics are analytically and politically crucial for reinforcing neoliberalism.

Talkin' 'bout My Generation

More than half of our interviewees ($N = 39$) talked about generations when discussing their job loss experience. These comments, which were unprompted, are perhaps not surprising given the ubiquity of generation-talk in our culture and the reality of our current multigenerational labor force. Minnesota's Department of Employment and Economic Development recently identified six generations coexisting in the state's workforce: Generation Z, millennials, Generation X, baby boomers, and the Silent and Greatest Generations.[37] When interviewees addressed generational differences, however, their comments mainly focused on three specific groups from this list: themselves, baby boomers; their parents, the Silent Generation; and their younger colleagues, the millennials.

Our Study Interviewees: Boomers

Demographics put the *boom* in the baby boom. Between 1946 and 1964, seventy-six million babies were born in the United States,[38] far more than in the periods immediately before and after. This population explosion led to a twentieth-century demographic pattern commonly, if rather distastefully, described as "the python that swallowed a pig." Just look at the dramatic curvature of the line on any chart tracking age trends in the United States, and the baby boom undeniably sticks out.

Even Philip Cohen, a harsh critic of generational labels,[39] would concede that the boomer cohort shared several formative sociocultural experiences. Many boomers, especially those who are White, benefited from post–World War II economic prosperity and grew up to enjoy widespread material comforts and broad access to higher education and employment. As young adults, they often possessed an expectation that things would continue to get better,[40] and they tried to make it so themselves through a variety of social movements—think hippies and flower power, feminism, and the Civil Rights Movement. They also weathered the Vietnam War, a presidential assassination, and the first Moon landing[41]—moments of great triumph and terror that shaped how they saw the world as they built their own careers, formed families, and began to move toward middle age.

But there are lots of differences across this cohort, too. Age is the easiest to recognize since the boomers' births span nearly two decades. Experts often distinguish between the "leading-edge" boomers, born 1946–1954, and "trailing-edge" boomers, born 1955 and later.[42] In our study, 40 percent of interviewees were between sixty and sixty-eight years old at the time of our original research, making them leading-edge boomers, while the remainder were between the ages of fifty and fifty-nine, the trailing edge of the generation. These two cohorts differ dramatically in rates of military service, with more than twice as many leading-edge boomers being veterans. There is also a difference in marriage rates, with trailing-edge boomers being somewhat less likely to marry.[43] Moreover, older boomers report engaging in a narrower range of online activities than younger ones,[44] which could be detrimental at a time when LinkedIn and online job applications are central to searching for new employment.

However, the entire boomer cohort is experiencing or has experienced life course challenges we would expect to be compounded by job loss. Given that they are now in middle adulthood, boomers are often sandwiched between their children and at least one of their parents. They face the pressures of caring and providing financial support for both older and younger family members, even beyond the time when their children are minors (we explore some of the implications of this life stage for interviewees' job searches in chapter 5).[45] And, while boomers were often associated with optimism and idealism in their youth, they more recently have been labeled "gloomy" and "glum." The Pew Research Center reveals that 80 percent are dissatisfied with the direction the country is heading,[46] a majority feel that their children's standard of living will be worse than their own, and they report the lowest self-rated quality of life of all age groups (though younger boomers are slightly more optimistic on some measures than older ones).[47]

Beyond what the statistics and scholars say, we are most interested in our interviewees' own interpretation of generational categories and their features. Indeed, while we asked interviewees to provide their year of birth, they often spoke about their own generational identities as the conversation unfolded. A few interviewees referred to themselves as baby boomers or called themselves "older workers" or "the older generation." Some also described themselves in relation to defining events or motivations associated with the boomers. For example, Benjamin stated that "the dawning of the Age of Aquarius" informed his youthful desire to seek employment that would make a "difference" in the world. Similar sentiments were expressed by Isaac: "For those of us who grew up in the sixties and seventies, we wanted to change the world . . . and some of us did." Helen reminisced about key events of her formative years, including the Vietnam War protests, the Civil Rights Movement, and her participation in student activism. She and Stephanie and Meg also referenced the implications of women's increasing labor force participation rates as they were beginning their own careers. Stephanie, a former creative director, had fond memories of this time: "Women were just hitting strides and it was great. It was great. Yeah, really good." For Helen, who also immersed herself in the feminist movement in the 1970s, this time was particularly empowering: "I was literally, in my mind, invincible. I literally had a sense of invincibility. . . . And I just remembered, you know, just thinking, 'I can do *anything*.'"

Significantly, some interviewees reflected on how privileged they were, either when they were seeking jobs or when they were at the height of their earning power. Kaleb recalled, "In 1979, when I graduated from college, every time you applied [for a job], you would get an interview. That was so cool. No matter where you applied, you would get an interview. And you could probably get an offer that you could accept or turn down." Helen also painted a picture of her generation in the heady days of the 1990s, which she labeled "an amusement park ride" and "a candy store," when "we saw nothing but blue sky." Her own economic situation was particularly prosperous: "Oh God, I remember the nineties. Oh what a sweet rise that was. That was crazy. I was spending money like water. I had the dual income, no kids . . . we would go out and buy an antique piece of furniture for a thousand dollars. We had so much money piled up. It was ridiculous. We really did a lot of uh, acquiring during that period." Certainly, as we noted in chapter 2, such privilege can set up a harder-they-fall dynamic, something to which Helen herself alluded: "And then it just crashed. And we were not prepared for this. We did not have this in our script."

A couple of interviewees also displayed an awareness of intragenerational variation among boomers. During her interview, for example, sixty-eight-year-old Meg noted how the job loss struggles of some in their fifties would be different from those of someone in their sixties, in part because the latter would be eligible for Social Security and Medicare. She also noted a divide between those boomer women who were married with children and those who were single and without kids. That said, the overwhelming majority of our sample did not make such distinctions. They were comfortable referring to "we" and "our generation" when they spoke about the boomer cohort.

Nowhere was this sense of shared generational identity more evident than when interviewees compared their own generation with those of relatives and workers both older and younger. Such comparisons also showcase the generationalism in interviewees' interpretation of their (un)employment experiences and give us a further glimpse into how they saw themselves and others in an environment that had shifted from the age of security to the age of flexibility during their lifetimes.

Depression-Era Parents

Most of our study participants' parents would have been members of what is commonly labeled the Silent Generation. Born from 1928 through 1945, the Silent Generation lived through the Great Depression and World War II as children.[48] In part, this is why our interviewees most commonly referred to their parents as the "generation that grew up in the Depression." Before reviewing comments in more detail, it is important to restate that interviewees identified as White. In this regard, their perceptions of a former time period are filtered by the various advantages and opportunities Whiteness offered specifically to their parents, such as homeownership in safe and attractive communities, preferred job opportunities, and wages that exceeded those available to BIPOC or racialized individuals.[49] In our conversations, these boomers were sometimes grateful for, sometimes resentful of, and sometimes in awe of the older generation's experiences and positions, but they all clearly understood their own situations against the backdrop of their parents' privileges. Some interviewees spoke about the financial assistance their Depression-era parents provided after their job loss. For example, when Isaac was unable to secure steady employment after his 2008 dismissal, his wealthy father subsequently "passed on a sizable amount of money" that funded a comfortable early retirement for Isaac and his wife. Christopher, a project manager who lost his job in 2011, received financial support from his widowed mother. He attributed his mother's generosity in part to her experience of living through the Great Depression: "Coming out of the Depression . . . many of them put things together in a way so they could retire . . . comfortably . . . and help their kids, [and] keep helping their kids." Christopher additionally acknowledged the lucrative salary his father earned in the post–World War II economy, which he discovered after his father died: "My father . . . had done what some tax attorneys will tell you to do: he had every tax return from 1948, their entire marriage. It was kind of fascinating to look at those, at least briefly, and to see what a small sum of money he made in 1950 . . . but then at the end, he was in the $200,000 to $300,000 range. He was doing incredibly well." Christopher, like other interviewees, was painfully aware of how different his own situation was shaping up to be from that of his parents'.

Not every interviewee had parents who were, or could be, as generous as Christopher's widowed mother. Sara was furious that her mother and father, "Depression-era babies," refrained from providing any financial assistance after Sara's 2011 layoff due to economic restructuring. Two years later, at her 2013 interview, Sara reported she was earning $13 an hour at a job she acquired through a temp agency; this meager income was a considerable departure from her former middle-class salary. Sara's resentment toward her "selfish" parents was visibly apparent during her interview.

Other interviewees spoke about the disciplined mindset their parents instilled in them regarding money management. For example, Tad's parents, whom he identified as "children of the Depression," influenced his savings habits to the extent that he could embark on an early retirement after his 2012 downsizing: "My parents are both children of the Depression, and that's rubbed off in a major way. The house is paid off, I had the money for my kids' college.... Maybe we need to make a few choices going forward, but we're fine." Felix, a fifty-eight-year-old former data manager who was effectively retired after his dismissal two years earlier, also benefited from the financial habits his Depression-era parents modeled. In the following quote, Felix expresses gratitude for the "very simple life" he experienced as a child: "I remember when I was young, my dad just started his own business in the early sixties, so I was about seven, eight, nine years old.... One thing I do remember is having oatmeal for dinner, or an egg and toast. And I didn't feel like I was missing out on anything. And then, you know... my dad fixed everything." Felix's comment, "I didn't feel like I was missing out on anything," suggests a nostalgic view of the prudent ways of a previous generation.

Helen likewise crafted a romantic account of the leisurely retirement her working-class father had in his final years: "[My father] retired at... sixty. He spent twenty-five years on a railroad pension just hanging out. Because it was like, oh my God, all [he] did was just hang out—for twenty-five years. [My parents] went to Ireland, they went to Hawaii.... All they did was play for twenty-five years.... His gross income was probably $30,000 or something. I mean, everything was paid for; it's... completely fascinating... that anybody could live like that."

The awe Helen expresses conveys an awareness that her father's retirement experience is unfathomable from a contemporary standpoint. Many interviewees recognized the extent to which their financial standing was diminished in the current socioeconomic context, regardless of their white-collar backgrounds and educational credentials, a sense that was amplified in comparison to the prosperity they perceived in their parents' later years. As Dawn stated, "It's bleak; it is comically dark; it is depressing. I'm of the generation that was supposed to have it better than my parents... [but] this generation does not have it as good as the one before. It is really sad."

Some interviewees acknowledged stressful interactions with parents who were unaware of the employment landscape negotiated by older, unemployed white-collar workers from 2007 to 2014. Mark, a former account manager who had difficulty securing steady employment after his 2009 dismissal, was particularly annoyed by his mother-in-law's frequent question: "Well, how many jobs have you applied for today?" Mark's irritation stemmed from a series of constraints he and other interviewees reported: limited job opportunities for older white-collar workers like himself; frustratingly tedious and time-consuming online employment application systems; the necessity of making time for networking; and employer responses that suggested a preference for hiring younger workers. When contrasting her father's thirty-five-year career with the same employer to her own "ricocheting around," Marie noted that her parents would naively ask, "Why can't you just get a job and stay there?" "Well," she responded, "it's not in my power to do that." Stephanie summarized a similar lack of comprehension when commenting on her own parents: "They've been retired for thirty years and they have pensions and they have, you know, all the things we all thought we'd have. So, um, they kind of don't understand any of this. They've always had the same job, they had the same job throughout all their life. They got the gold watch, the fruit basket, retired at fifty-nine. . . . They don't understand things like not having health care because you can't afford it. And they don't understand moving job to job either." Through such comparisons, interviewees demonstrated their awareness of how the employment context had transitioned since their parents were in the labor force.

Charles fleshed out this argument by drawing on the example set by his father-in-law: "My father-in-law . . . worked at [his employer] for forty-two years. Forty-two years. And you don't see that anymore. You don't see people staying with one company [for] more than two or three years now. And I think that's the accepted role of employees today. I think the expectation is employees are not going to stay. And I think the companies . . . in turn treat the employees as temporary." Charles's acknowledgment of the flexible employment contract, one that treats employees as "temporary," was repeated by Margaret, a clerical worker who was downsized from a job she loved in 2012. Margaret began her commentary by sharing some employment advice once offered by her father: "My father always said, 'you find a good job [and] you stay there,' because that's the generation he was from. You find one, you stay there. And I think nowadays you don't. You get your experience, you get what you can from that company, learn as much as you can, and you move on and take your experience and get more money."

Margaret's transactional view—"you get what you can" from your employer and then "move on"—is revealing. At sixty-one years of age, Margaret's career began in an era characterized by job security and the still relevant memories of her father's employment experiences. She and other interviewees now appear to have internalized the idea of a short-term employment relationship, which emerged with the neoliberal flexible economy. Overall, our interviewees' experiences in the aftermath of the Great Recession reinforced the stark contrast between their own lives and those of their parents who, although they might have had difficult childhood experiences during the Depression and World War II, experienced an adulthood of relative security and stability.

Younger Workers

Kids these days! Regardless of your generation, chances are, you have a few ideas about how the younger generation goes about their lives. For our interviewees, those "kids" were the younger workers in their midst—most of whom were millennials. According to the Pew Research Center, this group was born after 1980 and thus were "the first generation to come of age in the new millennium."[50] None of our respondents used that term; however, sometimes they mentioned "Generation Y" (an alternative moniker for the millennials) or even Generation X. Most often, our interviewees preferred "the younger generation" or "kids today," with a generally disapproving tone.

At the most superficial level, we heard off-the-cuff remarks that belittled or diminished younger workers, often by reducing younger people to their ages. Vanessa and Sally, for example, each shared a specific fear of finding jobs that required working "with a bunch of twentysomethings." Kaleb mentioned a job opportunity that also attracted the attention of "two young whippersnappers," while Cat referred to "the one little thirty-year-old in the room" who was downsized at the same time as Cat. Along with labeling adults in their twenties and thirties "kids," such dismissive phrasing hints at the more significant judgments of the younger workforce our interviewees expressed.

Many of the people we talked to felt that, especially when compared with themselves, younger workers were missing appropriate life experience and the skills to perform their jobs well. Our interviewees often characterized these former coworkers as "clueless" or "lacking expertise." Cat, downsized from her job in health care in 2014, spoke at length:

> And we're now letting policies [be] made, that are gonna be about fifty- or sixty-year-old people, are now being made and implemented by thirty-year-olds who have no life experiences and who have no, no insight into life and who don't have a clue what a sixty-year-old needs in terms of managing their health.... So they are clueless to the reality of life.... They don't have, they don't have any expertise and they don't know what they don't—they don't know what they don't know. And they're not *interested* in knowing because if they knew, if they went out and did that, they'd find out how incompetent they are.

Other interviewees spoke about how younger workers were not "masters of their craft" or how productivity has diminished because, as Kirk asserted, "that's what we lost four years ago by firing all the old people." Lyle had a remedy for such situations, however. The former sales director was particularly agitated that his "thirty-plus years of work experience" could not compete with "some kid [who] comes out of college with great grades and a marketing degree." But, as he said, "let me bring my experience. Okay, you hire a bunch of kids fresh out there. 'Come on, you little kids, let's go. Let me, let Grandpa show you how to sell something.'"

Interviewees' comments about different generations' use of technology were more mixed. Lyle continued his rant by mocking a young person's imagined sales approach: "'Can I just text him?'" After an eye roll and a pause, Lyle responded, "No, you can't; you have to go out and sell it." On the other hand, Kirk described finally learning how to text—well before his 2014 interview—because his boss did ("It's not that hard"), and Marie celebrated her ability to "work right alongside people much younger than me and be right there with the technology, the software... the understanding." Still, Martie appeared concerned that her employment prospects might be jeopardized because she was "part of a generation that wasn't born to technology, where it's just a part of how I think," and Kaaryn lamented how online employment workshops were less accessible to her: "I mean, maybe the younger generation can get it—I can't." This range of attitudes is a reminder of the complexity beyond popular assertions about digital divides and generalizations about boomers and technology.[51]

There were other comments that aligned with some popular but unflattering stereotypes about the workplace attitudes of millennials.[52] Sally, for example, echoed a common assumption about entitlement when she critiqued younger colleagues: "They're not willing to spend the time to—how do I want to say this? [sigh] They don't see that they have to pay their dues in any way, shape, or form. [They say,] 'If I don't like it, I'm going to move on to the next thing.' And then the other piece of it is, 'Well, I've been here six months, and I've done a good job; now I need a raise, or I need to be promoted.' They want to go through those stages quickly." Similarly, Lyle referred to "these kids" as "little butterflies" who flit from job to job rather than loyally staying in a position and learning to master it.

When casting these aspersions, interviewees revealed an us-versus-them stance fortified with resentment. Margaret's comments are illustrative:

> The older generation, we have so much [more] to give than the younger people. We have experience, we have the loyalty—if someone can back us up on that. We have the "We're gonna be there every friggin day"... and they don't care. They don't put [in] 100 percent. "It's a job, it's money, I'm going home, that's it." It's not like what we can offer. We have so much to offer. And what are we doing? Being greeters at Walmart. Or being receptionists. Volunteering our time at the hospitals and stuff like that. [sigh] It's sad... the older generation has so much more to offer than the younger people.

Margaret continued in this vein, stressing how older workers put in more effort and how, although the "younger ones" might have more "get-up-and-go," people her age have the mentality of "Yeah, let's get up and get this done, you know? Let's move!" Whereas younger colleagues, she said, would respond to a request by asking, "Really? You want me to do that?" Margaret noted someone like her would simply "get the job done. Tell me what to do and I'll do it."

Beyond echoing the generation-talk frequently heard in the media and popular culture, these comments both reveal and help construct our interviewees' characterizations of themselves and their own generation. We learned from these remarks that our interviewees saw not just themselves but their entire generation as dedicated, experienced, hardworking, and skilled workers. Such a self-understanding not only was inspired by their dismissals but, in being tied to the employment expectations they had gleaned earlier in their careers and from observing their parents, made their job loss and continued unemployment all the more difficult to tolerate.

Interviewees' own experiences with ageism (a topic we explored in chapter 2) added to the mix, and discussions of it sometimes surfaced more generation-talk. Sara, for example, voiced a complaint about a younger "HR person" who appeared to lose interest in hiring Sara after reviewing her résumé: "She asked me to send her a résumé, and I did; and she said, 'I want to talk to you early next week,' and I said, 'Your schedule is busier than mine, so just give me a couple of dates and I'll respond as quickly as possible.' And then I never heard [back].... I think this happens with a lot of Generation Y—she's Generation Y—and I think she looked at my résumé and went, 'Oh, well, she's kind of older.'" Sara's conclusion that she was an individual victim of ageist hiring practices was complemented by others' observations that members of their own generation were replaced en masse by younger workers. This certainly was Margaret's experience: "They hired again when they let us go. They hired all of the younger people, because that's all the company is now, is younger people for innovation." Believing that such replacements were to the detriment of the company never dampened the hurt that came with feeling ousted by young, inexperienced "whippersnappers." Whether "twentysomethings" were the architects of ageism as human resources reps or simply the undeserving beneficiaries of such discrimination, our interviewees' stories were pockmarked with a sense of intergenerational conflict.

From Conflict to Compassion and Commonalities?

In some cases, the people we spoke with pulled back from generationalism's blame game to reveal a degree of compassion for and commiseration with younger workers. Sometimes people talked about the financial difficulties of the younger generation or about "feeling bad" for college kids who would graduate into a constantly changing labor market. And Kirk could not bring himself to blame younger folks for their lack of initiative, expressing with empathy that "they don't stick their neck out. They don't. Why would they? We are shifting into apathy and fear, because you're always looking over your shoulder like, 'I could be downsized at any moment, at any time.'" Here, Kirk recognizes that younger people's ability to live up to a valorized work ethic forged in the age of security has been diminished by neoliberal change.[53]

Also notable was the advice some interviewees offered, at least rhetorically, to the younger generation. Stephanie, for example, "would tell any young person today . . . if you work for a corporation, don't be loyal. Just do a great—do your job the best you can. Be an excellent employee, but don't give a rat's ass. *Do not be loyal.*" Sally similarly spoke about advising her own kids to "move from place to place, because you're not going to make better if you don't broaden your experiences and become more versatile so you can kind of slide into a variety of things." She expressed that what she called this "jaded view" stemmed from experiencing firsthand how hard work and commitment were no longer valued. Others came to the same conclusions, with Isaac's numerous job losses teaching him that "it's really dangerous to tie yourself to a specific job, to a specific set of tasks and commitments" and Margaret saying that she no longer took her computer home with her to check in while on vacation and that she would never again give a company her 100 percent loyalty.

It can look a lot like hypocrisy when some of these interviewees advise others to embrace the same attitudes around loyalty and commitment that they often judged in the younger generation. But the insights people shared with us are not moot.[54] We think, instead, that these comments reflect their internal back-and-forth, containing both a culturally common generationalism as well as a hint of a critique toward the culture of neoliberalism. Their sympathies and advice for younger workers and admission of their own attitude changes stem from their experiences and observations of layoffs and lack of employer loyalty in the era of flexibility. As Roberta understood, "I don't really think that anybody feels secure anymore, which is sad. It's a statement on our society that money is more important than people." Here, Roberta is not saying that the problematic generational shift involves the changed attitude or expectations of those she labeled "the young people." Instead, she implies the issue is the changed societal contract—and that it is affecting everybody.

Indeed, some interviewees avoided judgmental generation-talk and spoke about how the different generations were in the same socioeconomic boat. Caroline talked about how her "heart goes out to young college graduates as much as it does to older people." She broached this subject when she described what she called her "aha" moment in 2008, when she realized that what is frequently denigrated as entitlement should actually be considered a justified call for the rights of all—young and old—to have access to housing, a living wage, and the ability to support a family. Nathan, for his part, was very clear about who was to blame and who benefited when he was "replaced with someone half [his] age who made half [his] income." Tellingly, Nathan did not point fingers at the newer, younger employees but instead at the "millionaire" and the "independently wealthy shareholders" who were robbing people his age and their grandchildren of their financial security. As he elaborated,

> We continue to transfer wealth to the one percent by laying off people who would work until they're sixty for their grandkids, not for themselves. Laying off people in my age group. When private firms do it, they're not owned by poor people [laughs], you know what I mean? We're indirectly transferring wealth to the wealthier. Whether that job is outsourced to India or Vietnam or whatever, it continues that wealth transfer to the one percent. So, it's not about me. I don't look in the mirror and go, "Poor me." It's a much larger social pressure that continues to happen as wealth gets transferred to the wealthy.

We see in Nathan's reflections a salient recognition of neoliberalism's true nature, involving the upward redistribution of wealth.[55] Alongside Kirk's and Roberta's comments, these reflections also contain insightful allusions to macro-level forces that underlie the conditions other interviewees were experiencing and judging in the workplace.

A Generation Misplaced

In this chapter, we have reviewed the ways our interviewees understood themselves as part of a distinct generation, the baby boomers who came of age in the 1960s and 1970s. They frequently defined themselves and narrated their employment experiences by looking back at their parents' generation with nostalgia and forward to the generation of their offspring with disdain. In so doing, they reflected and reinforced the assertions of generational difference and conflict found in management handbooks and popular culture. By sharing their experiences and interpretations, our interviewees also revealed how both actual generational change and a more ideological generationalism are entwined with their experiences in the neoliberal era.

Recall that the rise of neoliberalism entails a shift away from the age of security, with its expectations of employer and employee loyalty, to an age of individual flexibility and responsibility. For our interviewees, the consequences of this progression often involved downsizing, long-term unemployment, and financial precarity—unpleasant to all but worse for the unprepared. The comments interviewees shared demonstrate their recognition of this unexpected but seismic shift toward an employment contract now emphasizing a short-term relationship between employers and employees, one that offers very few of the employment benefits that once afforded financial agency and security to many White families in the post–World II economy.

Interviewees' comments also revealed a paradox. On the one hand, their observations regarding the career trajectories of both older and younger generations demonstrate their awareness of the flexible employment relationships that emerged with the rise of neoliberalism. On the other hand, they criticized the younger workers who modeled the autonomy, individual self-interest, and narrow pursuit of economic gain that neoliberal actors are socialized to embrace.[56] As their comments make evident, the employment socialization our interviewees received during their formative years colored their judgments of present-day work values and employment relationships. In fact, only Kirk recognized that the oft-maligned work ethic of younger colleagues might be an appropriate response to the employment conditions of the neoliberal flexible economy. And with his diatribe against the 1 percent, only Nathan came close to recognizing that the real enemy was rooted in the neoliberal elite and not the younger generation. Other glimpses of compassion and understanding aside, most of our interviewees played the generational blame game.

It is important to recognize that generational rhetoric actually works to bolster neoliberalism. We all know the saying "divide and conquer." Well, neoliberal ideology is recognized for its self-serving ability to divide and isolate socioeconomic groups from one another.[57] Generationalism and its concomitant claims of generational discord fit here, too. Academic librarian John Buschman emphasizes the centrality of the market in neoliberalism. He helps us see that promoting generational characteristics as real (so that they can be marketed to) solidifies our cultural understanding of generations and reinforces the socially constructed differences between them.[58] Others have demonstrated that denigrating the older generation as overly privileged and selfish, often under the guise of intergenerational equity, simply provides an excuse to reduce state welfare and social services for all.[59] For their part, and despite the intergenerational sympathy and solidarity a few of our interviewees displayed, much of our interviewees' generation-talk revealed how they saw themselves as competing with the younger generation. This perception has both material roots in and cultural resonances with the neoliberal era, in which competition is always a prime value.[60] Each time our interviewees cast their blame at the younger generation, neoliberalism is buttressed.

Management gurus claim that the conflict between baby boomers and millennials in the workplace is a natural reflection of their clashing group personalities. That is a neat way of obscuring the fact that employer responses to the neoliberal economy—the downsizing of loyal long-term employees and a preference for young, technologically savvy, and untethered workers—are themselves partly culpable for driving a wedge between workers of different age cohorts. When attention is directed to mapping and managing the competing mindsets of different generational groups, it is also diverted away from addressing age-based and other forms of inequality, scarce resources, and the now-apparent shortcomings of the economic system in which all groups work. Put differently, neoliberal generationalism conveniently inhibits the kind of coalition building that might bring much-needed structural changes for all workers.

4

In God We Trust

"My husband and I are very faith filled," shared sixty-two-year-old Nadine at her 2014 interview. A Christian, like nearly all the *American Idle* study interviewees who mentioned a religious affiliation,[1] she admitted, "Sometimes it's been hard to consistently feel like it's going to be okay, but thank God, we are. I don't know what people rely on if they don't have some sense outside of themselves that things will be restored. Maybe not the way they were, but they will be restored." We met Nadine, matriarch of a large family, seven years after what she sardonically described as the moment "when my whole life started tanking." She was referred to the study by an employment counselor at her job club, located within a Twin Cities Catholic church, and came to us eager to tell her story to a new audience.

Nadine began by describing herself as a reluctant "primary breadwinner" whose husband of forty-one years worked in "a dying trade." Her three middle-aged children and nine grandchildren were not financially dependent on the couple, nor did they offer financial support when the couple needed it most. When the first job loss hit in 2007, Nadine was completing her master's degree in nonprofit leadership with an emphasis on ethical decision-making and theological reflection. She had chosen the program to build on her prior leadership roles and because it aligned with her strong moral compass and unwavering faith in God—neither of which was shaken as her successful career seemingly dissolved before her eyes.

When the company that employed Nadine was sold off, her management job of seventeen years disappeared. It had been, in her words, "the ideal job." She continued, "Somebody said it—'do what you love and you'll never work a day in your life.' That's what that job was, and I loved it." Her faith kept her going, but Nadine would lose her next managerial job to redundancy just four years later, in 2011. The second time around, it was easier, she said, because the company had not ever fit with her stalwart sense of right and wrong. She described the men who ran it as "immoral," "arrogant," and "demeaning," and her eyes widened as she spoke of a young co-worker who "was having an extramarital affair with one of the executive managers."

This time around, though, Nadine's earnest job-searching was not enough to land another managerial position. She ended up bouncing from one short-term job to another before enacting "plan B": temp work. The job conditions were "horrible," the industries had nothing to do with her career employment, the work was physically difficult for her aging body, she had "cruel" bosses and co-workers, and when her cumulative hours approached the full-time hiring requirement, she endured repeated sudden dismissals. Explaining how, at one company, temps could work up to ninety days before the company had to offer full-time employment, she bitterly recalled, "I was like four hours away from that requirement, and then the temp service called and said [the company] didn't want me to come back." Nadine broke down in tears.

Her current temp contract, which Nadine referred to as "a shit job," was "forty hours a week, ten dollars an hour, and . . . forty-seven miles each way" in a neighboring state. The assembly worker position felt like a considerable demotion, just years out from doing a job she loved for over $100,000 a year plus five-figure annual bonuses. The series of "ten- and eleven-bucks-an-hour" temp jobs that came after it were not just galling because they represented such steep downward mobility but because they required Nadine to embrace a work persona inconsistent with her graduate education and managerial experience. With a laugh, she told us, "I'm a leader," but "you gotta know when to lead, and you gotta know when to follow. And this is one of those areas where I gotta be more of a follower." Always one to find a silver lining, she added, "I'm learning a lot [on the assembly line] because I want to get my point across in ways that would be helpful but without appearing like I'm a know-it-all or I'm arrogant or—you know what I mean?"

The effects of job instability and poverty were clearly taking a toll as Nadine found herself unable to afford health insurance. She was living "paycheck to paycheck" and had narrowly escaped losing her home to foreclosure. "When you're just sitting there waiting for the phone to ring, waiting for the email to show up, waiting, waiting, it gets the best of me, oh yeah." Musing toward the end of her interview, "I don't know what people do that don't have [faith], I don't know," Nadine insisted, "I don't think I'd be here if I didn't have that." Then, chuckling, "Seriously, you can only take so much."

"Where we find trauma and tragedy," write psychologists Kenneth Pargament and Crystal Park, "we often find religion."[2] Indeed, though we only directly asked about religion once in our conversations with respondents, usually toward the end of the interview, mentions of God, religious congregations, and personal faith were sprinkled throughout our interviews. Some 71 percent of interviewees (twenty-six of the men and eighteen women) spoke in religious terms. Clearly, many respondents' coping strategies drew on faith and/or intersected with their participation in faith-based organizations like job clubs. Before delving into personal beliefs, practices, and communities of support, we first examine the phenomenon of job clubs affiliated with Christian congregations. Offering practical job search help as well as emotional support, the Twin Cities–area job clubs many of our interviewees attended were nonetheless strikingly neoliberal in their assessments of the problems of and solutions available to their members. Throughout this chapter, we discuss how our respondents' reliance on religion and religiously inflected support organizations during the significant life course transition of job loss both resonated with and reinforced a neoliberal lens of personal responsibility.

Faith-Based Job Clubs

Unemployed Americans have had access to job search support through publicly funded workforce agencies since the Great Depression. The Workforce Innovation and Opportunity Act of 2014 was, in fact, a replacement for the 1998 amendment of the 1933 Wagner-Peyser Act, which established the nationwide network of employment offices now known as the Employment Service. These legislative changes have resulted in the nearly century-old Employment Service offices being hosted alongside American Job Centers (AJCs) nationwide.[3] Today these centers offer a variety of reemployment and training services, including job search support groups commonly known as "job clubs," though on ever-shrinking budgets. With a long period of government retrenchment—the removal of funding for public programs and benefits—these job clubs have become ever more automated and reliant on self-serve programming.[4] A temporary budget increase for these services following the Great Recession proved entirely insufficient to handle the volume of newly unemployed Americans.[5]

As direct funding to public workforce programs dwindled over time, federal programs turned social problems like unemployment over to perennially underfunded nonprofits and religious groups. In fact, under what some label the "Newer Deal," religious organizations became increasingly important providers of many types of social services in the United States.[6] An early facilitating mechanism of faith-based social interventions was the Clinton Administration's 1996 Personal Responsibility and Work Opportunity Reconciliation Act. This act included so-called Charitable Choice legislation and other provisions circumventing the separation of church and state by allowing tax-exempt, faith-based organizations to receive government funding to provide social services even without compromising or concealing their religious mission, practices, or hiring preferences.[7] After George W. Bush established what is now known as the White House Office of Faith-Based and Neighborhood Partnerships in 2001, faith-based organizations became even more central. For instance, those involved in reemployment services including hosting job clubs became eligible to receive funds accessed through the Department of Labor's Welfare-to-Work program. These shifts are emblematic of the broader neoliberal transformation of U.S. society, in which responsibility for social welfare has been shifted from the federal government to lower-level jurisdictions, private sector and nonprofit organizations, and, ultimately, individuals.[8]

Politically, the religious right was at the fore, lending the ideational legitimacy of evangelical Protestantism to neoliberal aims. Urban geographer Jason Hackworth details how some conservative religious "logics" enhance the credibility of secular neoliberal policies, whether or not their Christian proponents intend to do so. Biblically based teachings, such as those against government intervention or in favor of libertarianism and maximizing personal prosperity, can have the effect of sanctifying neoliberal principles centered on individual responsibility. Pairing Christianity, a system with its own cultural sway, with neoliberalism, Hackworth's work suggests, can imbue policies of neglect with a sort of righteousness that discourages critique.[9]

Thus the significance of the Job Clubs Initiative (JCI), launched in 2011 under the Department of Labor's Center for Faith-Based and Neighborhood Partnerships. The JCI provided funds, information, and technical assistance and training to community- and faith-based groups or individuals interested in starting or expanding job search support groups.[10] According to one former Obama White House staffer, more than 1,100 American congregations created job clubs as a result of the JCI; as of our interviews, roughly a quarter of the estimated ten thousand U.S. job clubs were affiliated with the Department of Labor's effort.[11]

Seeking to build a "community of practice" while linking the clubs and the public workforce system, the center mounted a website. There, job clubs could register with a "State Job Club Directory" and access curriculum resources and tool kits to launch or support their programs. Only a fraction of the country's job clubs registered with the site, but Minnesota was a leader with sixty-two listed clubs.[12] Although this website is no longer maintained, careeronestop.org still has a job club finder on its site, and Minnesota faith- and community-based job clubs remain well represented.

Within this context, faith-based job clubs are both similar and different in important ways to those operated by AJCs and the secular community-based job clubs.[13] Most job clubs, regardless of location, host guest speakers, facilitate peer discussions, provide networking opportunities, advertise employment openings, and generally help interviewees refine their job-seeking skills. They offer workshops on résumé writing or practice interview sessions as well as weekly or biweekly meetings (typically outside business hours). Club membership is typically open to all job seekers; rarely do even church-sponsored groups restrict their services to congregation members or those from similar denominations. "Nobody's checking your credentials at the door, which is really nice," commented Victor, a Catholic who had attended job clubs associated with three different Christian congregations.[14] That said, some groups cater to certain subpopulations. During our study, we found Minnesota clubs targeting women, veterans, members of the Latino community, and individuals with particular occupational backgrounds, such as IT professionals or those in sales and marketing. Compared to AJC clubs, faith-based and community-based job clubs tend to attract more middle-class and older, white-collar job seekers.[15] They also differ from AJC clubs and those run by large nonpublic organizations, such as Lutheran Social Service of Minnesota, in that they are not led by professional paid staff but by volunteers working with shoestring budgets (if any at all).[16]

And then there is the main difference between the faith-based job clubs and other clubs: faith. Generally speaking, clubs affiliated with congregations are hosted as a partial means to fulfill religious dictates to help those in need—hence the number of faith-based job clubs founded after the economic downturn.[17] The degree to which Christianity is interwoven with club activities can vary widely, however.[18] At one extreme, a congregation may simply make its meeting space available to job club facilitators for free. At the other, spirituality is a club's defining feature; these groups offer explicitly faith-based curricula, emphasizing scripture, God's will, and the "Christian way" to find a job. In between, there are many variations—some groups invite club members to voluntary pre-meeting Bible study sessions, while others bookend their meetings with prayers but have no other spiritual content in their curricula. The variety makes it difficult to generalize about the faith-based elements of these job clubs, yet there is some indication that faith-based clubs emphasize personal encouragement and emotional support more than AJC and other community job clubs.[19]

Of the ninety Minneapolis-St. Paul metro area community- and faith-based job clubs operating at the time of our study, thirty-five were located in Christian churches.[20] Many indicated they were nondenominational groups, open to all, though some specifically offered prayer, spiritual support, or a focus on such things as "Biblical workplace values" or "combining the Word with real-world job hunting." Three job clubs were particularly popular with our interviewees: the Easter Job Transitions Group at Eastern Lutheran Church in Eagan; the Wooddale Job Transition Support Group at Wooddale Church in Eden Prairie; and the Basilica Employment Ministry at the Catholic Basilica of St. Mary in Minneapolis (only the first is no longer operational).

Perhaps not coincidentally, the affiliations of these clubs align with the three largest denominational groupings in Minnesota (the population of which is nearly three-quarters Christian overall): mainline Protestant, evangelical Protestant, and Catholic, respectively.[21]

"Wooddale," as our interviewees called it, describes itself as specializing in "networking, accountability, encouragement, and prayer support, [as well as offering] a job search process workshop."[22] The club's website (jobtransition.net) prominently features Christian beliefs alongside standard job search advice about topics such as dressing for success or composing effective résumés. Its centerpiece is a section on the "6 Steps" to finding a job (Attitude, Assessment, Marketing Strategy, Marketing Materials, Interviewing, and Follow Up). Step one, Attitude, foregrounds job seekers' positivity and faith as key drivers of success. Here, popular Texan evangelical pastor Charles "Chuck" Swindoll is quoted: "Attitude . . . is more important than facts. It is more important than the past, than education, than money, than circumstances, than failures, than successes, than what other people think or say or do. . . . I am convinced that life is ten percent what happens to me and ninety percent how I react to it. And so it is with you. We are in charge of our attitudes." In other words, "so much is going to depend on your attitude," the site counsels. Unemployed workers are encouraged to believe in themselves and let go of their negative feelings about their job loss. "The right attitude will diffuse or eliminate those negatives that stand in your way." Calling the six-step program "a wonderful tool kit," one interviewee in our study was a champion of the Wooddale job club.[23] There, he learned the importance of forgiving those responsible for his layoff so that his negative attitude would no longer "cast a shadow" over his interviews. In his words, Wooddale's "focal point" was that "you really gotta clean that brain and find that forgiveness and move on and not look back and look forward."

Wooddale also emphasizes the Bible. In its website resources, chapter and verse are commonly cited for specific situations, such as "if your pocket book is empty," "if you are depressed," "when you grow bitter and critical," or "for a great intervention/opportunity." Other passages underscore prayer along with faith and trust in God, who has a purpose and plan for job seekers: "We have an all-powerful, loving God who desires the best for us and who has a plan for our lives. To only pray for a new job while not pursuing job search activities is not what God expects of us. Depending on our own efforts and not praying about the matter is worse."

If only for the camaraderie and social interactions, the emotional support from peers also struggling with job loss, Wooddale and other job clubs have lots to offer the unemployed. There is even some evidence that such groups help job seekers to repair or sustain their professional or work-related identities, so often damaged when a worker is fired or laid off.[24] At Wooddale, club members are described as "working on their marketing materials" and are told, "You are not out of work. You already have a full-time job as the president of 'You Incorporated.' You will now be working full time marketing yourself to prospective employers."[25] Such businesslike lingo and job search approaches can help interviewees feel as if they are still working professionals. In the face of the identity-threatening experience of white-collar job loss, this rhetoric provides mental health benefits.[26]

Some research finds job clubs do indeed facilitate reemployment.[27] The job search training and resources offered by these clubs may be especially valuable to older workers, particularly those who were long-term employees with a single employer before dismissal (as some of our interviewees were), who had been socialized into the labor market's job search expectations in a much different era, or who otherwise may be unfamiliar with the contemporary rules common to what sociologist Ofer Sharone calls the American job search "game."[28] Indeed, our interviewees could not rely on the job-seeking strategies they once used, which was a source of frustration. For example, more than one interviewee mentioned the people in their networks were now retired or dead. When some interviewees last applied for jobs, they dropped off hard-copy résumés with prospective employers. The online application systems replacing this approach were "horribly designed," as Kai described them, and the indignity of never receiving a response was a further insult. Job clubs, our interviewees confirmed, offered valuable guidance for those who were navigating this modern context perhaps for the first time.

The linguistic framing and strategies job clubs use are not just reminiscent of corporate culture; they also reflect and reinscribe neoliberal ideals.[29] Aptly, sociologist Madison Van Oort refers to job clubs as "engines that help animate the neoliberal discursive shift from the social to the individual."[30] As we will discuss in chapter 6, positivity and self-determination devolve the burden of joblessness to the individual rather than blame corporations or the state, while also minimizing, if not entirely dismissing, collective attempts to critique or change the systemic problems of capitalist labor markets.[31] When Wooddale members are told that step one is Attitude, they are being told, in effect, "It's not the world that needs changing... it's you."[32] The fact that club members are counseled to work full-time on the "daily minutiae" of the job search further reinforces this perspective.[33] Sharone goes to metaphor here: "The focus on strategies draws attention away from the larger context of rules and constraints that structure the game. An absorbed chess player contemplating how to move her pawn does not simultaneously question the rules governing the pawn's mobility."[34]

Sharone further suggests, if an individual sees themselves as wholly responsible for winning the job search game, they will logically see themselves as wholly to blame should they fail.[35] Such self-blame may be augmented in the case of older workers when it intersects with ageism. As we saw in chapter 2, ageism and age-based discrimination are common in the workplace, as in our culture at large. To the extent that ageist stereotypes become internalized, self-blame and its adverse mental health effects can be exacerbated in older workers.[36] Importantly, this can hold true even if the reality of ageism is acknowledged. The Wooddale website, for example, provides "Help for the Older Worker" via a *Wall Street Journal* article that acknowledges market biases against older workers, while offering individual "hacks" to circumvent the bias.[37] In encouraging older workers to do things like cleverly construct résumés to downplay age, the piece once again foregrounds personal diligence and allows structural barriers to reemployment to evade attention.[38] As more generally in the neoliberal era, individual responsibility is prioritized in job clubs, too.

To be fair, these observations might equally apply to a range of job club types, not just faith-based groups. We still have not dealt with the *faith* in the faith-based job clubs, which can also be linked to neoliberalism. Before delving deeper into the "God talk" component of faith-based job clubs, let us first consider what scholars know about religious coping when life takes a turn for the worse.

Religious Coping

Psychologist Kenneth Pargament has devoted a large part of his career to studying how religion helps people cope with life stressors.[39] He and other scholars have examined the interplay of religiosity and life challenges/transitions such as illness, the disability of a family member, bereavement, divorce, and in the aftermath of terrorism and natural disaster.[40] These investigations often include a discussion of how religion functions as a framework for creating meaning, both in terms of an individual's beliefs and expectations about the nature of the world and how it operates and in terms of an individual's attempts to reappraise traumatic events that might be initially viewed as discrepant with their global meaning system.[41] In what is termed "benevolent religious reappraisal," for example, a tragedy or illness that might otherwise challenge an individual's global belief about fairness in the world might be reappraised as "part of God's plan." Other religious coping strategies include seeking a connection with forces that transcend the individual or waiting or pleading for divine intercession.[42]

That said, Pargament and his colleagues distinguish between such positive religious coping and negative religious coping.[43] Examples of the latter include the individual's reappraisal of the stressor as a punishment from God or expressions of discontent with God, clergy, or religious congregation members. Psychologist Julie Exline and her colleagues also show that anger at God—what they describe as "religious and spiritual struggle"—is actually quite common.[44] Their research on the psychological dimensions of "divine struggles" reveals individuals may also feel abandoned, punished, or let down by God when negative events occur.[45] Perhaps understandably, positive religious coping methods are associated with better mental health outcomes, while negative methods or religious and spiritual struggles are associated with worse mental health outcomes and emotional distress.[46]

We now know that job loss and prolonged unemployment can be especially harmful to and stressful for older adults. We also know that older adults are more likely to be religious than younger ones,[47] and that older people are more likely to use religious coping in the face of negative life events.[48] With these facts in mind, we will explore how religious coping worked in the lives of our interviewees. Although little existing research focuses directly or extensively on religion and job loss, some psychologists have shown that religiosity (expressed as service attendance or religious values held) plays a buffering role that mitigates some of the negative psychological effects of unemployment.[49] It is important to add to the quantitative work of such scholars, however, by seeking out qualitative data that highlight the voices and experiences of individuals in richer detail.

This is where the work of sociologists like Marianne Cooper comes in.[50] In her book *Cut Adrift: Families in Insecure Times*, Cooper examines how Silicon Valley families from different socioeconomic backgrounds navigate the economic uncertainty and emotional weight of the neoliberal era or, in her words, our "safety-net-less, go-it-alone age."[51] Her interviews revealed that it was the people who were dealing with the most extreme economic hardships who most often turned to their churches and their faith in God to cope. In insecure times, Cooper found that not only did many working-class and poor respondents depend on their congregations for material assistance like food, financial assistance, and dental and medical care, they also exhibited religious coping behaviors in line with those Pargament finds. In particular, she shows how her low-income interviewees took comfort in prayer and found security in a highly insecure world by believing that God has a plan and will intervene to provide for the faithful.[52]

But what about the unemployed older workers in our study, a group objectively less vulnerable than those whom Cooper documented as coping with insecurity by relying on religion?[53] While Cooper did not find significant evidence of Pargament-style coping among the middle-class individuals in her sample, we certainly did. In particular, we found extensive evidence of positive religious coping techniques. Time and again, our interviewees spoke unprompted on the themes of *faith as solace and sustenance, God's plan*, and *gaining strength from religious community*. We also found *spiritual discontent*, or negative religious coping/spiritual struggle, in the accounts of some interviewees. This range of coping techniques reinforced the primacy of faith in the ways older workers weathered the hardships of unemployment.

Faith as Solace and Sustenance

Almost half ($N = 21$) of the forty-four people who referenced religion in their interviews used phrases such as "walking the road with our Lord," "relying on faith," or, to echo Cooper, "turning to God" when talking about their unemployment.[54] For them, faith was a means to get them through the fear, anxiety, depression, or what they simply labeled the "down times" of job loss and un- or underemployment. Our interviewee Brian, an adult convert to Catholicism, was downsized from his customer solutions management position in 2012. What helped him sustain hope? "My faith in God. I just call on Him when I need Him," Brian said. "I pray to Him, and I tell Him how I'm feeling, you know? 'I'm scared God,' or 'I'm concerned, please help me through this one. I'd have no right to expect it, but if I don't tell you so. . . .' I do that. I reach out to Him first, and I've got a couple friends out there I can go to, but He's the first call. He's on my . . . speed dial. Number one."

Kaleb, who replaced the IT support job he lost in 2013 with a similar but much lower-paying position, lamented that he now only earned enough to "eat, . . . exist, and keep my home." Despite this setback, Kaleb viewed his faith in God as sustenance. He said that "testing" in the form of "health issues, or economic issues, or maybe even relationship problems" came into everyone's life and that "if you don't have something bigger to fall back on, it can be devastating. And fortunately, I have a faith strong enough to help me ride out this difficult period that I'm still kind of in. . . . If I didn't have a faith or a faith in God, it would be very depressing. . . . There would be really no reason to continue at my age." These statements are simultaneously filled with gratitude and despair—a conundrum tinged by faith.

Religious backgrounds became foregrounds for some who lost their jobs. For Sean, the faith orientation of his job club fit well with his "very strict" Lutheran upbringing and his belief that he was "not alone and that you can put your trust in the Lord." As he further explained, "I also feel like, let the Lord help fight your battles . . . He doesn't want you to despair, and it's kind of reassuring to have some of those sound bites when you go to those [job club meetings]. They always start out in prayer or saying positive affirmations or things like that. It just kind of reminds you and grounds you." Timothy also talked at length about his religious upbringing and Christian beliefs when asserting that he is "well insulated" from worry. In the parlance of life course theory, Sean's and Timothy's method of coping with job loss was consistent with their relatively stable faith trajectories over time. And in Teresa's case, the devastating double whammy of job loss and a breast cancer diagnosis motivated her to "pick back up" the Christianity of her childhood. These adverse transitions influenced the curvilinear pattern of religiosity over her life course.[55]

Not every interviewee who evoked faith expressed a firm commitment to a specific religious denomination or Judeo-Christian religious beliefs. Sophia, for example, described herself as a "lapsed Catholic" yet admitted to praying to St. Jude, her "go-to guy," when she unexpectedly lost her job at age sixty-five. Dawn referred to the potential of "the universe" to offset the "bleak" situation created by her job loss at age fifty-three. And Caroline referenced both Buddhism and Jesus's teachings as healing, telling herself that "all is well. All is well. All is eternally well," and cultivating the belief that worry and anxiety "are useless emotions or useless time."

Our interviewees' reports line up quite nicely with what Pargament and his colleagues discovered in all sorts of other stressful situations, as individuals "seek comfort and reassurance through God's love and care."[56] In fact, it makes perfect sense: having a divine "go-to guy," God on your metaphorical speed dial, or even just the touchstone of beliefs from your past and present all constitute sources of stability and succor in what is otherwise an uncertain and distressing economic situation.

God's Plan

On the Wooddale website, Christian career consultant Nancy Branton reassures job seekers that "God has a vision and plan for you" by quoting from the Old Testament: "For I know the plans I have for you, declares the Lord, plans to prosper you and not to harm you, plans to give you hope and a future," (Jeremiah 29:11).[57] In a similar vein, almost half of those respondents ($N=21$) who referenced religion used a religious coping technique that involved surrendering to God or otherwise placing trust in God's larger plan for their lives; one even cited the same chapter and verse from the Bible during his interview. Interviewees using this frame emphasized deferring to God's plan, waiting for God's plan to reveal itself, or hoping and praying that God would take control of the job loss situation.[58] What is clear is that interviewees adopting this frame viewed God as a just and merciful force capable of rectifying an unsuccessful search for reemployment.

Katherine, for example, was an unemployed nurse practitioner and divorced. She spoke of a year's worth of "emotional trauma," endured without the assistance of a spouse, family members, or close friends. Only God. There were dark days, Katherine reported, when "I felt like I couldn't even move. . . . I remember one day, I'm on my knees praying. It's like, 'Dear God, [you have to] bring this job.' You know? I'm crawling up the stairs, and it's like, 'I can't get up the stairs today.'" Despite such low points, she believed that "my job would come in God's timing and He would find the place where He wanted me to work."

Recounting how she did receive another nurse practitioner position, she declared, "The Lord will lead, His timing is perfect, and the love for my Father is the strongest it has ever been.... The Father knows exactly what we need."

Other interviewees were not as lucky in their job search, but their faith remained steadfast. Kenneth had recently lost his IT support job at the time of his interview. He was relatively straightforward when asked how his faith in God helped him: "Well, I believe that there's a better life than here, and if God wants me to have a job, He'll present it to me. And as long as I'm open to seeing it, I'll see it, and if He wants me to see it." Martin, an unemployed jeweler living in a rural area, understood his own job prospects as slim. Nonetheless, he affirmed, "God's going to work something out." With patience, he believed, God would provide: "At first, especially when you're at the peak of depression, there's nothing good. There's ... no good in anything. And you, you question why live. But as I work my way through ... the Book of Psalms, particularly the first half of it ... that David wrote, and you read ... the things that David went through, and how he cried out to God and ... how God answered him—that made a big difference."

Divine plans did not have to be Christian. Keith, for example, shared a four-year attempt to locate stable, secure employment after downsizing and succinctly expressed his hope for some beneficent intervention: "I told you that I am not religious, [but] you just have to hope at the end that God comes out of the clouds." Lars, an interior designer downsized in 2012, was similarly forthright when referencing this transcendental frame: "I feel fortunate. I think there's somebody that watches over me." He was indeed fortunate. In less than two years, Lars secured a new job with a large, stable employer. He made somewhat less than his previous salary, yet Lars believed "it kind of panned out nicely."

A final set of interviewees invoking the "God's plan" framework seemed uncertain about what it might be, but felt sure there was some larger meaning to be found in their job loss. Former sales account manager Charlotte cried when she shared that "I really believe that I will end up someplace. I'm not sure where, but ... like I said, I really believe that God put me here for a reason, and he'll let me know what that is." Still unemployed six years after his 2008 dismissal, Timothy was puzzled but faithful: "You know, to everything there's a reason for its existence. And it's, quite frankly, befuddling me to understand why that's the situation. Am I learning something by this? Is there something to be gained by being unemployed? I have empathy—it's one of my strengths. However, I don't know what I'm learning by it. Being patient? ... I do trust the Lord that there's something that'll come out of it." Cassandra did not self-define as "a traditionally spiritual person." Yet she too framed the loss of her human resources consulting business in the Great Recession as part of God's unseen plan: "When I went through the depression, I would lay on my bed sometimes and think, 'Okay God,' like, 'just kill me now.' Like, 'just take me now because I can't do this.' And then I kept living and I wasn't sick, you know? I mean, I was depressed and I did take antidepressants and stuff, but I was like, okay. I guess I'm here for a reason, and I don't know what that is and damn it, I guess I haven't finished my chore." Whether out of deep faith or cautious optimism, all these interviewees expressed some form of trust that a divine design would eventually reveal itself.

Low-income respondents in Marianne Cooper's study relied heavily on their beliefs that God has a plan as part of their "security projects," or their approaches to finding stability when their lives felt out of control.[59] We can now confirm religious coping mechanisms are also key to managing precarity in the lives of those further up the socioeconomic ladder. Indeed, evidence of religious coping was distributed all along the continuum of hard falls and soft landings we reported in chapter 2. And, even though those who experienced soft falls (who generally had more resources and support) were less likely to employ God talk,[60] there appeared to be no consistent relation between the degree of the fall and the extent of religious coping reported. Before the Great Recession and its uneven recovery, our interviewees had not worried about economic insecurity, but when it came, they also put faith in God's plan.

Once again, the fact that our respondents were older workers also comes into play. Some scholars have shown that older adults may be more likely to believe in God-mediated control; this sense of control, in turn, is associated with greater psychological well-being, including optimism about the future, in later life (on a related note, we discuss the neoliberal emphasis on positive thinking in chapter 6).[61] Regardless of social and life course location, however, a belief that everything happens according to a divine plan can provide a sense of coherence to the ups and downs of the job search process.[62] Notions of divine control also bring a heartening promise that, thanks to a loving and benign God, everything is going to work out in the end.[63]

Gaining Strength from Religious Community

For our interviewees, job clubs and religious congregations also helped with coping on a personal level. Seventeen of our interviewees talked about the importance of prayer, social support, or more tangible forms of assistance from their fellow believers.

Kenneth, for example, recounted feeling down about not getting any work. He asked others at his job club's prayer group for "some prayer to get me back up—to get my spirits back up so I can get back out there." Katherine's faith-based job club also provided prayer, as well as crucial personal interaction that helped her feel not so alone as a divorcee. She spoke frequently of the significance of the connections she made at the club: "It was connecting with people within the job search group, it was connecting even for coffee outside of the job search group, it was finding somebody . . . who'd be a volunteer, who was willing to work with me, and just support me when you felt like you were kicked in the shin again and again and again. It was finding Christian people to pray for me, attend my Bible study, maybe go for runs, go work out, pray." This type of interpersonal support was also observed by sociologist Dawn Norris in "FaithWorks!," a religiously affiliated job club that some of her middle-class interviewees attended.[64] The community part of a religious community should not be underestimated.

Much like one of the profiled Mormon families in Cooper's study, our interviewee Kaleb reported a wide breadth of support from fellow church members: "There were lots of friends in the faith community who would pray for me, encourage me, and . . . sustain me [with] their provisions of blessings. . . . There were monetary gifts and resources that were offered to us [and] that helped us. . . . That was important."[65] A similar accounting of instrumental support received from fellow congregants is provided by Norman, whose 2012 downsizing was paired with a degenerative disease that left him using a wheelchair. He reported that church members provided monetary assistance and numerous home repairs that made living with his limited physical mobility a bit easier. As Norman stated, "They did a lot of things for me. I thought it was a little bit over the top, but . . . I appreciated it."

Some interviewees who employed this theme talked about providing comfort and lending support to others within their religious community. Charlotte, who attended "a very small, very strict Lutheran church," emphasized reciprocal care: "I'm in their prayers and they're in mine." Cat, a former health coach downsized in 2014, found that volunteering at her church gave her "a busy work project to do" that she found "helpful" in her own struggles. As these two examples suggest, faith communities served as an outlet for activity by providing a venue for volunteer participation while congregation members simultaneously offered expressions of caring and concern, a form of reciprocity also acknowledged by Pargament and his colleagues.[66]

Interviewees did not need to belong to a congregation to acknowledge how helpful a church community could be. Cassandra's job loss loneliness drove her to reconsider joining a faith practice: "After I lost my job, people drifted away and then I became very lonely. . . . Now I'm coming back to myself and I'm trying to think about it again. Like, how do I reintegrate parts of that that would work for me? The same thing with . . . the religious thing. . . . Would it be useful or beneficial for me to join an established community because I've never been much of a joiner? And so, I'm kind of analyzing that with my life." A similar sentiment was expressed by former creative director Stephanie, who was laid off in 2008. "I sometimes wish I had belonged to a church," she said, "because I see the churches... pulling together to help their people.... [P]eople... who have faith, I think, get through... the unemployment easier." Like other respondents, Stephanie recognized that "having that community is a good thing."

Religious practice helps situate individuals within larger social networks of care. These networks consist of fellow believers who share similar perspectives and values (including charity and helping one's neighbor) and are thus likely to offer instrumental and emotional support.[67] This is a good thing for citizens, too: the more the neoliberal state sheds the responsibility of caring for people, the more such networks become central to their well-being.

Spiritual Discontent

Understandably, some people's joblessness led them to become angry, dissatisfied, or resentful toward God, religious beliefs, and job club teachings. Eight of our interviewees voiced such forms of negative religious coping or spiritual struggle, which stand in contrast to, and alongside, the consoling or supportive functions of religious coping most of the interviewees discussed.[68]

Lyle, who had lost his sales director job two years before our interview, was a cheerful man who nonetheless vented his frustration in religious terms: "I believe in... God, and yet... God ain't paying my mortgage, you know? If God's got a plan for me, step it up, pal! This has been going on too long." Along the same lines, Charles had endured a "roller coaster" of job losses, which we describe in detail in chapter 5. When asked directly about faith, he said, "I try to maintain the faith because... I think it does help me. Brings in doubt sometimes too because I'll say,... 'I'm good, why is this happening to me? Throw a bone my way once in a while.'" In expressing these sentiments, interviewees like Lyle, Charles, and several others in our study appeared to believe that God was capable of personally intervening in their lives—making it all the more maddening that God had not yet done so.[69]

For others, discontent was directed at faith-based organizations and, in particular, the job clubs hosted by churches in the Twin Cities metro region. Kaaryn, a former counselor, objected in particular to some of the ideas espoused at a Lutheran faith-based job club. She rejected the notion of a beneficent God who directly assists the unemployed: "I'm Christian, but I'm not necessarily born again, and it feels like the [job club] is more... 'born again.' And it isn't that [I]... don't believe.... I can trust God, but I just don't see. He's not just going to pluck me up and give me a job, you know?" Since losing her career, Kaaryn explained, she had experienced something of a crisis of faith: "I don't trust God as much.... I think that this [job loss] kind of pulled the rug... from underneath my belief system."

Kirk had tried job clubs run by Catholic, Lutheran, and evangelical congregations and concluded that the Catholic church "sucks" at providing employment counseling, while the other two relied on God's plan so much that he felt they saw Him as a wish-fulfilling "Santa Claus." He has a plan? "I want to go, 'No—He does not!'" Kirk said, while Martie cautioned, "You can have a lot of faith, but one should not be naive. Faith can only go so far, but it can't pay the bills."

Importantly, even our spiritual discontents could find some sustenance in their faith. It was not that they lacked belief, only that they recognized and were frustrated with the limits to what God or religious organizations could provide in their situation. Employing both positive and negative coping techniques simultaneously is reported in other research; in ours, interviewees commonly called on multiple themes when discussing their experiences, with none being mutually exclusive.[70] We conclude that religious coping itself is multivalent.

Christian Coping and Neoliberalism

A lot is going on at the nexus of religion and joblessness. Some of the people we interviewed expressed disappointment and frustration with God's inaction and with the religious rhetoric of the job clubs and their members, while also, like the majority of respondents, finding their faith in God or their religious networks both emotionally consoling and concretely helpful. In parsing these interviewees' statements, we have to acknowledge that it would be difficult to disentangle exactly how or from where their religious framings of job loss arise. There are certainly strong similarities between the teachings of some of the faith-based job clubs and our interviewees' comments, but those comments might also align with the tenets of their personal faith and/or religious backgrounds. Would job club attendees have coped with their unemployment in religious terms if they had not learned to do so at the club meetings? Would interviewees seek out, stay in, and speak in the terms of the faith-based organizations if the religious teachings did not resonate with their already-held beliefs? It is hard to say, but the mutually reinforcing parallels between the two are hard to ignore.

Also hard to ignore is the neat dovetailing of religious coping techniques and neoliberal agendas. Turning to inner spiritual resources to cope with joblessness, as it centers on the individual's belief in and relationship with the divine, does not present a challenge to the politico-economic order. Here journalist Barbara Ehrenreich, who posed as a job seeker to observe the inner workings of both faith-based and secular job clubs for her book on white-collar unemployment (*Bait and Switch*), makes the astute observation that both types of club teachings lend themselves to the "fantasy of [individual] omnipotence."[71] As Ehrenreich explains, unemployment can be overcome, with no need to confront the broader structural forces shaping one's life, as long as the individual does the right thing, including praying hard enough or having sufficient faith in God and God's plan. Rather than a narrative of secular, institutional, and structural forces shaping and occasionally torpedoing livelihoods, God's plan itself becomes the story, an explanation of the trials and tribulations that precede promised resolutions to individual problems.[72] Doing the right thing faith-wise and leaving matters in God's hands does not render the individual completely inactive, even though research by Kenneth Pargament suggests this can happen (effectively turning a positive religious coping technique into a negative one).[73] Far from it: as we discussed, job seekers at Wooddale still need to work diligently on the myriad of tasks involved in the 6 Steps, because, "to only pray for a new job while not pursuing job search activities is not what God expects."[74] Indeed, every job club participant we interviewed recounted all the hours and techniques they spent trying to find new employment. Moreover, those who expressed uncertainty about God's plan or anger at God's inaction, while not necessarily receiving the same comforting benefits as other religious job seekers, nonetheless maintained the belief that God could, would, or should intervene, restricting their expectation of assistance to the nonpolitical realm. Finally, even those like Kaaryn and Kirk, who expressed disdain at the belief in a "Santa Claus" God who would swoop in and solve their unemployment woes, directed their negativity toward the relatively circumscribed realm of the faith-based job clubs, not to religion or religious teachings or labor markets writ large. In relation to religious coping, then, action and critique were not absent from our interviewees' stories; they were simply not directed to challenging the broader structural factors underlying their job loss and preventing their reemployment.

It bears emphasizing that, as much as U.S. society is presently neoliberal, it is also predominantly Christian. Increasing religious diversity and numbers of nonaffiliated individuals aside, self-identified Christians still account for more than 60 percent of the population, and the total is more than 70 percent in Minnesota.[75] Further, many political and cultural institutions in the United States remain deeply influenced by the Christian tradition and its adherents.[76] Considering this socioreligious environment, and the largely Christian affiliation of our sample, it is not surprising that so many of our interviewees employed an interpretive frame informed by Christian beliefs.

Earlier, we touched on how Christian theology serves to independently legitimate neoliberal policy directions via the teachings of influential figures affiliated with the religious right. But such legitimation need not always be facilitated by high-level movers and shakers; our interviewees' reflections on their joblessness show that the faith expressions of everyday believers help corroborate the neoliberal enterprise from the bottom up. Faith-based job clubs are simply one arena in which these two influential worldviews coincide, further reinforcing the neoliberal hold on our era and its unemployed older workers.

Still, none of this implies that neoliberalism, much like Christian beliefs or faith-based job clubs, is inescapable or impervious to challenge by our interviewees. In the next two chapters, we unpack the resistance to neoliberalism that arose when our interviewees discussed the material realities and relational ties of their life course stage. First, we turn to stories of job seekers' reluctance to embrace the neoliberal ideal of the flexible worker. Then, in chapter 6, we see how interviewees' positivity discourse, while reinforcing some of the very same tendencies toward individualism as their God talk, often simultaneously contained a trenchant critique of their former neoliberal workplace environments.

5

"Here's Where I Am, Here's Where I'll Stay"

Charles leapt into his 2013 interview eager to share the story of a career path routinely thwarted by job loss. The tragic account began ten years earlier when his employer shut down operations and filed for bankruptcy. Charles was forty-eight years old and confident he would recover quickly. And he did: at first Charles opted for self-employment, creating and publishing a successful magazine. Then he was recruited to serve as vice president of a retail firm, a position, Charles said wistfully, that came with "the highest salary I've ever made."

After just two years in the new position, in 2005, Charles encountered another setback: his employer sold the company and the new owner moved operations to a different state. With his wife's support, Charles declined the relocation offer, which was fortunate because nine months later this company was shuttered. Charles opted to revive his magazine, but the onset of the Great Recession soon meant the small businesses his publication served were unable to afford advertising expenses.

When it became clear in 2008 that the magazine was no longer financially viable, Charles accepted a salaried position that required relocating from his home terrain in the Northeast to Minnesota. With four children all under twelve years of age, a wife who was a stay-at-home parent, and an economy in severe contraction, Charles believed he had no choice but to accept this job offer and relocate his family. In return, Charles landed a salary that supported a comfortable, middle-class lifestyle: "We were able to go out to eat; we were able to take small vacations; we were able to buy things for the kids; we were able to put them into good schools." However, within two years of relocating to Minnesota, Charles had again lost his job, this time to a staff restructuring.

By now age fifty-five, Charles was having difficulty finding employment. There was an unexpectedly brief stint in 2010 with a company that recruited him back to the Northeast—remembered as "the happiest six weeks that we've had." In that short time span, he and his wife met with a realtor, listed their Minnesota home, selected new schools for their children, and were making other arrangements for returning to a more familiar environment when these plans came to a sudden halt. "My boss got fired," Charles recounted, "and they let me go."

Charles entered a new career phase: long-term unemployment. Having endured two relocations, both ending in unexpectedly sudden job loss, had, however, led Charles to an important realization: "My wife and I decided that [Minnesota] is where we're going to plant our roots. We've got to stop all the stops and starts; we're just going to stay here now. The kids are happy here. We just want to stop moving around." It took three years after that point before Charles secured full-time employment. This time, when he lost his job after just a few months, fifty-eight-year-old Charles found it downright familiar. He was among hundreds of employees dismissed in his employer's nationwide downsizing effort.

Real life bore no resemblance to the expectations Charles once held for his career or his current stage of the life course. As a young man, he admired big business, and in both his career path and retrospective analysis of job loss, he still readily embraced neoliberal ideals like personal responsibility and taking ownership of one's circumstances. Yet while Charles once also accepted the terms of the flexible employment contract, he was becoming aware of the deficits embedded within this lopsided bargain. Approaching age sixty, Charles was seething with anger at a tumultuous marketplace and contemporary employment practices: twin forces that had uprooted his family, overturned their middle-class existence, and left them in a financially perilous position just when he should have been thinking ahead to retirement. About the only certainty was that Charles was no longer willing to move for a job.

Our larger sample of interviewees similarly understood the business logic behind their dismissals: employers, they agreed, must prioritize market forces over labor costs. For approximately 71 percent of the sample ($N = 44$), however, their list of career nonnegotiables included short commuting distances and a strong desire not to uproot themselves for the pursuit of continued employment. In other words, they put the brakes on the notion that workers seeking employment must be flexible to the point of being geographically untethered.

In this chapter, we dig into the motivations behind the ways interviewees—people who had endured job loss and extended unemployment—restricted their employment options. As workers in midlife, our respondents were deeply rooted to home and community. They were also embedded within networks of relationships that created human interdependencies and offered crucial social support. Their middle-class and upper-middle-class social standing provided access to resources, opportunities, and a mindset that facilitated the ability to stay in place. Because these insights depart considerably from previous research on job relocation, it is useful to examine some of the prominent themes emerging from this scholarship.

Making Sense of Job Relocation

Who is more likely to relocate for a job? Researchers across varied academic disciplines—sociology, demography, psychology, and management studies, for example—have answered this question by administering hypothetical relocation scenarios to groups of survey respondents. Their goal is to assess which sociodemographic groups are more amenable to relocating, and results focus on variables including marital status, family status, age, and community attachment that correlate to relatively high or low likelihoods of considering relocation.

Around marital status, the focus has been historically limited to studies of heterosexual marriages and, in particular, the decisions of working wives. In one analysis of survey data collected in the late 1970s, for example, working wives were found to be less willing to support a hypothetical job advancement that involved relocation. This correlation was strongest for wives who subscribed to traditional gender role ideology and whose husbands were employed in well-paying jobs.[1] Evidence from a more recent German survey finds working wives less willing to relocate for their own career advancement.[2] And a 2017 qualitative study of couples who participated in corporate relocations demonstrates the powerful effect of the male breadwinner model on wives, who, in this study, prioritized their husbands' careers and relinquished their high-status professional jobs.[3]

Other research draws attention to the importance of spousal salary in relocation decisions. Specifically, survey respondents with spouses who earn the greater share of household income are more reluctant to relocate, regardless of whether they identify as wives or husbands.[4] This finding speaks to the experiences of trailing spouses, or those who follow a spouse for their new job (and often encounter reduced earnings for doing so).

How does the presence of children in a household affect a person's willingness to relocate? In some studies parents, especially those parenting younger children, are less willing, though in other studies, children have no discernable impact on the decision.[5] These latter findings are puzzling given the potential for a residential relocation to disrupt a child's academic achievement, social ties, and community connections.[6] However, in one survey of employees who accepted a job relocation, workers with children were especially motivated by a desire to avoid being unemployed; this desire could mediate concerns about the potential upheaval in children's lives.[7]

Age stands out as a variable that produces more consistent results. Several studies find younger workers are more willing to relocate for a hypothetical job advancement, as well as for an actual employer relocation or as a means for career advancement in a professional occupation.[8] One economic analysis of the U.S. Panel Study of Income Dynamics, a nationally representative household survey, helps explain this finding: men under age forty saw their annual earnings increase after a relocation, while their older counterparts faced an income drop.[9]

At the same time, it cannot be assumed that older workers are always less willing to relocate. For example, only the oldest respondents in one survey sample, those close to retirement age, were unwilling to relocate for a hypothetical employment opportunity.[10] In a survey of public sector employees, younger respondents were more willing, but not when the proposed relocation required moving to a dissimilar community.[11] Still other studies find that a willingness to relocate declines as the number of years lived in a particular community increases, suggesting that age interacts with community attachment.[12]

Additional measures of community attachment, specifically satisfaction with a community and the presence of parents in the same community, also yield negative correlations.[13] Respondents who perceive their spouse as having strong community ties report less willingness to relocate, but the effects are more pronounced for women.[14] Strong friendships within a community also appear to enhance a feeling of embeddedness, which inevitably strengthens attachment and decreases the willingness to move for a job.[15]

One important factor informing these studies is that the data were largely collected by surveying individuals who were presently employed; in other words, reemployment was not a pressing concern when they took the survey. Further, most of these studies appear to be premised on the now-outdated notion that job relocation will yield career advancement and financial gain.

We took a different methodological and theoretical approach to studying willingness to relocate for employment. Rather than administer surveys regarding hypothetical scenarios, we sought out the ways our focal group responded to open-ended questions. Asking things like, "How long have you lived in Minnesota?" "How many jobs have you applied for?" "Were these jobs located in Minnesota?" and "Have you looked for jobs in other states?" does away with the assumption that individuals faced with relocation decisions are choosing among many options or that relocation is an economically rational behavior. Instead, it allows us to focus on the question of whether, for this group of workers, relocation is a feasible response to job loss in a destabilized economy and during a life course stage known as midlife or middle adulthood.

Our Interviewees' Answers and Their Life Course

Nadine's proclamation, "No, no, no. It's Minnesota, it's gotta be," was among the most emphatic in our study. After experiencing two major job losses in four years, Nadine believed her only option was to accept a minimum wage temp job in a neighboring state while continuing to reside in her rural Minnesota home. That meant a time-intensive round-trip commute. "Probably five counties and two states, and they're all back roads," Nadine explained, "and they take forever and you're already working twelve hours, so you're taking two-and-a-half hours to get there, and two-and-a-half hours to get home." Still, the huge trade-offs felt worth it: "I love Minnesota. I want to stay here. It's what I know."

Not everyone was as intrepid as Nadine. Carl, for example, was seeking employment within ten miles of his home. Olivia was searching within a thirty-to-thirty-five-mile radius, and Marie was willing to travel one hour "in almost any direction." Nicole initially looked for employment within a fifty-mile radius but avoided commuting by accepting a part-time job close to home that paid "just barely more" than her expired unemployment benefits but allowed her to regain and maintain her health. When explicitly justifying their geographic boundaries, several obvious factors were mentioned, including hazardous winter roads, fuel expenses, wear and tear on their vehicles, and traffic. While it might appear that job opportunities were sacrificed by self-imposed restrictions, the distances specified by our respondents are not far off from the average distance U.S. workers traveled to work in 2014: twenty-six minutes each way, or slightly less than a one-hour round trip.[16]

A handful of interviewees mused about looking for employment in select locations outside of Minnesota, though in a way that appeared simply to embrace a kind of compromise; if they could not find jobs locally, then they would at least consider some preferred locations. For example, Kaaryn, an alcohol and drug counselor, claimed she was "looking for jobs anywhere" but then expressed a preference for Fort Myers, Florida. Newly unemployed Cat mulled over the idea of relocating to some of her preferred destinations—a warmer climate, "but not hot," or a more cosmopolitan environment such as "out east"— but did not appear to be taking steps to make relocation a reality.

Lyle emphasized the need to be geographically flexible, and indeed lived up to this expectation by accepting a job in the Southwest. It lasted a mere eight months. Lyle's rationale for his continued flexibility after that disappointingly short period was informed by his perception that employment opportunities for senior sales managers were extremely limited in Minnesota. He ran through a list of possible destinations, noting those he would (and would not) consider: "I'm not moving to Detroit. I'm not moving to Des Moines. Not moving to Omaha [or] Fargo. Would we move back to Houston? Maybe. Dallas? Maybe.

Kansas City? Probably. Colorado? Maybe. East Coast? Maybe, but for the right opportunity." In the end, however, Lyle preferred to stay in southern Minnesota, where he grew up.

It might be tempting to conclude that our more inflexible interviewees were fickle. However, we should not jump to conclusions before understanding what else the data show. When answering additional questions about the effects of job loss on their relationships, finances, and self, respondents' replies yielded several additional justifications for geographically restrictive job searches. They mentioned their advanced age and how comfortable they were in their homes and in their neighborhoods. They talked about the bonds, benefits, and obligations that came with living near friends and family. And they revealed how their social class shaped their job search and mobility options. In these instances, a life course perspective continues to offer valuable insight.

Historical Times

If we wish to understand why our sample of older unemployed workers was reluctant to relocate, we must revisit the two divergent labor markets spanning the careers of baby boomers: the era of job security into which they were born, and the neoliberal era of employment flexibility into which they were cast. Although interviewees did not specifically mention this overarching context, it nevertheless appeared to inform their decisions to not relocate for a job.

As we outlined in chapter 1, the era of job security began shortly after World War II, at the same time as the baby boom. The postwar economy was marked by a shortage of workers and a surge in job openings; together, these factors solidified an employment contract that today we would call "worker-friendly." To attract and retain a loyal and committed workforce, employers offered financial and career incentives that, for most white-collar workers—and, indeed, White male workers—included internal career ladders. For workers who were committed to staying put, these ladders offered a means of climbing upward within the organization toward more lucrative, in-house opportunities.[17] When job relocations occurred, these were typically at the behest of an employer seeking to staff expanding regional, national, or global offices, and they tended to involve generous relocation packages including pay raises, bonuses, and stipends for moving expenses. All this support dampened the disruptions and difficulties of transitioning to a new place.[18]

While the post–World War II employment contract fostered a "bounded" career model, one based on lifetime employment with a single employer, by the mid-1980s this idea was growing obsolete for most categories of workers.[19] Routine personnel reductions, initially introduced to improve a company's survival prospects in a global economy, helped establish a "boundaryless" career model.[20] With a boundaryless career, white-collar workers must anticipate a rapidly changing series of jobs, companies, occupations, and even geographic locations in the pursuit of continued employment. The underlying assumption is that the job seeker can and will operate as an ideal flexible worker, thinking of themselves as a "company of one" or the proprietor of "self as business."[21] Employee mobility, however, is more likely to be lateral in this system. Think back to Charles, who moved across companies, industries, and geographical areas without any guarantees of job security, let alone career advancement. Because relocations are now pursued as a strategy to maintain continued employment, the financial burdens have shifted from the employer to the individual, and companies rarely offer support for those who must move.[22]

Coming back to the life course tenet of historical context, our interviewees entered the labor force when mutual commitment, compromise, and obligation were etched into the employment contract. By the time they were dismissed from their jobs in midlife, these values were no longer upheld by employers. Does that mean our interviewees fully abandoned them, too? Likely not. As sociologist Dawn Norris observed in her study of job loss among middle-class workers, "Simple awareness of a changing job market may not lead people to immediately abandon the values and expectations that have been cultivated throughout their lifetimes."[23] Our interviewees' reluctance to embrace the new geographically flexible worker ideal is no doubt tied to a mindset developed at the beginning of their careers, when workers and their families tended to plant roots in a single geographic location.

In addition, some interviewees astutely saw through the fiction of the geographically flexible worker. Sally, for example, identified an important risk to her personal well-being: "I don't particularly want to move for a job because of the nature of jobs these days. I mean, I can move and then that will disappear and then what? I'm stuck there." Luke, a former senior telecommunications manager, shared a similar concern: "Last thing I'd want to do is move somewhere and then I get downsized in a year or something. I don't want that." These respondents understood that without reciprocal loyalty between employer and employee, relocating in response to unemployment was simply too risky. They knew people like Lyle, whose move out-of-state lasted only eight months; if that happened to them, they would be out all their relocation costs, just to get back to where they started.

Wendy, whom you will recall from our first chapter was still struggling to recover financially from two extended bouts of joblessness, said directly that the costs of relocating would come out of her purse, and that was something she could no longer afford. Another woman, Sara, was enraged when she made it to the final round of interviewing for a distant job, but rather than being flown out, she was summoned to a Skype interview: "You are asking me to move out to the East Coast, to a town I've never been before, to work at a company where I don't know anyone, without ever having seen the area or met anyone beforehand? And I said, 'That's simply not acceptable to me, especially when it's at my own expense. And I'm taking the risk here, so no, I don't agree to a Skype interview.'"

As each of these latter quotes demonstrate, relocating older workers have to assume considerable risk, yet (as we note in the next section) they have only so many working years to recover financially and establish a sense of home in a new place. Many interviewees were unwilling to play along with these expectations. No matter how desperate the search for reemployment was, they prioritized human dignity, which for them meant staying put rather than accepting choices offered from an employment model favoring profit over worker well-being.

Rooted in Place by the Timing of Lives

A second tenet of life course theory is that the impact and meaning of a life event depends on the age of the person experiencing this event. While some events and transitions gracefully coincide with age norms, others, like late-career job loss, are poorly timed and consequently more difficult to navigate.[24] A considerable number of interviewees explicitly referenced their life stage when speaking about being "too old to pick up and leave." Lars, for example, was reluctant to "pull up roots" at age fifty-seven, so he concluded, "Here's where I am, here's where I'll stay."

Lars was one of twenty-nine interviewees who discussed having a strong attachment to home, city, or state. Such deep allegiance and sense of belonging reflects decades of residing in a single place. Another man, Carl, had never left the small southern Minnesota community in which he grew up. He recounted an idyllic childhood full of sports, long summer days spent at the local swimming pool, and "lots of friends." And he described this enduring attachment while sitting in his home, right across the street from his childhood elementary school.

Also born and raised in Minnesota, Tammy moved out of state early in her career but was eager to return in the late 1990s when a local job opportunity became available within her company. Tammy mentioned that her family's Minnesota roots stretched back to the 1870s, when Scandinavian immigrants flocked to the state in search of available farmland: "My relatives from Norway came up from Canada and then to Minnesota.... My family homesteaded farms down around—if you remember the old TV show *Little House on the Prairie*, all those little towns they talked about, that was the area where we had our farm ... Ulysses S. Grant was the president when they got their land signed over to them." Not that our interviewees were unfamiliar with the wider world, of course. A few interviewees mentioned living or traveling extensively outside of Minnesota, as if to convey they had not been homebound. "I've lived in San

Jose [California]. I've lived in Kentucky. I've lived outside of Minnesota and I wound up coming back here," Kenneth remarked. "Why would I wanna go do it again? I already learned my lesson; my lesson is this is where my heart is."

Why were interviewees so passionate about Minnesota? Dylan noted he had lived in the state for almost three decades, yet he was lively with the enthusiasm of a newcomer when describing everything he appreciates about the Twin Cities: "I just love this place.... There's no place better... I also like the winters. I like the parks. It's just fantastic, it's a fantastic city. I love biking, walking. It is very comfortable. And I like the snow... I have a big snowblower, and I love the snow." Other interviewees drew attention to Minnesota's favorable employment qualities, which made leaving inconceivable. Sally, for example, had been working in the financial services industry when she lost her vice president job. She mentioned "a lot of opportunities" for white-collar workers in the Twin Cities, due in part to the presence of several Fortune 500 companies headquartered in the region. Victor pointed to what he saw as Minnesota's unique workplace culture; he believed that culture made it possible for employees to balance job and family responsibilities: "There have been times where I've been able to slip away to go to a kid's Christmas program in the afternoon, and I remember being in meetings where we had a hard stop at five o'clock because people had to get to... soccer practice. Parents had to go because they were the coaches. In other places that would never happen.... The meeting would go until whenever... we were... done. Could be seven o'clock."

While it is true that Minnesota consistently earns top scores in popular media rankings of "best states to live in," the qualities and characteristics interviewees emphasized are not limited to the North Star State.[25] Perhaps what is reflected in their allegiance is, instead, a sense of Minnesota as home. Human geographers point out that the places we designate as home offer comfort, continuity, and a sense of control,[26] qualities that might alleviate the "ontological insecurity"[27] of an ill-timed life course event such as late-career job loss. Indeed, Dawn reinforced this idea when mentioning her "fear of moving" after her 2009 downsizing. "I have my comfort level here. This is my home."

Vanessa, now self-employed, drew attention to something quantifiably different about Minnesota: its social safety net is far more comprehensive than what is offered in most other U.S. states. She was particularly grateful for state-funded health insurance "for people like me who can afford to buy insurance but have been turned down." And Mark said he was grateful to live in a state he characterized as "incredibly progressive when it comes to unemployment," observing that life had "been a lot harder" for unemployed friends living elsewhere in the United States. In keeping with Vanessa's and Mark's comments, a 2018 report published by the Economic Policy Institute demonstrated that Minnesota's recovery from the Great Recession had been faster and more robust than Wisconsin's. This discrepancy between neighboring states was attributed to the innovative policy agenda instituted by Minnesota's Democratic governor Mark Dayton after his 2010 election victory.[28]

Respondents' social class standing, both middle- and upper-middle class, also appeared to intersect with age to influence their decision-making about whether to stay or go. They were financially and emotionally invested in—and understandably reluctant to leave—homes and other properties, like the "dream house" Luke and his wife had recently built; Kai's lake home, a real source of pride; or the rural properties that brought Margaret and Nadine such great joy. However, recall that our interviewees experienced job loss in the wake of the 2008 Great Recession, a downturn that was accompanied by a collapsing housing market. The resulting mortgage delinquencies and foreclosures led to the devaluation of homes across the nation. These economic forces certainly informed Cassandra's decision not to relocate: "I would've moved a long time ago from here, but I have to sell a house. The economy isn't the greatest for selling a house. I probably could now break even." At age sixty-one, Cassandra's concerns about her dwindling nest egg were valid; statistics show that unmarried women like herself are at greatest risk for living in poverty in old age.[29] By holding on to her home, she joined others in the hope that the housing market would eventually see an upswing and bring back some of the security that vanished when housing prices tanked. Indeed, in an era where job loss is all too common, houses can function as an alternate retirement account for the middle class,[30] making the timing of selling a home all the more crucial in the second half of life.

Linked Lives

According to life course theory, people exist not in individual isolation but rather within networks of interdependent relationships that inform how they experience and respond to life course transitions. When elaborating on their rootedness to place, forty-six respondents, approximately three-quarters of the sample, specifically referenced how their lives were linked to spouses, parents, children and grandchildren, and friends.

More than a dozen interviewees identified their spouse as the person who anchored them to Minnesota. Some of these respondents were married to people who had their own opinions about where they would and would not wish to live. Frank, for example, reported that Google had seemed interested in recruiting him after his 2011 job loss, but he did not pursue this option because "my wife was never interested in moving to California. [She] doesn't like California that much." Mark, who had been unsuccessful in finding stable employment since his 2009 job loss, described something similar as he quipped, "Well, my wife would tell me, 'Mark, you have to write if you're going to live somewhere else; be sure you write a letter once in a while,' because there's no way she's going to move."

Interviewees also referenced a phenomenon that academics call the "two-body problem," defined as the difficulty dual-career couples encounter when choosing a single destination to satisfy both partners' employment needs. From the perspective of linked lives, the misfortune of late-career job loss is thus inadvertently shared by spouses and other family members. Our interviewees believed their partners were unlikely to find comparable employment in a new location. While Victor would move if the "right opportunity" presented itself, he also noted, "My wife has got a really good, good job, and it would be hard for her to replicate what she's got somewhere else." Consistent with previous research, we met those reluctant to relocate because their spouses currently earned a significant share of the total household income, which helped to maintain the couple's standard of living.[31] It was hard to forgo that sure thing for the gamble of a move. By way of contrast, however, Bruno explained that his wife was also unemployed and in the process of starting her own business. They were unwilling to relocate because Bruno and his wife were committed to "trying to get that going."

Another perspective arose with Brian, who had only moved to Minnesota in 2005. He secured a midlevel managerial position that lasted until 2012, when his employer initiated a corporate downsizing. Two years later, Brian was still unemployed. When we asked whether he could use his social network to find a new job, Brian said with a touch of bitterness, "I don't have one here." Later he jokingly commented that this absence was his wife's doing—after all, it was she who insisted they relocate to her home state. The move, which made sense at the time, in Brian's eyes, ultimately destabilized his social network, crippled his job prospects, and introduced financial tension into his marriage: "We're okay financially, we're not in great shape, but it certainly is a stress on the relationship because we'd like to do more, and [my wife] would be really happy if we could double our income to where it was."

Stability matters for care work, too. Workers of all ages are embedded in networks of relationships, but some older workers are rooted in place because of caregiving roles they assume for parents in the life course stage scholars call late adulthood.[32] Downsized in 2009 and unable to find stable employment, Bruno was financially managing his ninety-year-old mother's estate in addition to performing property maintenance and repairs on the house in which she still lived. Nick, downsized in 2014, described running errands with his mom, who was at the time being treated for cancer.

The burdens of eldercare were more intense for some of our female respondents, a finding that fits with Aliya Hamid Rao's 2020 conclusions in *Crunch Time: How Married Couples Confront Unemployment* and with the wider literature on unpaid family caregivers.[33] Roberta's ninety-year-old mother lived with her, in an arrangement that was becoming increasingly challenging because "she has dementia, early stages, so she's still able to laugh and talk, but some things are difficult." After her 2013 job loss, Katherine stopped pursuing a job in Florida "because my mom and dad were falling and I had to stay here." Her siblings, noting that Katherine was the eldest and, after a divorce, currently single, thought it made the most sense for her to care for their parents in old age. She outlined all that went into the day-to-day management:

> It's the caregivers, the medication, it's the people at the memory care. It's the doctors' visits, it's the chiropractor appointments, it's the dental appointments, it's caring for the one at home—he's depressed. It's the meals, it's caring for him, it's making appointments for him, it's checking in on him, and I have to say that the hugest piece is the expectation of constantly doing without any compliments or positive reinforcement. It's just the reality of . . . aging and the belief system of, "I raised you, I gave you a roof, I paid for your education, now you be front and center for me."

Looking ahead in her own life, Sally acknowledged that she was open to relocating after her father died, but the prospective move would be limited to just one place: where her oldest son resides. "[My older son] is living out in New York City, and if the younger one decides that he wants to . . . live out there, I said, 'Once my dad isn't with us, then maybe we'll pick up and move out there.'"

Like other midlife adults, our interviewees were altering their work trajectories both in response to the needs of their aging parents and in terms of the best interests of their adolescent and young adult children. "The sandwich generation" is the term social researchers apply to the phenomenon of midlife adults sandwiched between caregiving duties.[34] Helen, a human resources consultant, experienced a series of job losses both in the months leading up to and during the Great Recession. Each took a toll on Helen's mental health, but she was primarily concerned for her two daughters, one enrolled in a local college and the other still in high school. When one of her brothers-in-law, invoking the logic of the flexible worker, implored her to widen her job search—to the "entire continent" if need be—Helen was floored: "And I said, not a chance. I am not going to uproot my children and transplant them anywhere in the country because I need to find a job. . . . He could not even understand that, that made no sense to him whatsoever. It was entirely, for him, 'Where do I go—anywhere—in order to have the most rich and profitable career experience?' And my whole brain was, oh no, no, no . . . I'm living in the environment that I want to live in, in terms of where my family unit is." Helen discussed why familial ties are so important for older workers like herself, disclosing her own personal realization about the human lifespan: "You're actually seeing yourself now, 'Oh, shit, I'm going to leave the planet.' You . . . start to get that, because you buried your parents. At about my age . . . we're burying our parents, so now we are the parent, we are the generation. So, you . . . go, 'Oh, wow, there is an end to [my time on this] earth.'"

Decisions about when the search for new employment could begin were also informed by the linked lives of older workers. Charlotte, a former sales account manager downsized in 2012, had to focus in the short term on caring for her widowed father. When he died unexpectedly, overwhelming grief combined with the responsibility of closing her father's estate left her still unable to focus on the search for new employment. Sure, life course transitions such as the death of a parent can disrupt anyone's employment search, but the rhythm of the human life course means that older workers are more susceptible to these losses. Nick, for instance, experienced a broad combination of events that coincided with—and hampered—his search for new employment: "I spent the first two months [of unemployment] really focused on Mom and some other issues in our family. I have a brother . . . whose wife probably will be dead in the next month or so from breast cancer. And I've been going down there frequently. I have a sister whose husband is going to be dead in the next couple of weeks, . . . also from cancer. And then another sister-in-law who was just diagnosed with stage 4 lung cancer, and . . . my dad died." As these examples illustrate, older workers are at a stage of life where their relationships have the potential to complicate the search for new employment. These same relationships, however, also offer crucial social support when late-career job loss upends things. For example, after her 2012 downsizing, Margaret received frequent phone calls and welcomed lunch invitations from a sister who lives nearby. Sean did not want to leave Minnesota in part because of his "aging parents" yet also described his dad as "my best friend who is always there for me." Adult children offered support to their unemployed parents, too: Norman was having "lunch once or twice a week" with a son who lived in the same neighborhood, and Teresa drew attention to the financial assistance she received from her children, who were covering her monthly car, cell phone, and utility payments.

Given these intimate examples of linked lives, it is little wonder the idea of relocation was overwhelmingly rejected by our respondents. This sentiment is succinctly captured by Meg, a lawyer who had not recovered from her 2007 job loss: "[Minnesota] is where home is, that's where my support system is, that's where my tiny family is." With unanimous resolve, interviewees spoke of the strategies they would use to avoid leaving Minnesota. In doing so, they invoked options available only to socioeconomically privileged workers like themselves.

Human Agency through Socioeconomic Status

In life course theory, the tenet "human agency" serves as a reminder that individuals actively respond to situations by drawing on the range of possibilities they perceive as open to them. Nearly all respondents provided multiple examples of the choices and compromises they made to stay in place after late-career job loss. What stood out was the degree to which their agency was enabled by advantages accrued from social class. For most of these individuals, a middle- and upper-middle-class social standing granted resources, opportunities, and a mindset that allowed them to manage unemployment without being forced to leave home. As Colin confirmed, "I guess we [weren't] desperate enough to . . . start casting out a net further."

Isaac, the senior marketing manager introduced in chapter 2, was downsized in 2008 and struggled to find permanent employment for the next five years. By his 2013 interview, Isaac had decided he was now "retired." This life course transition, from seeking steady employment to becoming retired, was possible because Isaac's wealthy parents had transferred "a sizable amount of money" to him and thus, "money's no longer an issue." The support that flows between middle-aged children and their parents, after all, is not only about the younger caring for the older but is frequently symbiotic.[35]

After the 2009 loss of her managerial job, Nicole found a job, but it came with some trade-offs. The new job came with less prestige and less pay, though it was, happily, stripped of the ninety-minute, round-trip commute she had endured for her previous position. Luckily, Nicole described, her husband's financial savvy allowed the couple to maintain their middle-class standard of living: "He charts what we spend every year, and we've stayed pretty steady, and we're . . . spending less than what we're bringing in, and that's his big worry, . . . if we're overspending—and we're not. . . . It doesn't even feel like we've really made some cutbacks. . . . And in fact, we're doing more travel than we were doing while he was in school. So it feels like we're actually better off than we were then, but it's more just keeping things in balance."

Marie, a former office manager and legal assistant, took a different approach to managing her 2011 job loss. She sold her stately Twin Cities home in a desirable neighborhood and relocated to a nearby rural community. Her romantic partner already lived there, and she would be able to offset a potentially longer commute with the lower cost of living—in fact, she could live mortgage-free outside the city.

Certainly not all interviewees were as well positioned as Isaac, Nicole, and Marie, yet the benefits of social class remained visible in others' strategies taken to manage job loss. Helen, whose job loss brought about existential reflection, realized that her lifespan had an expiration date: "You do think about the fact that you're going to die. I mean, you can't miss that message . . . because they're giving you lots of those clues." With this epiphany, Helen accepted a part-time professional job in a nearby suburb and redefined her life priorities. She invoked the rhetoric of personal choice: "So now what is valuable to you? What's important to you? How do you want to spend your time? Is it on a train going up to

Minneapolis? No, no, it is not. So if you can figure out a way to . . . downsize it, reduce your costs of existence, then you give yourself more choice."

Helen's decision was aided by her middle-class resources: the safety net provided by a new husband who was financially secure and generous with his support; the retirement savings Helen "dipped into," much to the chagrin of her financial planner; and some financial assistance provided by a college friend who had "married a multimillionaire." In other words, Helen's range of possible choices was broadened by her social connections to security and wealth.

Vanessa, who did not have the financial benefits that may come from being married, assumed the role of freelance editor after her job loss from the newspaper industry in 2011. While this employment decision was not financially lucrative, it was strategic. Vanessa claimed the shift would help her avoid the entry-level positions she was convinced an extensive job search would yield. Two resources made Vanessa's adaptation possible: the inheritance she drew on when her editing work did not generate enough income to pay her monthly bills, and the knowledge that if she sold her Twin Cities home in a trendy neighborhood, the sale would generate a profit large enough to sustain her. "That's one huge asset," Vanessa exclaimed.

For some, job loss upended their financial position, but here, too, we found those who expressed financial vulnerability also shared stories that demonstrate a different type of middle-class resource: the strength and conviction of their self-efficacy. In contrast to individuals who view themselves as "powerless, helpless, and fatalistic," individuals with a sense of self-efficacy believe they possess control over their environment and see themselves as "architects" of their life path.[36] This form of human agency is best expressed by Sara, a social media specialist who experienced a job loss in 2007 and another in 2011.

After eventually finding a contract position, which meant substantially reduced pay and no benefits, Sara devised a strategy to recover her previous financial standing: "I will probably now, every six months to a year, be sending out more résumés so I can find out if I [can] get a better paycheck [or] if I'm still desirable." In other words, she was not content with her contract work and had adopted the idea of self-as-business. Having applied for "over eight hundred jobs" since 2011, Sara had refined her job-searching skills and was confident the effort would help her land a position that would allow her to reclaim a middle-class standing. A sense of self-efficacy was expressed in a different way for Luke, who felt able to turn down a job offer in another location because he was confident that "there's opportunities here." Sally also decided against accepting a job in Chicago that "fit like a glove" because the prospective employer was "not bending" when she inquired about working remotely. In her own words, "I had to put that one . . . on the shelf."

As these examples illustrate, personal savings, high-value homes, and spouses with sufficient earnings are not the only class-related resources interviewees used to manage their late-career job loss. A belief in one's self "as strong, active, confident, and competent" also informed how our interviewees approached their job search.[37] Evidence collected by other scholars demonstrates that occupations characterized by prestige, autonomy, and socioeconomic achievement—the very types of occupations most of our interviewees once held—are more likely to produce such personal beliefs.[38]

There's No Place Like Home

From the outside, it could look strange to see a range of unemployed older workers who stoutly refused to broaden the geographical stretch of their job searches. Did they not need work? Yes, but, still they restricted their quest for work. Was their reluctance somehow related to their age or the result of neoliberal shifts in the employment relationship that made relocating a risky venture? Well, it turns out it is a bit of both—and more.

With their career paths bookended by two distinct historic moments, our respondents are uniquely positioned. They entered the labor force under an implied social contract that bound employees and employers. This bounded career path was assumed to mean working in one company for an entire career, moving up the ladder into higher-prestige, higher-pay positions, and then retiring with benefits and maybe a gold watch. But by the time they experienced job loss, there had been an enormous labor market shift that nullified the contract and eliminated the bounded career model. With a new playbook came the boundaryless career—one that spans several employers, across indeterminate geographic space, with lateral moves and dwindling benefits. The underlying logic today is that the motivated neoliberal subject can and will operate as an ideal flexible worker. In place of the career ladder is a tightrope on which workers nervously balance. The promise for career advancement within a single employment setting no longer exists for most workers; the career goal now is simple survival. Add to this burden the complications of a global economic downturn and a mortgage foreclosure crisis, which caused a confluence of high rates of job loss, long stretches of unemployment concentrated among older workers, a stock market crash, and a housing crisis. This toxic environment would discourage relocation for workers of any age, but older workers have fewer years to recoup their losses should they make the wrong decisions at this crucial moment.

It is not surprising that our older, middle- and upper-class interviewees responded to limited local opportunities for reemployment with a distinct reluctance to leave home. After being rooted to a single location for decades, if not their entire lives, most respondents were unwilling to uproot. They felt connected in their communities and were protected by Minnesota's unemployment benefits in ways they would not be elsewhere.[39] For our interviewees, this safety net assistance helped them stay afloat when they were otherwise unmoored. Age and experience also afforded our respondents the wisdom to know that geographic flexibility had a huge caveat: they alone were responsible for the costs and risks associated with relocating. Their experience of job precarity made them all too aware that relocation would not safeguard them against being terminated again.

Interviewees commonly invoked their linked lives with immediate family and friends to further justify their geographically restricted job searches. In their comments, it is evident that the notion of the flexible worker is incompatible with the ways most older workers live their lives. The flexible worker may appear neutral, but embedded within this construct are myopic assumptions about who the flexible worker should be: a risk-tolerant individual immune from basic human needs for family, community, and a sense of place and magically unencumbered by age-specific constraints and responsibilities to others. In other words, a capitalist dream, but a societal nightmare. The social relationships of our interviewees revealed distinct, age-specific challenges to this possibility: spouses who were established in their own careers, ailing parents who required support, children entering adulthood, and aging siblings experiencing their own life course transitions. The relational responsibilities of midlife adults, which also provide the reciprocal social support interviewees needed after their job loss experience, were nonnegotiable.

In her 2015 book, *The Tumbleweed Society*, sociologist Allison Pugh captures the effects of frequent job relocation on intimate relationships. Her interviews with three groups of workers—those who experienced layoffs, those who had stable employment, and those who had relocated either for their own job or a spouse's job—reveal the impacts employment precarity can have on personal relationships. This was most apparent for the disadvantaged and financially insecure workers in her sample, the group Pugh calls the "laid off." These individuals were more likely to respond to discord in intimate relationships in ways that fit with the logic of the flexible employment contract that dominates their lives: they quickly detach and move on. This group stands in sharp contrast to Pugh's "stably employed" interviewees: public sector workers whose jobs continued offering a bounded career path. This latter group approaches interpersonal conflict in ways that fit with the values informing their work lives: commitment, compromise, and obligation.[40] Pugh's research helps us recognize that today's employment contract, mandating workers' flexibility, has emotional consequences for swaths of workers with fewer resources than the people in our study. So, what will happen to individuals who spend their entire careers chasing a job? Will they ever accrue the social, familial, and financial resources—and the corresponding ability to say no to a move—that buffered the older workers in our sample?

While most of our respondents resisted the neoliberal imperative of being a geographically flexible worker, as we will see in the next chapter, they nonetheless responded to the stigma of job loss by embracing the neoliberalist happiness imperative, with its emphasis on positivity, optimism, and second chances. The stories we review bear out what scholars Cabanas and Illouz call "emotional capitalism," or the modern demand that individuals cope with workplace stress and job precarity by achieving individual happiness, emotional intelligence, and resiliency.[41]

6

Silver Linings and Positive Thinking

"Attitude-wise, I've always been a positive guy. You know, people are like, 'glass half full, glass half empty'; I see a glass that's twice as big as it needs to be." By the time we met in late 2013, fifty-four-year-old Lyle's career had been in turmoil for at least four years—it started with a corporate restructuring just after the Great Recession—yet, like two-thirds of our interviewees, he scaffolded his experiences with the language of positivity and silver linings.

Lyle's job loss story was bleak, though peppered by optimistic comments and clichés. Sitting down with us Lyle laid out the facts: He lost his sales manager position in 2009 to a corporate restructuring. After a disheartening eighteen-month period of unemployment and job searching, Lyle decided to relocate so that he could accept a sales director position in a Southwestern state, a move of over one thousand miles. Then that position ended abruptly after just eight months. He returned to Minnesota, where his wife had remained, though the labor market had not improved. There just was not any full-time, salaried employment available to Lyle, and credit card debt and mortgage payments were threatening the couple's already tenuous financial stability. So Lyle took temporary jobs paying a fraction of the income he could formerly command. Now living on his thirteen dollars an hour, Lyle and his wife adjusted their lifestyle and withdrew savings from their 401(k) retirement accounts. Why not? Lyle conceded that their retirement plan had been reduced to two possibilities: "winning the lottery" or never retiring.

Sometimes in the same breath, Lyle confessed confusion and frustration about all this uncertainty and upheaval, and he espoused sentiments reflecting a positive mindset about it all. For example, he believed his last dismissal may have been "a blessing in disguise," a welcome release from a "toxic" work environment. Happiness, it seemed, was Lyle's unwitting sales pitch—perhaps an emotional defense against the sense of failure that late-career job loss can inflict. In one particularly revealing moment, Lyle strung together an unbroken series of tough-love motivational phrases with the determination of a high school coach: "The job hunt sucks, but you know what? It's a fact of life, stuff happens. Pull up your bootstraps; nobody wants to hear your pity party. Go out with a positive attitude."

This curious paradox of our interview data, in which older workers are demonstrably harmed by job loss and yet emphasize its bright sides, is actually common in articles and books written by fellow scholars. Alongside the negative repercussions on physical and mental health, family relationships, and personal finances, older white-collar workers consistently tell researchers that there are undeniable silver linings to their experiences of suspended retirement dreams and protracted unemployment.[1] Yes, there are people who are just more upbeat than others, and some may be trying to soothe their own worries or put interviewers at ease by saying the same kinds of worry-abating things they tell concerned friends and family. But they are not lying. Job loss can absolutely be a negative experience and lead people to see themselves as happier. The key to understanding the apparent contradiction, we argue in this chapter, can be found in the neoliberal socioeconomic and cultural transformations that have reconfigured the terms of Americans' relationships with employers, government institutions, and each other.

Making Sense of Job Loss

Conventional wisdom and scholarly research agree that job loss is a negative life event. In ways that align with important sociodemographic differences, the literature is definitive: unemployment takes a toll on physical and mental health, as well as familial relationships.[2] To recap chapter 2, late-career workers who lose their jobs are more likely than their employed peers to report poor physical and mental health.[3] While the financially vulnerable report more of these health problems after job loss, the more affluent, who often tie their identities to their careers, tend toward greater psychological difficulties and often experience feelings of self-doubt and self-blame alongside identity threat.[4] Making matters worse, older workers' chances of finding new employment are low, with age discrimination often thwarting their job search efforts.[5] During and immediately after the Great Recession, American workers aged fifty-five years and older reported the highest rates of long-term unemployment, increased risk of financial hardships, and, when they did secure new jobs, steep declines in earnings upon reemployment.[6]

Before this economic shock, the blessing in disguise narrative was already prominent in interviews with those experiencing job loss. Loring Jones, a professor of social work, heard it from the middle-class professionals he interviewed, and approximately half of sociologist Craig Little's sample of technical-professional workers similarly noted their positive reactions to job loss.[7] Financially comfortable midcareer folks told researchers they welcomed an opportunity to pursue new career directions, and over a third of the white-collar workers in another sample described their job loss as an "acceptable, if not positive experience" and a relief from stressful or otherwise unsatisfactory work.[8]

More recent social research finds managers reframing job loss as a new chance for self- and career exploration, or what a subset of professionals unemployed at the beginning of the Great Recession described as the opening of a new "chapter" in their lives.[9] In follow-up interviews in one study, conducted two years later, only one respondent still believed their dismissal had been a "blessing in disguise"; nonetheless, while the others had moderated their earlier optimism, some still said the experience taught them "life was possible and even desirable outside those [corporate] gates."[10] Another group of middle-class, postfinancial crisis job seekers extolled renewed confidence and a greater awareness of their own "creativity, adaptability, and entrepreneurial spirit."[11]

In a cultural context in which positivity is widely promoted by mass media, self-help gurus, psychologists, and others, Claudia Strauss applies an anthropological lens to the affirmations she heard in her sample of jobless interviewees.[12] In tandem with their "blessing in disguise" comments, respondents spoke about handling job loss by participating in activities that generated positive emotions and comparing their situations with stories of those who were less fortunate, a technique she labels "counting my blessings." And, while Strauss and other scholars view positivity as the dominant "emotional regime" of American society, the bright-sides approach also crops up in research in non-U.S. contexts and with other groups of workers.[13] For example, in one Australian study, almost half of the occupationally diverse interviewees had constructed a consistent narrative about breaking away from difficult job conditions and finding the freedom to re-create their personal identity.[14]

Employers are implicated in perpetuating the happiness imperative among job seekers as sociologist Ofer Sharone argues in *The Stigma Trap: College-Educated, Experienced, and Long-Term Unemployed*. This observation is derived from Sharone's in-depth interviews with twenty job recruiters involved in reviewing and vetting applicants to white-collar positions. These professionals routinely instructed job seekers to project positivity, because anything less would be a "deal breaker" for prospective employers.[15]

All this research confirms that our interviewees' upbeat framing of involuntary job loss is neither anomalous nor divorced from larger sociocultural processes. However, by situating interviewees in a neoliberal, flexible twenty-first-century economy, we can move beyond existing scholarship. We can begin to see neoliberalism as the driver of late-career job loss, as well as the seductive cultural script that insists on personal responsibility and bootstrapping. Individuals befuddled by the forces behind staff reductions and restructuring efforts are encouraged to make sense of their difficulties by looking for lessons learned and bullets dodged, not by directly critiquing changing labor demands, reduced employer responsibility, or heedless profit seeking. By framing our analysis this way, we build on current work examining the pervasive reach of neoliberal ideas about individuals and who (or what) is responsible for their welfare, broadly conceived.[16] First, we need to put our interviewees' positive interpretations of negative events in historical context.

Socioeconomic and Cultural Context of Job Loss

Baby boomers roared into adulthood starting in the early 1960s, when it looked like there was no limit to sustained economic growth. Some of their parents had weathered two world wars, with the Great Depression and the dawn of the Nuclear Age sandwiched in between. However, recently created social safety nets buoyed post–World War II prosperity and opened far broader access to the American dream via education grants, expanded home ownership, and the establishment of career jobs complete with breadwinner salaries that permitted a family to live on a single income with the expectation of pensions to fund well-earned retirements. Indeed, all this happy prosperity was only available to a slice of Americans—those who were White—but to the children they raised, this boon created an expectation of baseline security. In the workplace, employers used various enticements to attract and retain committed, often lifelong employees. Internal promotion systems incentivized job performance and single-employer loyalty for white-collar workers; robust unions ensured the same by securing adequate pay and seniority-based promotions for blue-collar workers.[17] Many workers enjoyed protections including health insurance and company pension plans.[18] In this particular social contract, companies rewarded their faithful and competent employees with stable employment, steady living wages, and a range of benefits to ensure continued commitment.[19] It is no wonder young baby boomers were an optimistic group.

The neoliberal age of flexibility operates under a different set of assumptions that have implications for the contemporary employment relationship. The first signs of this paradigm shift emerged in the early 1980s, when numerous structural factors coalesced in corporate efforts to reduce employment costs and redirect focus to profit and share price.[20] The euphemism "downsizing" was common vernacular by the end of the century, as business organizations routinely engaged in workforce reductions, targeting employees across industries, occupations, and occupational hierarchies.[21]

At the same time organizational practices were embracing dispensability, white-collar employees were taking notice of changes in their working conditions. Soon, they reported changes of the kind more traditionally reported by manual laborers: the pace of their work had intensified, workloads were increasing, they were expected to continually raise their productivity, and they were confused because management strategies were always shifting.[22] These conditions and the rising sense of job precarity have been linked to rising reported rates of poor physical and mental health among American workers.[23]

Today, staff reductions are considered a commonsense business strategy—both a justifiable response to unstable market conditions and a means to achieve strategic financial goals.[24] Shifting the burden of employment costs from employers to employees has also meant cuts to those enticements employers once offered. For example, the number of workers with employer-supported health insurance and pension plans has steadily declined since the late 1970s.[25] Defined-benefit pensions, which provide guaranteed predetermined financial disbursements to retired workers, have largely been replaced with nonguaranteed defined-contribution plans that require individuals to invest their savings in the stock market. Now, what financial advisors call "growing a nest egg" is contingent on individual investor savvy, market stability and continued growth, and plain old luck. In this new retirement model, a loss of social standing is always a possibility. During the Great Recession and its sluggish recovery, individuals nearing retirement lost significant personal wealth because their money had been invested in a crashing market—at a time when business publications thrilled at the news that ten thousand baby boomers were hitting the traditional retirement age of sixty-five every day.[26]

This ideological shift from the collective good to individual autonomy is evidence of the heartless neoliberal revolution.[27] Cultural and political notions emphasizing "personal responsibility" and "taking ownership of one's own life" paved the way for welfare retrenchment, spreading until they informed a variety of political, economic, and social spheres.[28] In the workplace, the consequences have shifted from an ethos of corporate responsibility for worker well-being to one privileging individual autonomy. No longer are white-collar workers being recruited and retained via employer enticements; today, employers demand that workers consistently (and preferably measurably) earn their keep and enhance their employability by building human capital and cultivating a positive attitude.[29]

Social scientists Edgar Cabanas and Eva Illouz refer to the neoliberal emphasis on positive thinking as "emotional capitalism."[30] Emotional capitalism inverts psychologist Abraham Maslow's hierarchy of needs, which specifies the achievement of individual self-fulfillment only when innate needs for personal security and stability are satisfied.[31] In contrast, twenty-first-century white-collar employees are implored to cope with workplace stress and job precarity by achieving happiness, optimism, and resiliency, by turning "setbacks into opportunities for self-improvement and personal development."[32] This reversal is attributed to positive psychology, an academic field created by Professors Martin Seligman and Mihaly Csikszentmihalyi in 2000 with the goal of studying personal well-being.[33]

Happiness discourse and the tendency to retreat inward when facing difficult life circumstances are American hallmarks. Author Barbara Ehrenreich traces the deep roots of positivity rhetoric far further back in U.S. history than even Norman Vincent Peale's famous mid-twentieth-century book, *The Power of Positive Thinking*.[34] Cabanas and Illouz point to several twentieth-century social theorists who noted that the rhetoric of individuality necessitates retreat and self-help in response to personal difficulties.[35] These foundational traits gained further credibility at the beginning of the twenty-first century, as positivity doctrines merged with the happiness mindset promoted by positive psychologists and gained reinforcement from self-help gurus, management consultants, job coaches, and other social actors.[36] Chronologically, this timeline coincides with the expansion of neoliberal ideas about individual autonomy and self-reliance.

Considering these factors, the optimism Strauss found in her sample of unemployed people is not unusual.[37] With constant exposure to happiness rhetoric, both in the workplace and society at large, individuals in a variety of difficult circumstances are encouraged to interpret their experience with a positive attitude.[38] Recall that, as we described in chapter 4, cultivating the right attitude was also step one of the Wooddale job club's faith-based programming for job seekers. Positivity, sociologist Allison Pugh argues, has become the culturally acceptable emotional response to negative life events.[39] When our interviewees talk about silver linings, we believe it is a genuine impulse based on both personal optimism and the demands of neoliberalism's happiness imperative.

The Silver Linings Playbook

Interviewees reported a wide range of painful impacts of job loss, summarized in chapter 2. Some spoke of severe financial hardship as they whittled their budgets down to the bare bones, and most everyone shared psychological distress, including "anger," "anxiety," and "depression." Their housing hardships ranged from deferred home maintenance and difficulty meeting mortgage payments to foreclosures and one short sale. Unable to afford medications and health insurance, some had forgone routine medical tests and necessary dental work. Ageism complicated both their dismissal experiences and subsequent job searches. Nonetheless, fully two-thirds (forty-two of sixty-two total interviews) of these conversations were animated by the ameliorative rhetoric of silver linings. It turns out that late-career job loss, like so many aspects of life, evokes a full range of emotions.

Most of the silver linings comments came toward the end of the interviews, when overall reflections were introduced by asking, "What, if anything, has changed about you since your job loss?" "Have any parts of this experience been powerful or profound?" and "What, if anything, is sustaining your hope?" Positive comments also emerged spontaneously, for example, when interviewees discussed their relief at exiting a stressful workplace.

Nearly two-thirds of the folks who talked about silver linings (twenty-five of the forty-two bright-siders) had been unemployed for at least a year, and a few declared themselves "retired" or "semiretired." Those with soft landings after job loss were either financially positioned to retire or, if they were still searching for new employment, had safeguards and resources that reduced financial hardship. The rest experienced the low wages (if they found work at all), food insecurity, or other difficulties that came with a hard fall. We were not surprised that the soft landings folks were more likely to emphasize the silver linings of their situation (thirteen of eighteen individuals), but it is notable that a sizable number of respondents with hard falls also employed this rhetoric (seven of fourteen individuals).

Broadly, and regardless of where they fell on the hard falls/soft landings continuum, interviewees' optimism coalesced around two themes. The first, quality of life, included both comments about *improved health and wellness* post dismissal and individuals' *critique of the former workplace environment*. In the second theme, personal growth, job loss is presented as a valued opportunity to pursue life-improving goals and possibilities that we characterize as *self-actualization*, *reevaluation of life priorities*, and *renewed focus on relationships*.

Quality of Life

Improved Health and Wellness. In defiance of the well-publicized negative impacts of unemployment on mental and physical health, a sizable number of our interviewees—sixteen of the silver linings subsample—said their health and wellness improved after their job loss. The positive transformations they described frequently started with better sleep.

A year into her unemployment, former publishing manager Beth reported no financial distress and stated that she slept "very, very deep at night" since her 2012 downsizing, while Carl specified his relief at having "no nightmares" following his 2013 dismissal as a general manager in the construction industry.

Nicole lost her managerial position in the middle of the Great Recession, spending fourteen months cobbling together part-time jobs unrelated to her training and previous employment. When Nicole eventually secured full-time employment close to her home, she lamented that the new job came with diminished occupational prestige, a significant salary reduction, and a loss of job responsibilities and decision-making power compared with her earlier career. Nonetheless, she relished the short commute and reported that her mental and physical health were improving. In addition to "not being always so sleep deprived," Nicole stated: "You never wake up in the middle of the night worried about things, you don't carry home stress with you, when you go on vacation you're really on vacation, and all that is a really good thing. So, I would say . . . the longer I'm at it, it leans to a really good thing. . . . I was headed for a diabetes diagnosis, and now my blood sugars are back to normal." Former copyeditor Vanessa remarked, "My blood pressure went down quite a bit" after job loss. Carl similarly referred to improved markers of physical health, boasting that "my blood pressure went down, my everything went down."

Having time to pursue healthy lifestyles was one reason for the improvements our interviewees reported. "I'm going to live to be one hundred years old," Cat declared confidently just two months after her 2014 downsizing from the health care industry. She was sixty-eight at the time of our interview and said, in unemployment, "I am taking care of my body physically better than I was; I get to eat and plan the food that I want." Upon his dismissal from a director position in the food industry, Tad pursued cycling with aplomb, telling us he had biked "2,500 miles this year; I did about 1,500 last year." The effects of this new hobby were apparent at his last checkup: "I'd lost probably between ten and fifteen pounds, my cholesterol is down twenty points, my blood pressure is at an all-time low, and I'm sleeping through the night."

It might be tempting to conclude that the economic standing of our interviewees played a role in their improved health and wellness. Tad, after all, had personal savings, a company pension, and a generous severance package; several other individuals expressing these sentiments also encountered a soft landing after job loss. However, not all the health and wellness improvements we hear about can be chalked up to interviewees' financial circumstances. Indeed, even those with financial struggles discussed their improved health and wellness. We believe these comments reflect interviewees taking on the self-care goals promoted by the neoliberal culture of happiness and contrasting them with their previous difficulty in finding the time and space for these therapeutic practices.[40] Typically, our respondents' mentions of improvements in physical and mental health were linked to other comments noting the stressful and all-consuming aspects of their former jobs and workplaces. In sharing this silver lining, workers contrasted their present health with the relentless, overwhelming demands of the contemporary white-collar workplace, where basic human needs were neglected in favor of corporate strategies, goals, and objectives.

Critique of the Former Workplace Environment. To emphasize the ways their lives improved after dismissal, sixteen respondents presented their job loss as bringing relief from anxiety, frustration, and other negative emotions. They described their former workplaces with words and phrases such as "dysfunction," "toxic," "a drag," "so much crap," "a nasty place to work," and "sucking the life out of you."

Notably, the specific aspects interviewees brought up are inescapable hallmarks of neoliberalism's push into the white-collar workplace. Henry, a self-identified retiree (though he was in the process of launching a new business venture at the time of our interview), was glad to be rid of "the meetings and the politics" and the "constant change." Charlotte knew a lot about constant change, having lost her account manager position in November 2009 because her firm's sales took a nosedive, then being rehired six weeks later only to see her position finally eliminated in a 2012 corporate merger. When Charlotte was interviewed in 2013, she was in her ninth month of unemployment and reported struggling to afford critical medication. Her savings account had a "minimal balance"; nonetheless, Charlotte expressed relief at having been terminated because "things had gotten very, very stressful" at work. When she elaborated, Charlotte emphasized the tight bind of meeting managerial expectations, insufficient resources, and ever-longer working hours: "You're expected to do more with less. And the . . . tools that they were expecting you to use weren't there . . . It was pretty much ten hours a day, seven to five. And I . . . rarely took a lunch to leave my desk. No breaks." Redefined corporate goals, former insurance underwriter Tammy said, had created "impossible expectations [that] everybody knew . . . were impossible."

Vanessa chose self-employment after her 2010 downsizing, a transition funded in part by an inheritance. She had seen her dismissal coming. Her employer was struggling with online competition, and waves of layoffs had started three years prior. Thinking back, Vanessa was unequivocal: she would not return to her former employer, even if she had the chance. "If I were to go back now, I think I would be miserable. For one thing, we'd have the managers breathing down our necks, knowing that the industry is imploding. Many of the people I like working with are gone. Many of the most talented people have quit and moved on to other things, and so there's a lot of reasons to be glad I'm not there." Roberta, a former marketing communications consultant, had been unemployed for about half a year when we spoke, but her career instability began with a downsizing back in 2008. Like Vanessa, Roberta's experiences with management, specifically a vice president who was perceived as challenging, reminded her that losing her job was ultimately a good thing. She remained in contact with some coworkers but eventually withdrew, citing: "They are still complaining about being there.... One friend suffered depression and had to go on medication and was having terrible stomach problems and stuff because of staying there.... And it's still very negative there. I just don't want to be a part of that energy anymore. I kept telling them: ... 'Life is so much better when you are out here, out from under this person.' I said, 'It's toxic where you are working, don't you realize that?'"

Tad explicitly connected his critiques to twenty-first-century corporate practices: "When you start seeing the kind of bonuses that some of these guys get... it's like, really?... You're kidding me. And you're telling me you earned it?" He gave an example, a blunder in which senior executives miscalculated the market, resulting in the downsizing of "850 people." Tad and his co-workers "ended up paying for that" with their jobs. He concluded, "I don't trust corporations.... I think American society needs to recalibrate a little bit." Tammy expressed a similar post-job-loss cynicism toward corporate work environments when stating emphatically, "No more cubicles." She continued: "I just know for my mental health, no cubicles, no corporate, no sales projections, no goals like that. I cannot do that kind of stuff.... I will never do that to myself again. I will never put myself in a position where I have to go, 'Yes, sir,' or agree to something I absolutely don't believe in." Amid pervasive dysfunction, job loss was reframed by interviewees as liberation from the workplace conditions of the modern era: unrealistic corporate expectations, incompatible management styles, and job insecurity.

Personal Growth

Self-Actualization. Job loss brought another set of realizations into focus: a number of respondents embarked on a series of postdismissal experiences they perceived, frequently in gender-specific ways, as enhancing personal growth. Much like how Maslow described self-actualization—an effort "to become more and more what one is, to become everything that one is capable of becoming"[41]—seventeen interviewees referred to job loss as an opportunity to embrace and expand their potential. Among those respondents describing personal growth after job loss, approximately two-thirds were women ($N=11$).

Self-actualization could mean having the time to fully embrace a valued personal attribute. For instance, Loren believed her "que será, será" attitude had become "more pronounced" in her three years without full-time employment, while Roberta and Helen both noted a stronger awareness of their inner "resiliency." Beth said her 2012 downsizing "opened up a different part in me that existed and that's a good thing.... Whatever was inside has broken out of its shell."

Exploring new personal interests or reviving existing ones was sometimes an end in itself. Tad, who took up cycling, also shared that he had started taking improv classes after his dismissal, while Pamela, whose multiple job losses since 2007 left her fearful of becoming a "bag lady," resumed a cross-stitch project she began decades earlier—before her daughter was born. Marie was downsized from her legal administrative position in 2011 and, after an unsuccessful employment search, decided to try building a skill set that had nothing to do with the needs of a white-collar workplace: "I bought a fixer-upper house [and] I've been fixer-upping... I ripped out twenty-four boards in my deck and went to a lumberyard and got them cut, and put the new boards in, and then I cleaned the deck, and then I stained the whole thing. I do stuff like that. I've painted all the rooms.... I take wallpaper down. I've cleaned the carpet. I've painted ceilings. I sew. I belong to music groups. I do a lot of good stuff. I paint. I have a self-portrait in [an art] show right now."

Pursuing passions was sometimes also about career reinvention, even if that was not necessarily the initial goal. Tammy had never been passionate about insurance underwriting, though she mentioned finding satisfaction in being "a creative problem-solver." After her 2009 job loss, Tammy used her pension from a previous employer and her 401(k) to pay the bills as she turned an artistic hobby into a career. In discussing the personal satisfaction derived from this career path, Tammy reached far back into the life course to establish consistency between her current career and past self. Artistic creativity, she commented, "I guess that's something that... has been in my brain cells since I've been a kid. I love looking at clouds and seeing things. I love looking at wallpaper patterns and finding things. So maybe that's something I've always looked at." Now she finally had the time and freedom to see it.

Dawn had an epiphany when she lost her enjoyable twenty-year job as a mechanical drafter to downsizing. She transitioned to caring for her mother, after which Dawn "found an affinity with elderly people, and thought I could go into nursing assistant kind of work." Indeed, she enrolled in a nursing assistant program and found commensurate employment. When we met in 2013, however, Dawn had been terminated due to performance issues following a workplace injury. Across our study participants, we learned that even personally rewarding career transitions did not always produce financially successful outcomes.

Several men referenced a different type of self-actualization but had similarly disappointing economic outcomes. These individuals sought to augment their education and skill sets to maximize their chances in a slack labor market. For example, Timothy completed a master's degree in design after a 2008 dismissal from a merchandising position, and Lyle, introduced at the beginning of this chapter, used funds provided through the Minnesota Dislocated Worker Program to expand his educational credentials past his high school diploma—he completed a "mini-MBA" certificate program. Though both men anticipated their self-investment efforts would boost their labor market competitiveness, neither succeeded in locating full-time employment.

Although Timothy and Lyle could not parlay their new credentials into new jobs, it was clear that these achievements were meaningful to them. Lyle was enthusiastic about his certificate, commenting that it had "reinforced ... I am good at what I do. I am a professional. I can do it." In a similar vein, Victor, a former director in the financial services sector, sought out consulting opportunities to expand his skill set and enhance his market value: "[I've] been in the ... same company, same job, same industry for thirteen years. In some cases, that's not attractive to a new employer. And, so what I've been able to do ... through contract work [is] broaden my skill set and also broaden the number of companies and industries I've worked in." Instead of lamenting the loss of his former position, Victor reframed his long tenure in a directorship as a liability and, despite his disappointment at not being able to find permanent employment, emphasized the benefits he was reaping from his more recent contract experiences. Each of these men spoke during their interview of struggling with no longer being the family breadwinner; their self-actualization strategies were one means of remediating their damaged identities.[42]

Reevaluation of Life Priorities. A second personal growth experience interviewees described involved taking stock and revaluating their priorities. Often, they reflected on how they moved past materialism to a more philosophical or spiritual focus for their lives. Of the eighteen interviewees whose experiences included these transformations, a little over 60 percent were women ($N=11$).

Commonly, interviewees' loss of income had compromised lifestyles, strained relationships, and often produced downward mobility. Yet several interpreted the change as a positive one. In an upbeat tone, Sophia explained that she lost her managerial position in 2012 and was unable to acquire gainful employment. She was sixty-seven when we met the following year, and said she considered herself retired. Now drawing on her Social Security benefits, Sophia announced that losing her career meant "I ended up in poverty level as far as money, but I realized money isn't everything." Repeatedly, she referenced the "money can't buy you happiness" cultural idiom: "I get up and I thank God. I'm so lucky, you know? I'm so blessed with all the things in my life that money doesn't buy.... I just realize how blessed and lucky I am, and I can do whatever I want.... I've realized that I can live on a lot less. There are a lot of things that I do without that I didn't need." Sophia's new perspective on conspicuous consumption was reiterated by other interviewees, many of whom drew distinctions between needs and wants.

Will landed as a bicycle mechanic after being downsized from his engineering position in 2011. He enjoyed the deeper connection to his passion for cycling, though he acknowledged it was less money and less prestige than his prior occupation: "It's probably changed our lifestyle a little bit and that's ... maybe for the better.... Found out that maybe some of that other stuff wasn't all that important, I guess." Fellow interviewee Kevin considered himself retired since his 2009 layoff and said similarly that he found "I don't need the material goods. I mean, at one point I had a cabin with pontoon fishing boats and all these kinds of things, but they aren't that important." In a reflective tone, he told us, "I really appreciate the kind of serenity that I have today."

Beyond serenity, several in our study described job loss as a spiritual journey. In the four months since her 2014 dismissal, Kaaryn reported becoming "more reflective and more of a 'human being' and not a 'human doing,'" while Katherine said twelve months of unemployment had helped turn off her preoccupation with productivity: "For the first time you can feel this incredible peace and calmness around being and not doing—and having gratitude." Teresa said, "You appreciate each day," and "I don't know that I'll take a lot of things for granted that I maybe did before," while Helen characterized a protracted period of repeated job and personal losses leading up to and during the Great Recession as "a gift of your strength and your resilience and your resourcefulness." Since each of these interviewees also shared stories of the destabilizing effects of job loss on their financial security and mental health, it is remarkable that they appear to embrace the experience with a certain holistic optimism.

Henry's blessing-in-disguise narrative is emblematic of the interviewees who said their job loss had given them new philosophical understandings of the greater meaning of life.[43] When he was dismissed in 2009, his only sibling was dying. "We were there when she died," he said calmly, noting that "my job loss" coincided "with my sister's loss.... I was glad to be available—and I would've made myself available if I was working, but, you know what I mean? It was like ... what else matters?" Likewise, sharing that a week after he was dismissed, a former colleague lost his daughter to suicide, Tad took up the count my blessings narrative: "I've got a problem? No way.... You start talking about putting things in perspective. This," he concluded of his own job loss, "is nothing."[44]

Renewed Focus on Relationships. Tad's and Henry's stories bring us to the third personal growth experience emerging from our interview data: renewed focus on relationships. Yes, job loss could mean losing work-based friendships, and the financial stress could sow discord in intimate relationships. But twenty-six interviewees referencing silver linings of job loss discussed new or enhanced existing relationships as a positive outcome. Especially for men ($N = 18$), this period of joblessness seemed to provide space in which their relationships could develop and thrive.

Lyle was also among those whose family relationships were reinvigorated. No longer tied to a relentless travel schedule, he celebrated the fact that "I've had ... more time [to spend] with [my daughter] and ... with my parents, and do some things that I normally wouldn't have been able to do if I was working sixty-eight hours a week." Seymour was frank about the stress of looking for employment that could accommodate his medical needs yet described the timing of his 2009 dismissal as "perfect... because I'm available to [my young son] and I can do things that I wouldn't normally have done, and I think I'm better off for that." Terrence, too, experienced hardships after his 2013 downsizing and still framed his protracted unemployment positively: "It's been a blessing in disguise. I would never have had this much time with my two grandchildren, and we've grown a lot closer. So that's the silver lining of this whole thing."

While Will shared that his 2011 downsizing motivated him to propose marriage to his long-term girlfriend, he admitted that his decision was affected by finances: "I'm not going to be able to make my house payment with what I'm making now," he said, indicating an intention to move in with his partner. The situation was not, however, entirely without romance: "I think [my job loss] also probably brought us closer.... I'm depending on her a little bit more, so it kind of knocked me down a notch or two [in] that I'm not so careless with my relationship." Carl's marriage benefited from his job loss, albeit in a different way. When he was a construction manager, Carl had developed some unhealthy habits. He tended "to stay up too late, have too many beers, eat too much pizza, eat unhealthy in general" and had become "not a nice person." He figured his wife benefited from his dismissal and release from all the stress and bad habits: "I think she likes me more when I'm not working. I'm more the way I used to be."

Late-career job loss could also help people nurture more expansive friend networks. Partially, this was a function of having more time. Mark said losing his job in 2009 gave him the chance to "get together with some buddies every week" for coffee, and Carl was having fun with a new group of friends: "I hang around with a pretty bizarre group of people on Wednesdays and play Ping-Pong; they're from all different backgrounds." Improved friendships also tied into narratives about personal growth when interviewees spoke about their newfound "tolerance" and "sensitivity." Kenneth thought he gained empathy when he lost his job in 2014 and found himself craving but not getting emotional support from his family. Choking up, he said, "I'm more sensitive to people that are hurt." Kenneth apologized as he began to cry, then continued, "Because there are so many people out there that are hurting and people on the other side don't care.... I think I feel their pain more now because I'm... in the same boat."

With these comments, interviewees convey that connections to family, spouses, friends, and acquaintances played a restorative role after job loss. The comments also indicate that interpersonal relationships and dependencies were easier to balance without the stressful demands of their previous work and workplaces. Given that a large proportion of men we interviewed spoke of seeking solace in interpersonal relationships when they lost their jobs, we further suspect these individuals previously labored under gendered notions that work ought to be a man's primary focus.[45] With time, and sometimes with greater emotional openness, job loss had revealed the benefits of nurturing valued relationships that link our lives together.

As an aside, when we last discussed gender (in chapter 2), we indicated that our female respondents were more likely to have fallen hard after job loss while our male respondents were more likely to have landed softly. In this chapter we find some additional gender differences related to how our respondents articulated their personal growth after job loss. Specifically, women were more likely to express self-actualization and a reevaluation of life priorities while men were more likely to articulate a renewed focus on their relationships. These findings add another layer of complexity to previous research by sociologists Sarah Damaske[46] and Alia Hamid Rao[47] demonstrating that gender, much like age, plays a critical role in shaping the unemployment experience.

Live, Laugh, Love?

Sophia teetered on the edge of poverty and said that job loss "changed everything." With a smile, she added, "I love it." The fact that two-thirds of our respondents spoke of job loss at least partially in terms of silver linings is surely influenced by factors earlier scholars have identified. Emphasizing the positive could be a coping strategy to help people avoid the demoralizing effects of unemployment or regain agency in the face of uncertainty. Portraying yourself as cheerful or optimistic, alternatively, might be an attempt to repair or allay the stigma attached to American unemployment.[48] Furthermore, a few interviewees reported employment counselors encouraging them to embrace a positive attitude with the intention of enhancing labor market success, a phenomenon the aforementioned sociologist Ofer Sharone explored in more detail in *Flawed System/Flawed Self* and *The Stigma Trap*.[49] Again, it makes sense that those who had the softer landings of our sample were also slightly more likely to use the silver linings frame; they objectively had more to be upbeat about. Recognizing these potential factors, we nonetheless assert that individuals' positive comments about job loss reflect their larger socioeconomic and cultural contexts, particularly in terms of generational experiences of employment and cultural scripts about individualism and the power of positivity.

As we have discussed previously, life course theorists assert that we need to understand individuals and generations as situated in their historical times. As baby boomers, our interviewees were socialized to participate in a post–World War II economy offering security. When they experienced economic insecurity in their fifties and sixties, the long-term commitment between employer and employee had been replaced in the neoliberal economy with heightened levels of personal risk and uncertainty. Subsequent generations would enter workplaces where they were socialized into employment instability, but these interviewees had been more intimately familiar with an earlier set of conditions more favorable to worker wellness, wealth-building, and job security. These previous employment expectations may well have informed the negative commentary interviewees shared about former workplaces and their apparent relief and quality-of-life improvements following job loss.

Additionally, interviewees are situated in a cultural context encouraging positive thinking in response to negative life events. Scholars argue that a happiness mindset is common within individualistic societies such as the United States. In these contexts, failure to project optimism may invite shame, guilt, and judgment from those responding to cultural conditioning.[50] Layered on top of this is the largely Christian socioreligious environment in the United States that, as we saw in chapter 4, may also promote the correct attitude as an antidote for personal woes. Thus, there are both social pressures to maintain a facade of happiness and a larger cultural "tool kit" informing individual responses to negative life events.[51] This inference is supported by the abundance of positivity vocabulary sprinkled throughout our interview transcripts: "serenity," "calmness," "gratitude," "appreciate," "gift," and "resilience."[52] As these examples suggest, even though the older workers we interviewed retroactively pushed back against the neoliberal workplaces they escaped through dismissal, the cognitive confines of neoliberal happiness discourse and the implicit requirement of personal responsibility, from the marketplace to one's own emotions, become apparent in their job loss stories.

Pop psychology cautions against "toxic positivity," the notion that always looking on the bright side requires individuals to avoid or suppress difficult emotions such as sadness, fear, and anger.[53] Seeking deeper meaning from job loss, however, is not a misguided endeavor. Late-career job loss is a multifaceted trauma for many, and it can take a long time to reassess personal and professional goals. Positivity discourse, much like the religious coping techniques we reported earlier, can provide necessary comfort and reorientation throughout this process. Still, similar to relying on the right combination of attitude and faith, positivity discourse remains foundational to neoliberal notions of personal responsibility for health and wellness and to the public health and welfare retrenchment they have been used to justify.[54] Moreover, when individuals frame job loss as an opportunity to fix themselves and focus on their relationships, they sidestep any recognition of or challenges to the neoliberal structure of the flexible economy, within which only organizations appear to benefit. When those harmed by this new paradigm focus on conquering their personal shortcomings rather than protesting the system's failures, the current age of neoliberal flexibility will continue unless we make a concerted effort to come together and challenge the status quo. We expand on this conviction in our final chapter.

7

Where Are They Now? And What Can We Do?

> In so far as an economy is so arranged that slumps occur, the problem of unemployment becomes incapable of personal solution.
> —C. Wright Mills, *The Sociological Imagination*

Continuing unemployment and age discrimination. Lounging in the sun by the pool at a second home. Death, disability, and divorce. A newfound artistic passion and inner peace. Cutting back on expenses and realizing that stopping work is not an option. Retiring to new hobbies, homes, and travel to, well, anywhere they wanted, when they wanted. When we recontacted our interviewees in the summer months of 2023, we discovered a broad spectrum of later-life experiences in our sample of older adults who experienced late-career job loss.

In this chapter, we update readers on where some of our interviewees have been and what they have done, personally and professionally, since our initial conversations roughly ten years ago. Twenty-five individuals from our original group responded to a survey we administered. We also conducted follow-up interviews with six people from the survey pool whose responses we wanted to explore further (a description of the follow-up study can be found in our methods appendix). Once again, individuals spoke with candor and insight, generously sharing intimate details of their lives and interpretations of their career trajectories over the past decade. Thus, we are able to reflect on how their ongoing stories intersect with the major themes of this book, pass along their advice, and review the latest social scientific literature to flesh out some ideas about what we—not just older workers, but all of us—can do about job loss in a neoliberal era.

Neoliberalism, as we have discussed throughout these pages, operates on multiple levels with multiple implications for older workers. There are the neoliberal political and economic policies that involve shrinking the state and social services while privileging free-market forces, corporate interests, and an ideology of individual self-reliance. We have also seen a shift in formal employment practices and informal employment expectations, which has been characterized as a shift from the age of security (involving job stability and benefits, plus mutual loyalty between employee and employer) to an age of flexibility (with its downsizing and job precarity often woven through with age bias). When combined with the shock of the Great Recession and its aftermath, these political and economic patterns were both the context and cause of our interviewees' job loss experiences. As these older workers told us their stories, we have also seen how their narratives were often couched in neoliberal framings and assumptions, revealing the extent to which neoliberalism has, to its own benefit, seeped into our workplace cultures and broader consciousness.

For instance, we have noted how interviewees called on assertions of generational change to narrate how much—and how distressingly—their working lives shifted over the course of their careers. Their emphasis on generational differences, advantages, and disadvantages served to place the blame for their woes on younger adults instead of the structures under which workers of all ages are struggling. We examined how religious coping strategies and Minnesota's faith-based job clubs, while important sources of solace and support for job seekers, became purveyors of a mindset that paralleled neoliberal calls for individualistic bootstrapping and downplayed the true nature of the unemployment obstacles interviewees faced. Interviewees were rooted in geographical place by age, life stage, and material realities and, as such, were unwilling and unable to fulfill the neoliberal ideal of the flexible worker who would obligingly relocate for new employment. Indeed, several interviewees who refused to move for new opportunities recognized from experience that, given contemporary labor relations, such a move would do nothing to protect them from yet more job losses. We also saw interviewees' critique of other elements of neoliberal workplaces—the stress caused by unrealistic management expectations and the unrelenting demand to do more with less—and how it allowed them to paint their dismissals as a welcome escape from toxicity. These latter framings hint at a dual consciousness among our participants: they recognized the harsh reality of job loss while also characterizing their unemployment within the familiar neoliberal framework of positivity and opportunities for personal growth and self-actualization.

Our interviewees' experiences and interpretations corroborate the observations of economic geographer David Harvey, one of the foremost chroniclers of neoliberalism. As Harvey once summarized, "Neoliberalism has become a hegemonic discourse with pervasive effects on ways of thought and political-economic practices to the point where it is now part of the commonsense way we interpret, live in, and understand the world."[1] However, to respond to Harvey and draw on the work of Antonio Gramsci (the political philosopher most often associated with the concept of hegemony),[2] hegemony is never total and neoliberalism is not necessarily eternal. In the latter half of this chapter, we turn to a discussion of those signs for the future we see as promising.

A Decade Later

Whereas our first set of interviews were conducted at a time when older job seekers were still feeling the effects of the Great Recession, the 2023 follow-up study occurred in an entirely different sociohistorical context. So much had changed a decade later, including that we were more than three years into a seemingly endless global pandemic. Masks and yearly vaccine boosters had become the norm for many of us as we, our families, and communities learned how to live with COVID-19.

The pandemic and the ensuing dysfunction it brought to the marketplace contributed to soaring rates of inflation in 2021 and 2022,[3] putting the brakes on a nascent post–Great Recession economic expansion. In 2023, inflation rates declined considerably, but financial belt-tightening continued for those whose wages had not kept pace. With groceries, transportation, housing, and energy costs remaining at record highs, many households across the nation continued to feel the pinch. This financial precarity was measured by rising rates of household debt, driven in part by expanding credit card balances.[4] As if this was not enough, rapidly increasing interest rates made borrowing money even more costly. Meanwhile, the stock market dropped precipitously in 2022. Individuals with retirement portfolios that included stock were once again nervous about diminished returns.

On the jobs front, official unemployment rates climbed to an astonishing 13 percent in the first year of the pandemic,[5] surpassing even the highest rates recorded during the Great Recession's recovery. These early pandemic-related job losses were soon followed by American workers quitting their jobs in droves, a phenomenon dubbed "the Great Resignation." According to a 2021 Pew Research Center survey, the three most popular reasons for moving on were "low pay," a "lack of opportunities for advancement," and "feeling disrespected at work."[6] Other unhappy workers remained with their employers but engaged in "quiet quitting," a historically documented phenomenon that suddenly came to the attention of the popular media in the pandemic years.[7] In this form of workplace disengagement, employees express their dissatisfaction by doing only the minimum amount of work required to retain their jobs. The good news for job seekers was that both national and state unemployment rates fell to unusual lows. Minnesota, in particular, was singled out by the media for its "record hot labor market,"[8] which plummeted to a historic low of 1.9 percent in August 2022.[9] Instead of laying off workers, employers were now desperately searching for employees, evidenced by the "help wanted" signs appearing everywhere we looked. Amid a historic labor shortage, workers were gaining leverage. Some of the concessions select employers made included signing bonuses, higher wages, and allowances for workers to perform their jobs remotely if they wanted.[10]

So how about our interviewees—where were they in 2023? How were they making sense of their job loss a decade later? Were they still working or had they retired? And how were they managing in this new sociohistorical context? As we learned in our follow-up survey and interviews, they continued to endure hard falls, enjoy soft landings, and adapt to a variety of ups and downs in between.

Follow-Up Survey: Findings and Insights

In June 2023, we attempted to recontact fifty-one of our original sixty-two interviewees with a request to complete an online follow-up survey.[11] We succeeded in reaching forty-three interviewees, and more than half of them completed the survey.[12] Our survey was populated with close-ended questions and predetermined response categories. Many questions also provided space for individuals to elaborate on their responses.

We asked the survey respondents about their employment history in the years since our first interview. Three-quarters of the twenty-five-person sample ($N=19$) found work, but employment challenges were common. Ten respondents met the criteria for long-term unemployment to the extent that it took them six months or longer to find a new job. Job precarity was another issue a few respondents encountered. While eleven individuals indicated they had "one or two jobs" in the past decade, eight had held "three or four" or "five or more" jobs. When prompted to elaborate, they indicated that this instability was the result of short-term contract positions or part-time jobs. We assume these respondents struggled to find full-time employment, as research suggests this was a common experience for older displaced workers during and after the Great Recession.[13] Perhaps respondents were stymied by the ageist assumptions they encountered on the job hunt: employers viewed them as too old ($N=4$), too experienced ($N=3$), too senior level ($N=2$), overqualified ($N=2$), and lacking in technical skills ($N=1$). One comment provided deeper insight into the age and career-stage frustrations encountered by older workers seeking employment: "I discovered age discrimination, and [a] gap between my knowledge and wisdom and [that of the] individuals interviewing me on professional jobs. Interviewers seemed intent on asking questions . . . with little interest in the knowledge, wisdom, and level of expertise I had to offer."

At this time, our oldest respondents were in their late seventies, and the youngest were in their early sixties. Given their ages, it was not surprising to learn that eleven respondents considered themselves retired. Most of these individuals reported enjoying their retirement, though the timing for those with an "early retirement" was not what they had planned. One respondent noted, "I had [foiled] plans to work until I was sixty," while another stated, "I'd hoped to continue working, but because of my age and experience, there were few options available." Retirement did not mean, however, these respondents were disengaged and living a life of leisure. For example, one male respondent was "cultivating a business idea," another was engaging in "some meaningful volunteer work that built on my job skills," and a third man became "a climate activist." In contrast, a retired female respondent was contemplating returning to the labor force because "high inflation has taken a toll on [my] retirement budget."[14]

Among those respondents who were not currently employed yet also not retired, one individual was on disability and another two were actively looking for work. Seven respondents indicated they were currently employed, but none of these respondents had full-time permanent positions. One employed respondent was now working a contract job, three were working part-time jobs, and three were self-employed. We do not know if these types of reemployment were the result of personal preference or an inability to find full-time opportunities that matched career stage, expertise, and salary expectations. In terms of earnings, a single currently employed respondent earned a salary consistent with their previous salary; the remaining respondents were earning less—"WAAAAAAY less!"—than they once had. (While other research shows that older workers in general tend to report earnings losses upon reemployment,[15] the earnings losses our respondents reported may also be due to self-employment or working part-time.)

Many of our interviewees were previously adamant that they would not move, so we asked respondents where they lived today. Most indicated they were still in the same place. The five individuals who relocated each selected one of the following response categories: "to be closer to family members," "to reduce housing costs," "to live in a different environment," "to have access to more job opportunities," or "to be closer to a new job." The one respondent who moved closer to a new job had an employer who "took care of the move-related details."

This support would have been a decisive factor. Given the findings we presented in chapter 5, many of our interviewees' earlier refusal to move was related to the fact that they could not afford to relocate.

Looking back a decade, respondents reflected on their job loss experience. Approximately half the sample ($N = 12$) was "very or somewhat satisfied" with how life turned out after job loss. One respondent indicated, "I . . . read my doctor's notes on MyChart recently and it said 'he [feels losing] his job is the best thing that ever happened to him.'" Another respondent in this category took the opportunity to share his disappointment "in the system." As he elaborated, "I'm fortunate, but others not so much." Four respondents were "neither satisfied or dissatisfied," and another eight were "very or somewhat dissatisfied." A retired respondent in the latter group, "very or somewhat dissatisfied," explained her response: "I would say being unemployed caused me to slip from middle class to poverty level by IRS standards."

We gained further insight into these responses when we delved into the emotional impacts of job loss. Many respondents were now experiencing relief ($N = 9$), happiness ($N = 5$), and/or personal fulfillment ($N = 12$). On the other hand, five respondents reported persistent financial hardships ("just to pay bills is bad"), and five indicated they struggled with their mental health as a result of job loss.[16] For some, the total experience of job loss was difficult and disheartening. One respondent described their job loss as "humiliating, frustrating, discouraging, painful, and a host of other adjectives." Another summarized their experience as "soul-crushing" because "it felt very personal, even though I was told, 'It's not personal.' Like hell it's not!"

Of course, we have no idea whether those interviewees who responded to the survey are representative of our larger original sample. Still, the fact that we touched base with over 50 percent of the original participants who were still alive (and for whom we had a current email address) provides some updated insight into how respondents had fared since we last spoke.

Follow-Up Interviews: Findings and Insights

We conducted in-depth conversational interviews with six of the follow-up survey respondents in July and August 2023. We reached out to Charles, whom we highlighted in chapter 5, because he had been determined not to leave Minnesota and yet he indicated on the follow-up survey that he had moved out of state. When we interviewed Charles in 2013, he was one of the few men who had experienced a hard fall. Ten years later, he was still having an objectively rough ride.

Now sixty-seven years old, Charles gamely reported, "I'm healthy, I feel great," but "I'm not ready to retire." The truth was, he could not. On top of several dismissals, Charles reported other costly and highly stressful life events, including facial paralysis that took away his ability to smile, a painful divorce, and the death of his youngest child. In 2013, Charles was adamant he would never move again; however, he did not anticipate his ex-wife and children relocating to the Northeast. By 2020, the first year of the pandemic, a sense of self-isolation drove Charles to quit a full-time job he loved and move closer to his children. In some ways, Charles had less to lose; he was not originally from Minnesota and thus did not have roots that ran as deep as some other respondents. Still, he was now living across the country in an unfamiliar city and in an expensive one-bedroom apartment that was a far cry from his previous home in a tony Minnesota suburb rich in amenities. With the understatement characteristic of his entire interview, Charles noted, "I wouldn't recommend what I've had to go through the last ten years."

Though Charles secured full-time employment in his new location, he soon encountered a familiar scenario: "The company started losing money, and they decided they couldn't afford me anymore. So, they let me go in January of '23, and I've been looking for a job since." Financially strapped and lacking the type of networking and social support Minnesota's job clubs had once provided, Charles accepted a physically strenuous part-time job at a shipping outlet. He spoke positively about his new colleagues. Generationalism sometimes arose when Charles contrasted his own work ethic with that of the "kids" with whom he now worked, but he also characterized them as "fun," "smart," and "ambitious," saying they "energized" him while he, in turn, provided a "stabilizing force" in their workplace.

Charles was also seeking a second part-time job to make ends meet. He understood that his age made him an unattractive candidate for full-time positions, especially when he was competing with applicants thirty or more years younger. No longer willing to mask his age as he once did, asserting, "No, this is who I am," Charles nonetheless felt powerless to challenge the age discrimination he perceived from prospective employers. As he recounted: "I've spoken to attorneys, many attorneys, about it, and they said it's the most difficult thing in the world to prove unless somebody blatantly comes out and says, 'You're too old for this job.' There's no way to prove that it's age discrimination. So, most attorneys won't even take that case."

At the other end of the spectrum was tanned and relaxed Felix, now aged sixty-seven. He was a valuable person to interview because his survey responses indicated that he continued having a fulfilling retirement and a soft landing after job loss. As you may recall from chapter 2, in addition to a relatively generous severance package and a defined-benefit pension, at dismissal Felix accepted a lucrative fifteen-month contract from his former employer before embarking on early retirement. Unlike all our other follow-up interviewees, Felix was lucky enough to receive such remnants from the age of security, and he felt that his dismissal did not affect his life in any negative way. As he told us, there was "no way" he would ever go back to work. He simply did not need the money and was not willing to give up his leisurely lifestyle. Moreover, the boredom he once feared had never materialized.

These days, Felix and his wife continue to spend their summers in Minnesota and then escape the state's infamous winters for the warmth of the Gulf Coast. "We have the best of both worlds weather-wise," Felix happily noted. He is surrounded by close friends he and his wife made in their coastal community, and he enjoys several new pastimes, including golf, cooking, and volunteering, with an occasional river cruise thrown in for a change of pace. Felix even joined the governing board of his new condo, until personalities and politics soured that experience for him.

As Charles's and Felix's contrasting stories demonstrate, how one is initially positioned at job loss can have long-lasting effects. Felix, who throughout his interview expressed awareness of and gratitude for his privilege, made the pleasant discovery that the benefits he received from working for a Fortune 500 company meant that he did not need as much retirement savings as financial advisors typically recommend. Charles, on the other hand, was in an entirely different position and certainly "nowhere near ready to retire."

Similar to the pattern we detected in chapter 2, not every job loss revealed as many trials as Charles's nor was as much of a triumph as Felix's. We originally labeled Mark, Victor, and Vanessa as "in-betweeners" on the hard falls/soft landings continuum, and now, all these years later, we can see that the moniker still holds.

We interviewed Mark, now sixty-eight years old, because his survey responses indicated that the resentment and depression he experienced after his 2008 job loss had been supplanted by an awareness that "I discovered myself." Financially, in the time between our two interviews and largely due to his wife's continued and increasingly well-paid employment, he had gone from a place that was "really tough" to amassing some savings and security in the knowledge that "we're not going to be homeless or anything like that." Mark had held a variety of short-term and casual positions in a variety of industries since our first conversation, including a stint as a manual laborer for a package delivery company. He tried his hand as an entrepreneur in health care when he started his own business in 2015, drawing on his expertise and previous experiences, not to mention his personal savings. He made a go of it for a while, despite making "every possible mistake you could ever make." Ultimately, Mark realized that both his money and his wife's patience would run out before he would ever get his business idea across: "It was a hard, painful lesson." He closed that business just as COVID-19 was starting to spread. Since then, he had found his silver lining: contentment and a small stream of income as an artist doing digital portraits, while continuing to pick up occasional temp work. Sure, he was not retired and sketching on an iPad by the lake (his original retirement dream), but Mark felt that things had turned out "reasonably well" and that his recession dismissal had opened the door to "some fun things that have come out of [my] experiences of change." Showing us some exquisite examples of his art from the digital portfolio on his phone, he described his current mindset. Mark was pretty satisfied with his quality of life, not by what he called the "traditional" measure (income), but by "the life measure": a supportive wife, good friends, and a job that, while by his own admission was not going to make him rich, was still fulfilling because, as he said, "I make people happy. It's a lot of fun."

Victor, now age sixty-nine, similarly experienced some employment challenges in the decade since his initial interview but, in the end, felt things had worked out. While Victor shared some of these details in his follow-up survey, we were eager to learn more. When we sat down with him, we learned that he had pieced together enough employment over the years to save adequately for retirement. Those positions, however, were not without their downsides. He found it particularly difficult when consulting jobs ended in the early years, throwing him "back to ground zero" and creating a state of financial and emotional turmoil along with marital discord. Throughout this process, Victor was keenly aware of his advancing age. An ardent networker who made frequent use of area job clubs, he realized that the attendees were not his contemporaries anymore: "I'd look around the room, and I was like the parent to these people." Victor also came to the realization that all his professional contacts had "aged out," leaving him without a network to access, and was further caught off guard by the young hiring managers he typically encountered. His luck turned around, however, in late 2015 when he was offered a permanent position. It was the "best Christmas present ever," Victor told us. The good news was that the company coordinated what Victor labeled a "traditional corporate move" and thus covered the costs for his relocation to their offices in the South. Like Charles, another non-Minnesotan, neither Victor nor his wife had any family ties or obligations tethering them to Minnesota. The bad news was that Victor sustained a painful back injury around that time. He hid the fact he sometimes needed a wheelchair, took "a lot" of painkillers, and soldiered on without revealing his discomfort, lest his new employers think he was too old and not fit for the job. Victor was not wrong to have such worries either: three and a half years later he felt that, due to his age, he was being "pushed out" of his position. By that time, however, he was ready to move on and spend more time visiting his children and grandchildren out of state. He retired in 2019, just before COVID-19 hit.

Since then, Victor has been enjoying better health and a life filled with family, travel, civic engagement, and volunteering. Reflecting on his career trajectory, and reprising some of the religious coping themes we discussed earlier in the book, Victor was convinced that "somebody was looking over my shoulder, helping me make the right decisions, the right smart moves. . . . Time and time again, when something needed to happen, it happened for me." A self-described spiritual person, he concluded that he was "very, very, very blessed" and that, despite some of the low points he encountered, "God [only] throws things at me that He knows I can handle."

Of all the in-betweeners, it was Vanessa, now sixty-five, who showed the broadest range of emotions in her survey responses. She was still "bitter" about her 2010 layoff from a newspaper job she loved, yet this job loss also helped her realize she was "more resilient" than she thought. When we interviewed Vanessa, we dug deeper into the sting of job loss. She described how the newspaper was now owned by "big capital investment" and "horrible, horrible, conniving people in New York" who just wanted to lay people off and who did not care about the state of journalism. Plus, Vanessa, who was single and "ha[d] to take care of [my]self," was let go while two other co-workers with employed spouses were kept on. "Definitely a case of favoritism," she concluded. Granted, she did have a bit of a cushion to land on in the form of a small inheritance from her mother (now spent), and she recounted taking fun trips with her sister, who generously paid Vanessa's way (until becoming too ill herself to travel). And she had gone into business for herself, cobbling together enough clients and contracts to amount to an average of twenty to twenty-five paid hours a week. While this was just enough to cover her mortgage and buy some groceries, she admitted that she was having to cut back: "The problem is, I don't make that much money." Having had some health struggles of her own in recent years, Vanessa also revealed that she was worried about a "catastrophic illness" in her future, an eventuality for which she did not think she would have enough savings.

Still, Vanessa's "deep Christian faith" provided the reassurance that God had a plan and that "God is going to take care of me because, I mean, that's what God does." In the final minutes of our interview, she acknowledged she was also lucky to have a network of "supportive friends, supportive family, a good boyfriend, and a really good therapist." Finally, Vanessa recounted the silver linings of her job loss aftermath in terms of both quality of life and personal growth. There was the indisputable upside of no longer having to work evenings and weekends, as she did in her former job: dinners out with friends, spending Saturdays and Sundays with her boyfriend and family, and watching *The Bachelorette* on TV. She had further come to the realization that she was now a "more well-rounded person." She continued, "because I did have the chance to travel more, spend more time with my family and friends, and focus on things besides my job. You know, the income isn't everything, really." Overall, did things work out for her? Vanessa waffled: "I guess I'd lean toward yes."

And then there was our follow-up interview with Cat, now seventy-seven years old. At the time of her original interview in 2014, she was still too fresh from the loss of her health promotion job to be classified as having experienced either a soft landing or a hard fall. For this reason, we interviewed Cat to understand the longer-term impacts of her job loss. We learned that she, too, had a mixed bag of experiences and emotions befitting those who ended up somewhere in between.

Like Vanessa, Cat was laid off from a job she loved and found very fulfilling. Ten years later, she still felt that loss "every day" as she struggled to re-create the fulfillment she got from her original position. Earlier on, there was some success. She earned a lump-sum payment after she was invited to publish a book related to her expertise, which gave her a bit of an emotional boost and a financial buffer while job searching. After that, however, there were a series of part-time and/or short-lived jobs. She quit some (e.g., because the commute was too long relative to the part-time hours she was working) and was laid off from others (e.g., due to the COVID pandemic). Like Charles and Victor, Cat also experienced age discrimination during her perpetual job search: "My 'grandchildren' would be interviewing me and they had no clue about . . . what I had to bring to the world." Once hired, she sometimes had difficulty with those she labeled her "millennial" co-workers (she found them disrespectful, resentful, and lacking life skills). Overall, Cat had struggled to find work that was "validating"—that is, to secure a job that matched her capabilities and made her feel valued.

On the surface, Cat's position at the time of her 2023 interview did not exactly meet these criteria. She was working part-time at a call center, and although she attempted to go above and beyond in her role, none of her supervisors ever commented on or even noticed her efforts. She was overqualified for the position and earning far less than she had earlier in her career, which put a question mark over her retirement plans. The one bright light of that position, however, were the connections she sometimes forged when chatting with the people on the other end of the line—she felt these conversations could "feed her soul." Indeed, she said she was working for both the money and "the meaning": communication and interconnectedness. Although her "broken heart" from not finding another dream job had never gone away and her retirement account was smaller than she intended, Cat remained grateful. She listed the positives of her current situation toward the end of her interview: "I like who I am. I still have the capacity to find hope in the world . . . and I am healthy. I mean, I have some health issues that are age related. I don't like having an old body and a young heart, but I know I can find ways to work around that." For Cat, what mattered most was that she could find some joy in her life by drawing on her relationships, her faith, and her community.

Where Do We Go from Here? Some Ideas, Advice, and Hope

Our follow-up interviewees had plenty of ideas and advice for individuals who are working and/or seeking jobs. First, our respondents caution others to be mindful of the impermanence inherent to contemporary employment. For this reason, some interviewees believe in the necessity of being proactive on the jobs front. Mark, for example, emphasizes always "thinking and learning and looking [for employment]." Felix and Charles stress the importance of networking and, even more importantly, having money in the bank. As Charles instructs, "Get involved with your company 401(k), max it out, and save whatever you can. I mean, just save, save, save, because you never know when you could use it." For those who are already unemployed, Vanessa believes, from personal experience, it is necessary to avoid spending "frivolously." She encourages unemployed workers to "take account of your finances and, if you have the talent for it, create a budget."

Interviewees also suggest a necessary reimagination of what it means to be employed. Looking back on their careers in relation to their lives, Charles and Felix now both understand that "work isn't everything." Charles reports that he once worked "ungodly hours" and thus "missed out on a lot at home." He cautions: "Don't sacrifice at home, because you never get those hours back." Charles shares another important epiphany about working in a neoliberal era: "I look back over my career right now, and I think, you know, all the hours I put in, and you wonder why you did it—because in the end, they didn't care about you personally."

Mark offers sage advice for reframing job loss. He believes it is imperative not to take a layoff "personally." He reassures: "You may not be a fit here, but you're okay. You're capable, you can still do these other things." Cat offers similar advice for moving on after job loss: "Let go of what didn't happen, [what] your dreams were, so that you can rebuild what you want to be doing with the rest of your life." Moreover, in keeping with her background in health promotion, Cat adds: "Take care of your health. Because once it's gone, it's gone."

Finally, Vanessa's advice for laid-off workers includes, "just because you lose your job, you're not going to die." Despite her initial fears of what a loss of income could do to her life, she discovered: "I'm still here. I still have my house. I still have two cats." Moreover, job loss does not have to mean losing your personal identity "even if your job is [as] super important to you as mine was." In the end, Vanessa believes job loss can provide an opportunity to become a "well-rounded person."

In the years since we began writing this book, several others have published their own books examining the issues we touch on in the preceding pages. Our closing recommendations for workers, the job clubs that support them, and society at large are informed by the work of these fellow scholars.

What Can Workers Do?

Many of our respondents accepted their layoff as a commonsense business response to market forces. With this framing, layoffs are portrayed as beyond the control of employers, which suggests individual workers have no other option than to accept their fate and move on. But is this framing accurate? Do employees facing layoffs have the capacity to fight back, and if so, will their efforts be successful?

The research of political scientist Sidney Rothstein responds to these questions. His book *Recoding Power: Tactics for Mobilizing Tech Workers*[17] examines two sites, one in Germany and one in the United States, where tech workers successfully challenged their layoffs.[18] While the collective responses to layoffs varied according to cultural context, the important point is that both groups of high-wage, white-collar tech workers launched successful campaigns against their layoffs.

The German workers were employed by Siemens' Information and Communication Networks division (ICN). In late 2002 and early 2003, Siemens proposed laying off thousands of ICN workers due to declining sales. The works council, a group of employees who represented workers' interests, was committed to ICN's profitability but critical of management's obsession with stock price and shareholder value. The council convincingly argued that this singular focus led management to abandon its long-term commitment to creating high-quality products and instead pursue a series of poor business decisions that undercut sales. ICN's workers, persuaded both by this counterargument and the council's proposed plan for reorganizing production, began contesting their dismissals in court. Employees additionally held several mass demonstrations that gained the attention of the press, political parties, and shareholders. These protests enhanced worker solidarity and inspired even more workers to submit legal claims to German courts. When these plaintiffs convinced judges that their layoffs were illegal, Siemens recognized that continued litigation would be costlier than the savings they could achieve from the proposed layoffs. The layoffs were called off, and workers who already had been laid off were reinstated. As this example illustrates, social change can occur when workers collectively mobilize and "discursively challenge" (a phrase used by Rothstein) explanations that appear to be common sense.

It is possible that our readers are thinking, "But that's Germany—workers there have many more institutional protections than American workers." Rothstein likely anticipated this response, hence his focus on a U.S. site where another group of white-collar tech workers successfully challenged their mass layoff. These American workers were employed at Burlington, Vermont's campus of IBM, the state's largest employer. The corporate campus and the state shared a mutually dependent relationship: IBM provided tax revenue and jobs, and the state offered workers and supporting infrastructure. Such reciprocity inspired a "normative" discourse emphasizing worker loyalty and dedication in return for secure and stable employment. This implicit promise was ultimately undermined by two rounds of downsizing early in the new millennium, with more than 1,400 workers laid off. When a group of terminated workers discovered statistical evidence demonstrating managers had in fact disproportionately dismissed older workers (a pattern several of our interviewees observed in their own downsizings), they launched a successful age discrimination class-action lawsuit. Their challenge demonstrated that, contrary to management's market-based explanation, the layoffs were driven by employer discretion. This second case study suggests that collective acts of resistance can be effective even in a place where comprehensive worker rights and protections are absent.

Rothstein's research shows workers can push back successfully against downsizing strategies. Some recent anecdotal evidence also suggests that specific groups of U.S. workers are beginning to assert themselves collectively. For example, though unionization rates remain exceptionally low in the United States, we saw some high-profile union activity in 2023. Corporate behemoths like Amazon and Starbucks were among those employers contending with unionization drives. Closer to home, doctors, nurses, and other health care workers at Allina Health, headquartered in Minnesota, voted to unionize in October 2023.[19] Meanwhile, U.S. autoworkers; Hollywood actors and entertainment workers; writers in film, television, radio, and online media; and workers from other health care systems were among the thousands of workers who had recently been or were on strike at the time.

Could this activity portend a larger shift in employment relations? While it is too early to answer this question, it certainly seems within the realm of possibility. Beyond broader unionization, we suggest that one key move in this direction is to spark the types of conversations and coming together that led some of Rothstein's American tech workers—who, like our interviewees, were not unionized—to collective action. One logical forum for such community-building could be job clubs.

What Can Job Clubs Do?

So many of our 2013 and 2014 interviewees shared positive comments about the assistance Minnesota's job clubs provided. In their 2023 follow-up interviews, Charles and Victor continued praising these clubs. Having now relocated to states where job clubs are virtually nonexistent, both respondents reflected on the valuable support they once received as Minnesota residents. Charles fondly recalled club-sponsored networking opportunities, which fully occupied his idle time: "I could literally have half-hour meetings all day long, five days a week." Victor, on the other hand, was grateful for the moral support these clubs once offered him: "What they did is kept my spirits up . . . gave me something to do that was related to what I was trying to achieve." As we noted in chapter 4, Minnesota's job clubs, many of which are faith-based, provide crucial resources to people seeking employment, including résumé writing workshops, practice interview sessions, guest speakers, and job postings. However, we remind readers that the self-help approach many job counselors embrace is problematic from a sociological standpoint. The emphasis on personal diligence, individual responsibility, and a positive attitude requires the individual to adapt and overcome while current employment practices and neoliberalism more broadly escape scrutiny.

In his book, *The Stigma Trap: College-Educated, Experienced, and Long-Term Unemployed*,[20] sociologist Ofer Sharone is critical of "you can do it!" job counseling for similar reasons. With this approach, job seekers are implored to hone their search skills, network exhaustively, and always display a positive attitude, as if these are the only factors that matter. However, as we discussed in chapter 2, variables like age, industry conditions, and available job opportunities can greatly hinder (or enhance) the ability to land a job. By centering the individual, Sharone argues, a self-help approach encourages job seekers to bear full responsibility for their unemployment woes, which in turn creates self-blame and social isolation. He recommends an alternative approach informed by the sociology of unemployment, a field to which we hope this book contributes.

A promising model for employment counseling was developed by Sharone himself. The Institute for Career Transitions (ICT) is a not-for-profit organization for job seekers. It offers many types of support, including small group conversations facilitated by career coaches, workshops for larger groups of job seekers, and focused one-on-one coaching—in other words, the very same services Minnesota's job clubs offer. Where ICT's progressive approach differs is that participants also explore sociological research on topics like job seeking, barriers to employment, and hiring practices in order to equip themselves with evidence-based strategies for both making sense of the circumstances behind mass layoffs and navigating a shifting labor market. This environment creates opportunities for candid discussions among fellow job seekers, facilitating camaraderie and a broader recognition that negative labor market experiences are not unique to the individual but rather common to most workers. ICT's multifaceted approach, as its participants reported in in-depth interviews, ultimately avoids "internalized stigma," thus enhancing personal well-being.

Could the ICT model be adopted and adapted by the types of job clubs—including faith-based ones—to which our interviewees were drawn? The power and potential of ICT's sociological approach, after all, does not simply rest in making workers feel better about themselves or in simply helping workers find new jobs. While such outcomes would certainly be welcome to anyone who frequents these employment counseling groups, a form of consciousness-raising could also take place in such forums, which, as Rothstein shows, is a necessary precursor to mobilization. Several of our interviewees were already able to discern that age bias played a role in their job dismissals, and a few detected the true nature of the one-sided neoliberal ethos. In chapter 3, for example, Nathan called out the 1 percent and a system that continually transfers wealth to that minority. In chapter 5, Sara raged against the potential employer who expected her to move to a new and unfamiliar town, sight unseen, on the basis of a Skype interview. Similarly upset, Tad in chapter 6 railed against the large bonuses for the corporate executives whose missteps cost him and more than eight hundred of his co-workers their jobs. And, in her follow-up interview, Cat called for a reckoning and more taxes for the wealthy who are "misusing" employees and threatening them with job loss while demanding "unkind" things. A more purposeful sociological approach that, in renowned sociologist C. Wright Mills's words,[21] links up personal troubles with public issues, could help others to develop a similar understanding.

While we would recommend an employment counseling approach that empowers job seekers to think beyond the individual to the larger social-structural realm, we have also argued (in chapter 4) that the faith-based job club teachings' consonance with neoliberalism would work against this application of the sociological imagination. That said, the history of religion is replete with examples that show us that it does not have to be this way. In the 1970s, for example, a faith-based movement known as liberation theology took direct aim at burgeoning Latin American neoliberal policies and their militaristic enforcers.[22] Combining a critical social scientific lens and elements of 1960s Catholic Social Teaching,[23] liberation theologians challenged a capitalist system that served to entrench both the wealth of the elite and the suffering of the poor. Crucially, this counterhegemonic form of religion was not restricted to theologians and progressive supporters with official roles in the church. It also emerged from below via small, grassroots discussion groups known as *comunidades eclesiales de base* (*cebs*; in English, "base ecclesial communities" or "basic Christian communities"). These groups often read the Bible's message in light of their current conditions of poverty and came to recognize the culpable political and economic structures as sinful—and therefore as legitimate targets of challenge on the basis of faith. In fact, some members of *cebs* played important roles in social change and even revolutionary movements across the continent.[24] Liberation theology in general and the *cebs* in particular show how Christianity can, in both theory and practice, challenge the powers that be.

While the United States in the 2020s is not 1970s Latin America, the lessons of the past show us that the future is not necessarily preordained, a hopeful theme that resonates with the latest work of Astra Taylor.

Something for All of Us to Consider

The research of Rothstein and Sharone makes it clear that we should not let neoliberal ideology divide us and make us think we are all alone. This is an argument Astra Taylor also develops in her 2023 book, *The Age of Insecurity: Coming*

Together as Things Fall Apart.²⁵ An author, organizer, and cofounder of the Debt Collective (a union of debtors), Taylor has a message for all of us—younger and older, employed and unemployed—to consider.

A harsh critic of the massive social inequality that capitalism breeds, Taylor notes that neoliberal capitalism is particularly pernicious. The fifty-year dismantling of the welfare state that has accompanied the rise of neoliberalism has increased social inequality. Growing numbers of people both feel and actually are financially insecure. But it is important to realize that even groups considered economically privileged are insecure in neoliberal capitalism. Job insecurity has grown in part due to routine downsizing and restructuring activities (with the constant threat of job loss keeping workers from demanding something more). At the same time, many full-time, permanent jobs have been reduced to short-term contracts and temporary positions lacking benefits and stability; these are the very same jobs some of our respondents turned to when they were unable to gain permanent employment. Moreover, the Great Recession showed us that the other systems and strategies that once helped middle-class people feel secure—education, savings, property acquisition, and investments—can no longer guarantee stability. Our interviewees' stories have amply demonstrated that on the individual level. More broadly, as Taylor argues in a *New York Times* opinion piece based on her book, "the stock in our 401(k), if we are lucky enough to have one, all too often supports industries that poison the planet; the tech company we work for undermines democracy; the rising price of the home we own makes it harder for others to stay housed."²⁶ Taylor's point is that we are all, one way or another, insecure in a neoliberal society.

Yet, therein lies the hope.

Granted, surveying the contemporary North American landscape, reasons for hopefulness may seem in short supply. We can see how insecurity has fostered individualism among so many, dividing them and causing a discernible "rightward tilt"²⁷ that has them blaming other vulnerable people for their woes. Taylor observes that neoliberal capitalism gets a pass while immigrants, religious minorities, Black people, trans people, people seeking abortions, and, we would add to the list, either boomers or "kids today" (depending on your perspective) are the scapegoats.

Nonetheless, Taylor argues, division and hostility are not the inevitable by-products of insecurity. For Taylor, there is hope in recognizing our common insecurity and its links to the intersecting crises of our time. We do not have to shrink into ourselves, blame others, and thereby guarantee security for nobody and nothing but neoliberalism itself. Instead, we can work—together— to foster new ways of relating to one another and to build new systems of mutual support and care, lessening both inequality and insecurity for everyone. After all, Taylor reminds us, the United States was far more egalitarian less than a century ago. As she points out, the expanded American welfare state that evolved after the Great Depression achieved widespread employment security and historically low wealth inequality via investments in old-age social insurance (Social Security), health care benefits, public higher education, unionization, and progressive taxation.[28] The COVID-19 pandemic more recently showed us the positive impacts expansive government assistance can make. We now know that three rounds of direct relief payments, extended employment assistance, a child tax credit, and emergency rental assistance demonstrably reduced economic hardship for many individuals and families.[29] Moving forward, we should consider the lessons of the past, which teach us that material and emotional security cannot be found in market-based principles and priorities, but rather in "policies and public investment that prevent markets from undermining everyone's well-being."[30] By enhancing our collective welfare through such means, we will be free to engage in the creative labor of building a more equitable and sustainable society, one in which beauty, self-expression, and creativity can flourish.[31] For Taylor, hope lies in collaboration, not competition, and in solidarity, not narrow self-interest.

Granted, American society may not be ready for Taylor's ideas. After all, one of the reasons for the widespread receptivity to neoliberalism in the United States is that ideology's compatibility with preexisting American cultural values based on individualism, self-reliance, and competition. As we have argued throughout this book, generationalism, conservative Christianity, and the sway of positive thinking variously function to reinforce those principles and once again neoliberalism itself. Still, if we look to the experiences and hard-earned lessons of our interviewees, we can find other glimmers of hope.

We find hope when Felix recognizes that he owes his soft fall into retirement to a company pension. We are heartened to learn that Kenneth has, through his own job loss journey, cultivated more empathy for others who are hurting. Recall, too, that Caroline and Kirk report sympathizing with instead of demonizing their younger colleagues, while Charles found great satisfaction in intergenerational workplace collaboration. In Sally's and Luke's refusal to leave family, friends, and their homes in Minnesota, because they understood it would only mean trading one insecure position for another, we realize that some have seen through the false promises of flexibility. These convictions, along with the occasional barbs at the neoliberal order we have seen throughout the book, lead us to believe that at least some of our respondents are piecing the problem of insecurity together. As such, we admire those like Cat, who understands that "we're so brainwashed by this need to acquire" that we neglect relationships, community, and health. She strives to live by her values of love and connection, and to "leave the world a better place than when I found it." These principles are ones that may be harder to nourish under neoliberal insecurity, but they are also ones that we, like Taylor, understand will be an integral part of a different path forward.

While our interviewees may not yet be banding together with others to forge this path, activists like the Gray Panthers and the Raging Grannies, groups who challenge ageism and other social injustices, provide ample evidence that older adults can mobilize for social change.[32] More immediately, insights from our interviews spur us to suggest that perhaps there is another silver lining to the experiences of our respondents, one apart from, or at least potentially separable from, the bright-sided optimism we dissected in our last chapter. Why should we allow a neoliberal framework to colonize the hope that rests in the alternative values and aspirations of our participants? Why must personal growth, self-actualization, and the reordering of priorities be associated with an individualistic positivity discourse when instead they can grow in tandem with new forms of social solidarity? We need to consider that, as opposed to an echo of the neoliberal happiness imperative, at least some of our interviewees are expressing sentiments that align more with Taylor's vision. If we ignore this alternate interpretation, we risk unwittingly giving too much power to neoliberalism and not enough to the wisdom of our elders. Instead of accepting the neoliberal hold on our society, we can imagine more. Maybe we should all pay closer attention to Cat when she says, "I still have the capacity to find hope in the world."

Appendix A

Studying Late-Career Job Loss
in the Land of 10,000 Lakes

This study is a collaborative effort between two old college friends: Annette, who lives in Northfield, Minnesota, and Dana, who lives in Guelph, Ontario, Canada. Annette, a sociologist who studies work, unemployment, and aging, created the research project and conducted the interviews. Dana, intrigued by the preliminary results and its connections to her own sociological research on aging, joined the project, assisting with data analysis and crafting this book's foundational argument while also participating in every aspect of the writing process. As tenured sociology professors, neither of us has experienced a career-ending job loss; still, in the early twenty-first century, even those without a personal understanding have witnessed these enormous upheavals affecting friends, families, and communities.

The stories, trends, and sociological insights we have presented in the preceding pages should serve as a layered warning—to scholars and students in our discipline, but also to policymakers and the public—that hazards lay ahead. In documenting how a specific group of older workers experienced and interpreted late-career job loss in the volatile economy of the Great Recession, we tap into the voices of people who, as one interviewee put it, found themselves at a troubling new stage of the American life course: too young to retire but too old to start all over. At the time of the original data collection, August 2013 to October 2014, news media had no shortage of such dramatic tales, frequently comparing the recession to the economic collapse of 1929 that unleashed the Great Depression. Yet these emotionally charged anecdotes were, of course, reported without broader context or theoretical perspective. Concurrent accounts produced by social scientists and government agencies were, on the other hand, overwhelmingly quantitative—facts, figures, and numbers devoid of lived experience. By weaving these approaches together, we have drawn a vivid picture of economic precarity and the emerging challenges proving insurmountable for too many in our aging population.

Sociological rigor demands methodological transparency—a careful accounting of researchers' choices with regard to selecting a research site, recruiting and winnowing participants, structuring interviews and data collection, and analyzing data. The sociological imagination further urges us to share our approach in the hopes that it will inspire our colleagues across disciplines to take up further investigations of late-career job loss, graying societies, and the wide-ranging effects of neoliberalism.

The Research Site

This study is based in Minnesota, the Land of 10,000 Lakes and the upper Midwestern home to more than five million people. Minnesota consistently receives top scores in popular media rankings of "best states to live in"; this distinction is due in part to several Fortune 500 companies headquartered in and around the Twin Cities of Minneapolis and St. Paul.[1] Some of these companies downsized their workforce during the time frame of this study, making Minnesota a good place to examine the effects of late-career job loss among white-collar workers. When the interviews were conducted, the Minnesota economy was rebounding from the Great Recession, but job opportunities remained limited for three demographic groups: BIPOC communities, young adults with limited or no job experience, and individuals caught in long-term unemployment.[2] In this study, we focused on the latter, a group increasingly populated by individuals over age fifty. By 2014, a startling trend was already apparent: almost half of older, unemployed workers reported having experienced an unemployment spell lasting at least twenty-seven weeks (or approximately six months). Those agonizing half years met the formal definition of "long-term unemployment."[3]

Minnesota is the nation's twelfth largest state by geographic area, and, owing to a 1755 mapping error, it is the most northern of the lower forty-eight.[4] Its 86,000 square miles are bordered by two Canadian provinces, Manitoba and Ontario; the world's largest freshwater lake, Lake Superior; and five contiguous Midwestern states. The individuals recruited to this study resided in thirteen counties and represented three distinct geographic regions (rural towns, suburbs, and the Twin Cities metropolitan area), though all resided within a seventy-five-mile radius of Minnesota's Twin Cities and approximately two-thirds lived in Rice, Dakota, and Hennepin counties.

Recruitment

There are no public lists of older, unemployed workers from which a random sample can be drawn. For this reason, individuals were recruited to the study via three acceptable nonprobability sampling methods: convenience, snowball, and site-specific sampling.[5]

Though we use "we" throughout this book, mostly when referring to our data collection effort, all the interviews were conducted by Annette. She began recruitment with convenience sampling in July 2013. The city of Northfield, Minnesota, is small and rural, with approximately twenty thousand residents spanning Rice and Dakota counties. Anchored by two respected liberal arts colleges, Carleton and St. Olaf, and a diverse array of industries that also includes light manufacturing, transportation, finance, agriculture, and food processing, Northfield has a rich mix of blue-collar and white-collar workers, making it a suitable location for initiating a recruitment process initially focused on assembling an occupationally diverse sample.

Posters, online advertisements, and a local radio segment all helped spread the word. From flyers dotting community bulletin boards in grocery stores, the public library, a bookstore, a senior center, a popular coffee shop, and a community resource center to online pleas spread through community websites, local LISTSERVs, and Facebook pages tailored to the colleges' faculty, staff, and alumni, these appeals urged locals to "tell your story" about job loss. They specified that the study sought any participant "age 50+ who has lost their job since 2008 as a result of a downturn in the economy." To increase the sample's reach, Annette distributed additional posters to a senior center located twenty minutes closer to the Twin Cities and to the Rice County WorkForce Office, which provides government assistance to job seekers and agreed to advertise the study in its monthly newsletter and among its clients. Subsequent snowball sampling played an equally important role in recruitment by leveraging the networks of our earliest respondents. The initial interviewees were invited to share recruitment flyers with family, friends, neighbors, and former colleagues who were similarly experiencing late-career job loss. In this way, Annette was able to increase both the sample size and the geographic reach of her interview pool.

Finally, to enhance the racial, occupational, and religious diversity of the respondents recruited through convenience and snowball sampling, Annette also undertook site-specific sampling. This approach meant distributing flyers among the following organizations: a Twin Cities nonprofit dedicated to assisting older workers undergoing employment transitions; a Minneapolis WorkForce center located in a racially diverse neighborhood; a WorkForce Center located in a Latino community in St. Paul; two WorkForce Centers located in the Twin Cities' outer-ring suburbs; a Minneapolis church with a predominantly African-American congregation; a Jewish Community Center; and four faith-based metro-area job clubs (some of which also provided opportunities to present the study to groups of their clientele).

The Sample

Nearly one hundred people responded to these study appeals. Of them, sixty-two qualified for an interview. These individuals were over age fifty and had experienced late-career job loss directly tied to the 2008 economic downturn. They were at various stages of unemployment, from less than a few weeks to more than three years of joblessness. To cope with financial insecurity, some interviewees accepted part-time jobs. Others accepted limited-term contracts or became self-employed. Many of these interviewees still considered themselves unemployed and thus continued looking for permanent full-time employment similar to the job they had lost. For these reasons, it is difficult to define and hence calculate which interviewees were short-term or long-term unemployed.

The thirty-three men and twenty-nine women in the resulting sample ranged in age from fifty-one to sixty-eight years at the time of their interviews (modal age fifty-eight), and all but one were technically baby boomers according to the Pew Research Center's classification.[6] The mean number of years interviewees worked for their employer was twelve,[7] and the most common year of job dismissal was 2011. Our interviewees worked full-time, and most had an employer who paid them wages, a salary, or a consulting fee. Also included in the sample were two individuals who classified themselves as "self-employed" independent contractors (neither had employees working for them); these respondents were forced to close their respective businesses due to the Great Recession. Forty percent of the sample were previously employed in occupations we coded as "manager/executive" (including marketing manager, sales account manager, vice president). The remainder had been employed in nonmanagerial positions in the following fields: sales and related occupations (11.3 percent); office and administrative support (9.7 percent); computer-related occupations (8.1 percent); architecture and engineering occupations (6.5 percent); knowledge workers (6.5 percent); health care practitioners and support occupations (4.8 percent); and self-employed (3.2 percent). Another 10 percent of the sample were in miscellaneous occupations that did not fit these occupational categories devised by the U.S. Bureau of Labor Statistics. Table B1 provides additional summary statistics about the sample. Table B2 provides select characteristics of individual interviewees.

No other personal characteristics were specified during the sampling stage, and yet, despite Annette's numerous attempts to recruit a diverse sample, the final sample is remarkably homogeneous. All but two of the interviewees featured in this book were employed in white-collar occupations,[8] and, despite claiming a mix of ethnic backgrounds, all the respondents self-identified as White. This racial homogeneity may be attributable to the racial composition of the state and its workforce. At the time of this study, approximately 84 percent of Minnesotans had selected "White" as their racial identifier in the U.S. Census, and approximately 90 percent of the working population identified as White.[9] It cannot, however, be discounted that the very approaches used to recruit participants may have inadvertently facilitated a sample of similarly situated individuals. For example, being asked to "share your story" may have dissuaded individuals who did not feel safe communicating personal information with a stranger or simply could not, given the study's need for English fluency in a state where major recent immigration flows originate in Mexico, Somalia, India, Laos, and Ethiopia.[10] Furthermore, individuals who have routinely encountered racial and/or class discrimination might feel less than enthusiastic about recounting the indignity of job loss, let alone with a White, middle-class interviewer. Further study is needed to determine whether the problem of late-career job loss is concentrated among the region's White and white-collar workers and, assuming it is not, to access the experiences of more diverse populations.

Our nonrandom sampling strategy prevents us from making broad generalizations. Instead, the findings offered here provide crucial insight into the experience of job loss among a select group of individuals who were receptive to a request for a face-to-face interview. These individuals generously shared their time—sixty to ninety minutes on average, if not longer given travel times—and discussed difficult experiences in detail without any compensation beyond a cup of coffee and a bite to eat. So, what motivated their participation? Some noted a desire to be a voice in a sociological study. Most everyone, however, indicated they wanted their stories documented so that a larger public could become aware of the deleterious effects of job loss on older workers. They wanted, if nothing else, the dignity of recognition.

The Interview

Annette's in-depth, semistructured interviews were designed to capture the voices and perspectives of individuals who had experienced late-career job loss and then identify themes and commonalities across their collective set of experiences. Exploratory studies of this sort are not guided by hypotheses, but by questions. Annette used prompts, probes, and follow-up questions, and her conversational approach allowed respondents to narrate their own stories and to pursue tangents. Across this sample of similarly situated individuals with few years left for financial recovery, Annette heard a surprising variety of interpretations of and reactions to job loss. Still, the study reached saturation, or the point at which new themes ceased to emerge in subsequent interviews, and hence, data gathering concluded by October 2014.[11]

The interviews were guided by forty-one open-ended questions grouped around the experience of dismissal; the effects of job loss on self, finances, and relationships; the job search experience; and large-scale reflections. After a series of sociodemographic background queries, interviewees discussed their occupations, typically sharing their dismissal and unemployment stories with little prompting. For comfort and convenience, interviews primarily took place at coffee shops, restaurants, libraries, and other public spaces where we could enjoy privacy, though some occurred in people's homes or in small conference rooms on the Carleton College campus. Because Annette completed every aspect of data collection, from recruitment through interviews, trust and familiarity were sown well before she came face-to-face with interviewees. Nonetheless, each interview began with a consent form that assured interviewees their identities and former employers would not be divulged, accompanied by small talk designed to place interviewees at ease and confirm their continued willingness to participate in this research study. Interviews were recorded with two digital audio devices and transcribed verbatim by a handful of undergraduate research assistants at Carleton College, each trained in scholarly requirements surrounding confidentiality and anonymity.

Interviewees appeared to enjoy the experience, often stretching the exchanges past two hours and commenting, at the close of their interviews, "That was like therapy," or "I feel better." Respondents shared their appreciation for an opportunity to discuss job loss with a listener who neither passed judgment nor offered trite employment advice in the ways that their spouses, adult children, extended family, and friends tended to do. Overall, there was no apparent hesitation or self-censoring among study participants.

This relative comfort and candor likely stems from several sources, including assurances regarding interviewee anonymity as well as homophily, or the tendency to feel comfortable and positive toward others who share our own social characteristics. Both Annette and the individuals she interviewed were White, middle class, (predominantly) college educated, and sometimes relatively close in age (while Annette was younger than some interviewees by as much as twenty-four years, in other cases she was only seven years younger). Studies aiming at extending our findings would be well advised to reach out to more diverse populations and use more diverse interviewers.

Data Analysis

Several undergraduate research students from Carleton College transcribed the interviews and participated in coding the transcripts, an effort aimed at identifying distinct patterns in interviewees' accounts of job loss. The data were analyzed in three separate stages, with each stage employing Glaser and Strauss's constant comparative method.[12]

Annette first began noticing certain codes during the interview process, and these codes became more visible when reading the transcripts multiple times. Twenty-two codes were eventually identified in this initial data analysis stage. These codes were defined and discussed at length to facilitate consistency across coders and reach consensus when disagreements arose. For this reason, the coding definitions evolved as we reviewed the transcripts. Each transcript was reviewed, at this stage, by Annette and two or more research assistants.

In the second stage of analysis, we grouped similar codes into themes. For example, when interviewees discussed being rooted to their community or neighborhood, or mentioned assisting family members with their medical needs, or drew attention to their selective job criteria or life stage–specific responsibilities, the quotations associated with these codes were grouped into the single larger theme "inflexible worker." Each quotation was placed in a shared excerpt file co-curated by Annette and Dana, who separately identified subthemes and sorting guidelines, then came together to resolve incongruencies and produce a unified thematic coding process.[13]

In the last stage of data analysis, Annette and Dana reread quotations and engaged in further discussion about the themes created, reflecting our assumption that qualitative research is an iterative (as opposed to a linear) process. By doing so, we also solidified both internal homogeneity and external heterogeneity in our themes, as well as our larger understanding of the themes detected within these interview accounts.[14]

The Follow-Up Study

In the summer months of 2023, we attempted to recontact the interviewees. The goal was to understand how our respondents, now in their sixties and seventies, were faring approximately ten years after their initial interviews. LinkedIn gave us a sense of who was still working and who had retired—at least for those using the social networking site—but we wanted deeper insights into the longer-term impacts of late-career job loss. This data collection effort was conducted in two stages.

Stage 1: The Questionnaire

In June 2023, we invited our respondents to complete a web-based follow-up questionnaire we designed with Qualtrics,[15] a cloud-based survey platform. Our intention was to recontact the entire sample of sixty-two interviewees, but for a variety of reasons,[16] we ultimately contacted forty-three. More than half this group, twenty-five respondents in total, completed our questionnaire, resulting in a 58 percent response rate. Additionally, we sent two reminder emails and provided modest compensation[17] to those who agreed to take the questionnaire. Our final analytic sample consisted of fifteen men and ten women who ranged in age from sixty-one to seventy-eight years old ($\bar{X} = 69$).

Our questionnaire was populated with closed-ended questions and predetermined response categories with space provided throughout for respondents to elaborate. First, we asked respondents for their current sociodemographic information, including marital status, residential location, educational level, and gender identity.[18] Then, based on their responses to the question "Are you currently employed?" respondents were sent to the next series of questions.

Respondents indicating they were "currently employed" specified their job title, annual salary, and how their total compensation differed from that of the job they reported losing in their initial *American Idle* interview. Respondents indicating they were "unemployed" selected the reason(s) why they had not found work: "I think my age is working against me"; "I have rejected jobs because of low wages, poor working conditions, difficult schedules, etc."; "My résumé or interview skills need to be improved"; "I am between jobs at the moment"; "Finding the right job takes time"; "I was retired but now I want to work again"; or "Other, please specify."[19] Unemployed respondents also answered a question about the type of job they were seeking (specifically, the occupational title plus anything else they wanted to mention). Respondents indicating they were "retired" specified when they retired and their age at retirement, then indicated if they "retired earlier than anticipated," if the retirement was "voluntary," if they were "enjoying retirement," if they were "financially prepared to retire," and if there was anything that would have helped them "be better prepared for retirement."

The questionnaire closed with responses to statements evaluating the long-term impacts of job loss. The first, "In retrospect, I am satisfied with how my life turned out after experiencing job loss," was answered with a five-category Likert scale ranging from "very satisfied" to "very dissatisfied," while the next three ("Job loss strengthened my familial relationships," "Job loss strengthened my friendships," and "Job loss strengthened my religious faith") were answered with yes, no, or maybe. A final statement began, "As a result of my initial job loss, I am now experiencing..." and prompted respondents to check all items on a list that applied: financial hardship; depression, anxiety, or another mental health issue; relief because I am retired; happiness because I have found satisfying alternative work; personal fulfillment because I have time for family, friends, hobbies, and/or volunteer work; and other.[20]

Our analysis of the questionnaire consisted of tallying the number of individuals selecting a particular response category and examining open-ended comments.

Stage 2: The Interview

In July and August 2023, we invited six of the questionnaire respondents to an in-depth interview with Annette. She conducted face-to-face interviews with the four respondents residing in Minnesota[21] and Zoom interviews with the two respondents living in other states. Participants were compensated for their time: $100 cash for those who did an in-person interview and a $100 Amazon gift card for Zoom interviewees. The interviews lasted from forty to ninety minutes, and, similar to the first round of interviews a decade ago, they were conducted conversationally, with interviewees invited to narrate their own stories. While many tangents were pursued, Annette followed an interview guide in order to gain information that allowed for comparison across interviews. Spontaneous probes and follow-up questions nonetheless helped achieve conversational flow and greater depth of response.

The interview began with a review of a detailed consent form assuring interviewees of their continued anonymity. It then progressed into twenty-four open-ended questions, organized around four themes. The first set of questions gave interviewees the chance to discuss their life and employment since their first interview. The next set asked about experiences with finding employment, followed by questions focused on the current socioeconomic context. The interview concluded with reflection questions about the overall job loss experience.

Each interview was recorded with a digital voice recorder, and a second recording device, Annette's iPhone, ensured a backup recording of each interview. The recordings were uploaded to Panopto, a video platform with the capability to produce a transcript.[22] In contrast to our first round of interviews a decade earlier, which took several years to transcribe, Panopto's caption function quickly provided a rough text of each conversation, much to our great relief. Both Dana and Annette reviewed the transcripts for accuracy and to identify relevant quotes for summarizing the story of each interviewee (as presented in the concluding chapter of this book).

We are immensely grateful for the generosity of our interviewees in providing us with their time and insights. Access to such intimate and detailed accounts of human experience are rare but nonetheless indispensable for our craft as social scientists. As we promised on the various consent forms, the quotes we share throughout this book are anonymized. We use pseudonyms for the speakers and omit identifying references to their places of employment and residential location, as is standard practice in social research. To enhance readability, we have streamlined the quotes to cut out some of the conversational fillers ("yeah," "um," "you know," etc.) that clutter the words of researchers and respondents alike. Ellipses (...) indicate that we have removed some words from a direct quotation, and brackets [] within a direct quotation indicate words we have added to a quote to enhance clarity.

Appendix B

Tables

Table B1
Sample Characteristics at First Interview (*N* = 62)

Interviewee Characteristics	N (%)[a]
Gender	
Male presenting	33 (53.2)
Female presenting	29 (46.8)
Age at interview (years)	
50–54	9 (14.5)
55–59	28 (45.2)
60–64	18 (29.0)
65–68	7 (11.3)
Marital status	
Married (includes common-law)	43 (69.4)
Single (includes widowed, separated/divorced)	19 (30.6)
Educational attainment	
Graduate degree (master's, PhD)	18 (29.0)
Professional degree (e.g., MBA, law degree)	7 (11.3)
Bachelor's degree	24 (38.7)
Associate's degree	8 (12.9)
Some college, no degree	4 (6.5)
High school diploma	1 (1.6)
Residential location	
Urban	15 (24.2)
Suburban	29 (46.8)
Rural	18 (29.0)

Table B1 (continued)

Interviewee Characteristics	N (%)[a]
Occupation at dismissal	
Manager/executive	25 (40.0)
Office & administrative support	6 (9.7)
Computer-related occupation	5 (8.1)
Sales & related occupation	7 (11.3)
Health care practitioners & support occupation	3 (4.8)
Architecture & engineering occupation	4 (6.5)
Knowledge worker	4 (6.5)
Self-employed	2 (3.2)
Miscellaneous	6 (9.7)
Job tenure at dismissal	
Less than 1 year	6 (9.7)
1–5 years	17 (27.4)
6–10 years	15 (24.2)
11–15 years	3 (4.8)
16–20 years	4 (6.5)
21+ years	13 (21.0)
Did not specify	4 (6.5)
Year of dismissal[b]	
2007	3 (4.9)
2008	5 (8.2)
2009	10 (16.4)
2010	2 (3.3)
2011	13 (21.3)
2012	13 (21.3)
2013	9 (14.8)
2014	6 (9.8)

[a] Due to rounding, some percentages do not add up to 100 percent.
[b] Because one interviewee did not specify a dismissal date, these numbers add up to sixty-one.

Table B2
Characteristics of Individual Respondents

Pseudonym	Gender presentation	Birth year	Age at interview	Marital status	Occupational category	Dismissal year	Outcome (hard fall/soft landing)	Where are they now? (in 2023)
Benjamin	Male	1951	62	Married	Manager/executive	2013	Too soon to tell	Don't know
Beth	Female	1958	55	Married	Manager/executive	2012	Soft landing	Don't know
Bonnie	Female	1962	50	Single	Knowledge worker	2009	In between	Don't know
Brian	Male	1956	58	Married	Manager/executive	2012	In between	Don't know
Bruno	Male	1951	62	Married	Computer related	2009	In between	Retired
Carl	Male	1958	55	Married	Manager/executive	2013	Soft landing	Retired
Caroline	Female	1944	64	Single	Self-employed	Did not specify	In between	Died
Cassandra	Female	1953	61	Single	Self-employed	2011	Hard fall	Don't know
Cat	Female	1946	68	Single	Health care practitioners & support	2014	Too soon to tell	Employed part-time
Charles	Male	1955	57	Married	Manager/executive	2010	Hard fall	Employed part-time
Charlotte	Female	1954	59	Married	Sales & related	2012	In between	Retired
Christopher	Male	1959	54	Single	Manager/executive	2011	In between	Don't know
Colin	Male	1950	64	Married	Manager/executive	2008	Soft landing	Don't know
Dawn	Female	1956	57	Single	Architecture & engineering	2009	Hard fall	Don't know
Dylan	Male	1958	56	Married	Computer related	2012	Soft landing	Unemployed
Felix	Male	1956	58	Married	Manager/executive	2012	Soft landing	Retired
Frank	Male	1957	56	Married	Architecture & engineering	2011	Soft landing	Employed full-time
Heather	Female	1955	58	Married	Office & administrative support	2007	Hard fall	Don't know
Helen	Female	1953	60	Married	Miscellaneous	2007	Hard fall	Retired
Henry	Male	1945	68	Married	Manager/executive	2009	Soft landing	Retired

Table B2 (continued)

Pseudonym	Gender presentation	Birth year	Age at interview	Marital status	Occupational category	Dismissal year	Outcome (hard fall/soft landing)	Where are they now? (in 2023)
Isaac	Male	1952	61	Married	Manager/executive	2008	Soft landing	Retired
Kaaryn	Female	1949	65	Single	Health care practitioners & support	2014	Hard fall	Don't know
Kai	Male	1960	53	Married	Manager/executive	2012	Soft landing	Retired
Kaleb	Male	1955	58	Married	Computer related	2013	In between	Retired
Katherine	Female	1955	58	Single	Health care practitioners & support	2013	In between	Employed full-time
Keith	Male	1954	58	Married	Sales & related	2009	Hard fall	Don't know
Kenneth	Male	1949	65	Single	Computer related	2014	Soft landing	Died
Kevin	Male	1945	68	Single	Sales & related	2009	Soft landing	Don't know
Kirk	Male	1955	58	Married	Manager/executive	2014	In between	Don't know
Lars	Male	1955	57	Married	Architecture & engineering	2012	Soft landing	Died
Loren	Female	1950	64	Single	Office & administrative support	2011	In between	Retired
Luke	Male	1960	53	Married	Manager/executive	2013	Soft landing	Don't know
Lyle	Male	1959	54	Married	Manager/executive	2011	In between	Employed full-time
Margaret	Female	1953	61	Married	Miscellaneous	2012	Soft landing	Don't know
Marie	Female	1949	64	Married	Office & administrative support	2011	In between	Self-employed
Mark	Male	1956	58	Married	Sales & related	2009	In between	Retired
Martie	Female	1954	59	Single	Manager/executive	2011	In between	Don't know
Martin	Male	1949	64	Married	Miscellaneous	2013	Too soon to tell	Don't know
Meg	Female	1946	68	Single	Knowledge worker	2007	Hard fall	Died
Nadine	Female	1952	62	Married	Manager/executive	2011	Hard fall	Don't know

Name	Sex	Birth year	Age	Marital status	Occupation	Year	Landing	Status
Nathan	Male	1962	51	Married	Manager/executive	2012	Soft landing	Employed full-time
Nick	Male	1956	57	Married	Miscellaneous	2014	In between	Don't know
Nicole	Female	1956	53	Married	Manager/executive	2009	Soft landing	Retired
Norman	Male	1959	55	Married	Miscellaneous	2012	In between	Don't know
Olivia	Female	1952	61	Married	Office & administrative support	2011	In between	Don't know
Pamela	Female	1949	64	Married	Computer related	2013	In between	Employed part-time
Roberta	Female	1952	61	Single	Miscellaneous	2008	In between	Semiretired
Sally	Female	1954	59	Married	Manager/executive	2011	In between	Retired
Sara	Female	1960	53	Married	Knowledge worker	2011	Hard fall	On disability
Sean	Male	1962	52	Single	Manager/executive	2014	Too soon to tell	Employed full-time
Seymour	Male	1950	63	Married	Office & administrative support	2009	In between	Died
Sophia	Female	1947	67	Single	Manager/executive	2012	In between	Retired
Stephanie	Female	1952	61	Married	Manager/executive	2008	Hard fall	Don't know
Tad	Male	1954	59	Married	Manager/executive	2012	Soft landing	Retired
Tammy	Female	1956	58	Married	Sales & related	2009	In between	Self-employed
Teresa	Female	1954	59	Single	Office & administrative support	2011	Hard fall	Don't know
Terrence	Male	1955	59	Married	Manager/executive	2013	In between	Employed part-time
Timothy	Male	1956	58	Married	Sales & related	2008	In between	Occasional temp employment
Vanessa	Female	1958	55	Single	Knowledge worker	2010	In between	Self-employed
Victor	Male	1954	59	Married	Manager/executive	2012	In between	Retired
Wendy	Female	1951	63	Single	Sales & related	2013	Hard fall	Retired
Will	Male	1958	55	Married	Architecture & engineering	2011	Soft landing	Small business owner

Acknowledgments

Some say it takes a village to raise a child. We have learned it also takes a village to write a book. So many people and institutions, in two different countries no less, were instrumental in helping bring this project to fruition.

First, we owe a debt of gratitude to our sixty-two interviewees. Job loss can be difficult to talk about, especially in a society that often frames it as an indicator of personal shortcoming. Yet these individuals bravely shared their stories with a level of candor and detail that gave us a visceral understanding of late-career workers' sudden unemployment. It was a privilege to bear witness, and we hope that each research participant finds solace and companionship in the stories and findings we share in this book. We also appreciate the kind support of several Minnesota job clubs; the opportunities they provided to advertise the study and present the initial findings were invaluable for connecting us with our participants.

At Carleton College, where Annette teaches sociology, several students transcribed the initial interviews, a necessary task when speech-to-text programs were not yet widely available. We thank Yijun He, Katie Shaffer, Porter Truax, Ankita Verma, Mo Vue, and JordiKai Watanabe-Inouye for the hours they spent meticulously turning hours of conversation into the written words that became our data, and for approaching this task with patience, diligence, and a high level of professionalism.

A number of students participated in coding the transcripts with us. At Carleton College, our research assistants were Eve Butler, Mallika Dargan, Camille Jonlin, Cecilia Kryzda, Vicente Bobadilla Riquelme, Quinn Schiller, and Natalie Slinger. At Wilfrid Laurier University, where Dana teaches sociology, Mina Ly also assisted with coding and library research for the project. In addition to the role they played in establishing inter-coder reliability, our research assistants established important connections and shared valuable insights. We also wish to thank Dylann Cullinane, who skillfully transformed many of our citations to Chicago-style endnotes.

We benefited tremendously from the technological support provided by Paula Lackie, academic technologist at Carleton College. In addition to guiding us through best practices for data storage and security, Paula helped us design a Qualtrics survey for recontacting our sample. Her student assistant, James Marlin, ensured that the survey successfully reached our respondents and could be completed with ease.

Carleton College's Humanities Center has been an invaluable partner throughout this project. In addition to providing several small grants to cover some of our research expenses, the center appointed Annette a faculty research fellow in the 2017–2018 academic year. This appointment provided an opportunity to explore neoliberalism among a faculty cohort dedicated to examining its widespread effects. Ross Elfline, Wes Markofski, Anna Moltchanova, Juliane Schicker, and Kathryn Wegner—thank you for the stimulating conversations that were so important for this book's development.

We are grateful to the Carleton College administration, specifically the former dean of the college, Bev Nagel, and the current provost, Michelle Mattson. They, along with the faculty grants committee, awarded Annette several internal research grants and sabbatical terms over the ten-year span of this project. The sabbatical terms were funded by a Hewlett-Mellon Fellowship, a Carleton College Roth and Presidential Faculty Development Grant, and a Carleton College Presidential Fellowship. The research grants included two Gilman Grants and a Carleton College Targeted Opportunity Grant.

Wilfrid Laurier University likewise provided or facilitated the acquisition of research and travel funding, sabbatical terms, and a course remission in support of this project. On that note, this research was supported by the Social Sciences and Humanities Research Council of Canada. The staff in the Dean of Arts Office deserve special mention for helping Dana wrangle the administrative processes related to these opportunities over the years.

We thank the American Philosophical Society for awarding Annette a Franklin Research Grant. This support, which came at a critical juncture, provided funding to compensate our follow-up interviewees. The grant also gave us an opportunity to meet face-to-face to analyze the follow-up interviews and write the concluding chapter of the book. The support of Carleton's Grants Office (and, more specifically, Christopher Tassava, Charlotte Whited, Dee Manning, and Quinn Arnold) was instrumental in ensuring that Annette's grant application was successful.

Several people were involved in editing and proofreading our manuscript. Danielle Schultz provided constructive feedback on chapter 5. Letta Page coached us through every chapter of the manuscript and then some. In addition to helping us maintain a clear throughline, she taught us the importance of translating complex sociological jargon into prose that is accessible to a much wider audience. We are also grateful to Robert Morrow, Annette's husband, for listening to many iterations of each chapter while also focusing on word choice and tone. Rob's remarkable vocabulary is augmented by his songwriter sensibilities and paired with a laser-like focus on the written word. Like Letta, Rob helped make this book readable for an audience beyond academic sociologists.

We also wish to thank our colleagues. Annette's colleagues in the Department of Sociology and Anthropology at Carleton College (Pamela Feldman-Savelsberg, Wes Markofski, Constanza Ocampo-Raeder, and Liz Raleigh) listened to our ideas, celebrated our victories, and even provided supplemental research funds. Several current and former colleagues of Dana's in the Department of Sociology and in the Faculty of Arts at Wilfrid Laurier University were similarly supportive. Lucy Luccisano, Glenda Wall, and Linda Quirke (aka The Motherhood) deserve special mention for their collegiality and friendship on campus and beyond. Diane Collier's (Brock University) daily accountability texts with Dana and her ongoing encouragement contributed more to the completion of this project than she could know. Jo VanEvery played a key role in helping Dana learn how to manage many competing professional commitments.

Beyond our respective departments, Ofer Sharone of the University of Massachusetts Amherst provided unwavering support that spanned from the inception of this project to its completion. Dawn Norris of the University of Wisconsin-La Crosse and Sarah Damaske of Pennsylvania State University reviewed our manuscript proposal and generously offered suggestions that greatly improved the finished product. Sarah Damaske also provided valuable feedback on the completed draft.

At Rutgers University Press, we are appreciative of the opportunity provided by Enobong Hannah Branch and Adia Harvey Wingfield to publish in the Inequality at Work series. We thank executive editor Peter Mickulas for his unflagging support and enthusiasm for our work, and for easing every step of the process. We also thank the Rutgers production team for their professionalism and efficiency. The responsibility for any errors or omissions contained within this book rests entirely with us.

Finally, Annette is grateful to Robert Morrow for the love, support, and sustenance he provided throughout this entire process. Dana is grateful to David Bryce for playing the same role in her life (once again!) and to Michael and Benji for being, well, Michael and Benji. Annette's aunt and uncle, Vida Juozaitis and Eugene Martynec, were a great source of both intellectual inspiration and media articles related to our project. Our parents, Irena and Waldemar Nierobisz and Kate and Don Sawchuk, have not only provided unending support throughout our academic careers; they have given us quiet spaces in their homes to think and write. Pooka and Pony, Annette's Alapaha Blue Blood Bulldogs, also deserve a shout-out for keeping the manuscript safe from marauding squirrels and rascally rabbits.

Notes

Chapter 1 "Broke, Unemployed, Downsized Again"

1. A national unemployment rate of 10 percent is considered abnormally high for the United States. If this rate were amended to include discouraged workers (those who withdraw from the labor force after protracted job searches) and involuntary part-time workers (those who desire a full-time job but must settle for part-time work), 2010's comprehensive unemployment rate is estimated to have been between 16 and 18 percent. David B. Grusky, Bruce Western, and Christopher Wimer, "The Consequences of the Great Recession," in *The Great Recession*, ed. David B. Grusky, Bruce Western, and Christopher Wimer (New York: Russell Sage Foundation, 2011), 3–20.
2. Alexander Monge-Naranjo and Faisal Sohail, "The Composition of Long-Term Unemployment Is Changing toward Older Workers," *The Regional Economist*, October 2015, https://www.stlouisfed.org/~/media/Publications/Regional-Economist/2015/October/unemployment.pdf.
3. Arlie Hochschild, *Strangers in Their Own Land* (New York: The New Press, 2016).
4. In 2019, millennials became the largest population group. This happened for two reasons. First, new immigrants to the United States are more likely to be members of the millennial generation. Second, the size of the baby boomer generation is declining due to deaths within this older population group.
5. Elise Gould, "Older Workers Were Devastated by the Pandemic Downturn and Continue to Face Adverse Employment Outcomes: EPI Testimony for the Senate Special Committee on Aging," Economic Policy Institute, April 29, 2021, https://www.epi.org/publication/older-workers-were-devastated-by-the-pandemic-downturn-and-continue-to-face-adverse-employment-outcomes-epi-testimony-for-the-senate-special-committee-on-aging/. According to a 2017 Special Senate Committee on Aging report, "The number of Americans over age fifty-five in the labor force is projected to increase from 35.7 million in 2016 to 42.1 million in 2026, and, by 2026, aging workers will make up nearly one quarter of the labor force"; Senate Special Committee on Aging, *America's Aging Workforce: Opportunities and Challenges*, December 2017, 3, https://www.aging.senate.gov/imo/media/doc/Aging%20Workforce%20Report%20FINAL.pdf.

6. C. Wright Mills, *The Sociological Imagination* (London: Oxford University Press, 1959), 3.
7. Marc Levinson, *An Extraordinary Time: The End of the Postwar Boom and the Return of the Ordinary Economy* (New York: Basic Books, 2016).
8. Women, immigrants, and BIPOC Americans were excluded from this type of employment relationship. These workers, as sociologist Arne Kalleberg writes, "have always been more subject to uncertain, insecure, and risky work relations." Arne L. Kalleberg, *Precarious Lives: Job Insecurity and Well-Being in Rich Democracies* (Medford, MA: Polity, 2018), 18. See also Beth A. Rubin, "Employment Insecurity and the Frayed American Dream," *Sociology Compass* 8, no. 9 (September 2014): 1083–1099 and Matissa Hollister, "Employment Stability in the U.S. Labor Market: Rhetoric versus Reality," *Annual Review of Sociology* 37 (August 2011): 305–324.
9. Arne L. Kalleberg, *Good Jobs, Bad Jobs: The Rise of Polarized and Precarious Employment Systems in the United States, 1970s to 2000s* (New York: Russell Sage Foundation, 2011).
10. A similar metaphor was employed by an interviewee in Carrie M. Lane's study, *A Company of One: Insecurity, Independence, and the New World of White-Collar Unemployment* (Ithaca, NY: Cornell University Press, 2011), 154.
11. George Monbiot, "Neoliberalism—the Ideology at the Root of All Our Problems," *Guardian*, April 15, 2016, https://www.theguardian.com/books/2016/apr/15/neoliberalism-ideology-problem-george-monbiot.
12. David Harvey, *A Brief History of Neoliberalism* (New York: Oxford University Press, 2007). See also Susan Dudley, "Jimmy Carter: The Great Deregulator," *The Regulatory Review*, March 6, 2023, https://www.theregreview.org/2023/03/06/dudley-jimmy-carter-the-great-deregulator/.
13. "The Chicago boys," a group of University of Chicago–trained economists who advised the Chilean government, subscribed to the neoliberal theories of economics professor Milton Friedman. According to scholar David Harvey, "The US had funded the training of Chilean economists at the University of Chicago since the 1950s as part of a Cold War programme to counteract left-wing tendencies in Latin America." Harvey, *A Brief History of Neoliberalism*, 8.
14. Harvey, *A Brief History of Neoliberalism*. As critic, essayist, and university professor Louis Menand reminds us, President Reagan stated in his inaugural address: "Government is not the solution to our problem. Government is the problem." Louis Menand, "The Price Is Right: The Rise and Fall of Neoliberalism," *New Yorker*, July 17, 2023, https://www.newyorker.com/magazine/2023/07/24/the-rise-and-fall-of-neoliberalism.
15. Michèle Lamont, "From Having to Being: Self-Worth and the Current Crisis of American Society," *British Journal of Sociology* 70, no. 3 (June 2019): 660–707; Massimo Pendenza and Vanessa Lamattina, "Rethinking Self-Responsibility: An Alternative Vision to the Neoliberal Concept of Freedom," *American Behavioral Scientist* 63, no. 1 (January 2019): 100–115.
16. Emily Oster, *The Family Firm: A Data-Driven Guide to Better Decision Making in the Early School Years* (New York: Penguin Press, 2021).
17. Jason Hackworth, "Compassionate Neoliberalism: Evangelical Christianity, the Welfare State, and the Politics of the Right," *Studies in Political Economy* 86, no. 1 (March 2016): 97.
18. Wendy Brown, *Undoing the Demos: Neoliberalism's Stealth Revolution* (Cambridge, MA; London: Zone Books, 2015).

19. Hila Keren, "Divided and Conquered: The Neoliberal Roots and Emotional Consequences of the Arbitration Revolution," *Florida Law Review* 72 (May 2020): 575–638.
20. Ilana Gershon, *Down and Out in the New Economy* (Chicago: University of Chicago Press, 2017), 2.
21. Gershon, *Down and Out*.
22. Kalleberg, *Precarious Lives*.
23. Kalleberg, *Good Jobs, Bad Jobs*.
24. Monbiot, "Neoliberalism."
25. Michael Peters, "The Early Origins of Neoliberalism: Colloque Walter Lippman (1938) and the Mt Perelin Society (1947)," *Educational Philosophy and Theory* 55, no. 14 (2021): 1574–1581, https://doi.org/10.1080/00131857.2021.1951704.
26. Lamont, "From Having to Being," 666.
27. Lane, *A Company of One*.
28. Michael Hout, Asaf Levanon, and Erin Cumberworth, "Job Loss and Unemployment," in *The Great Recession*, ed. David B. Grusky, Bruce Western, and Christopher Wimer (New York: Russell Sage Foundation, 2011): 59–81.
29. Pew Charitable Trusts, *A Year or More: The High Costs of Long-Term Unemployment*, addendum to the Pew Fiscal Analysis Initiative, May 2012, http://www.pewtrusts.org/~/media/Assets/2012/05/Long_Term_Unemployment_May2012_Addendum.pdf. In the first quarter of 2012, approximately 44 percent of unemployed workers older than age fifty-five had been without work for one year or longer; quoted in Pew Charitable Trusts, *A Year or More*, 3. Twelve percent was the equivalent statistic for workers under age twenty.
30. Grusky, Western, and Wimer, "The Consequences of the Great Recession."
31. Lori A. Trawinski, *Nightmare on Main Street: Older Americans and the Mortgage Market Crisis*, AARP, #2010–08 (Washington, DC: AARP Public Policy Institute, 2012), http://www.aarp.org/content/dam/aarp/research/public_policy_institute/cons_prot/2012/nightmare-on-main-street-AARP-ppi-cons-prot.pdf.
32. Richard W. Kopcke and Anthony Webb, "How Has the Financial Crisis Affected the Finances of Older Households?" working paper, Center for Retirement Research at Boston College, accessed September 25, 2021, http://web.stanford.edu/group/scspi/_media/working_papers/Kopcke_Webb_older-households.pdf.
33. Edward N. Wolff, Lindsay A. Owens, and Esra Burak, "How Much Wealth Was Destroyed in the Great Recession?" in *The Great Recession*, ed. David B. Grusky, Bruce Western, and Christopher Wimer (New York: Russell Sage Foundation, 2011), 129.
34. Wolff, Owens, and Burak, "How Much Wealth Was Destroyed?"
35. Pew Charitable Trusts, *When Do Americans Plan to Retire? A Brief from the Pew Charitable Trusts*, November 19, 2018, https://www.pewtrusts.org/-/media/assets/2018/11/whendoamericansplantoretire_final.pdf.
36. U.S. News and World Report, *Best States 2021: Ranking Performance throughout All 50 States*, accessed July 5, 2021, https://www.usnews.com/media/best-states/overall-rankings-2021.pdf.
37. Lisa Rowan, "The States with the Best and Worst Unemployment Benefits—and Why They're So Different," *Forbes Advisor*, March 17, 2021, https://www.forbes.com/advisor/personal-finance/best-and-worst-states-for-unemployment/.

38 Steve Hine et al., "State of the Economy," *Minnesota Economic Trends*, Minnesota Department of Employment and Economic Development, June 2014, https://mn.gov/deed/newscenter/publications/trends/june-2014/state-economy.jsp.
39 Pew Charitable Trusts, *When Do Americans Plan to Retire?*
40 Kalleberg, *Good Jobs, Bad Jobs*.
41 See, for example, Marianne Bertrand and Sendhil Mullainathan, "Are Emily and Greg More Employable Than Lakisha and Jamal? A Field Experiment on Labor Market Discrimination," *The American Economic Review* 94, no. 4 (2004): 991–1013; and Daniel Widner and Stephen Chicoine, "It's All in the Name: Employment Discrimination against Arab Americans," *Sociological Forum* 26, no. 4 (2011): 806–823.
42 Shannon Ridgway, "20+ Examples of Age Privilege," *Everyday Feminism*, January 24, 2013, https://everydayfeminism.com/2013/01/20-examples-of-age-privilege/page/3/.
43 Our methodological approach, detailed in appendix A, outlines the procedures followed to construct a sample of sixty-two older, unemployed adults. We provide a rationale for using a qualitative method and discuss the characteristics of Minnesota as the research site, and then outline participant recruitment and inclusion in the final sample. The appendix concludes with descriptions of the in-depth, semi-structured interviews conducted and an overview of how we analyzed the data produced by them.
44 Gould, "Older Workers Were Devastated"; Sarah Damaske, *The Tolls of Uncertainty: How Privilege and the Guilt Gap Shape Unemployment in America* (Princeton, NJ: Princeton University Press, 2021).

Chapter 2 Hard Falls and Soft Landings

1 Glen Elder, "Time, Human Agency, and Social Change: Perspectives on the Life Course," *Social Psychology Quarterly* 57, no. 1 (1994): 4–15. See also Glen Elder, "The Life Course as Developmental Theory," *Child Development* 69, no. 1 (1998): 1–12.
2 Glen Elder, *Children of the Great Depression: Social Change in Life Experience* (Chicago: University of Chicago Press, 1974).
3 For example, both the Great Depression and Great Recession began with a stock market crash. The two downturns were also characterized by steep unemployment rates and protracted recoveries. For more examples, see John V. Duca, "The Great Depression versus the Great Recession in the U.S.: How Fiscal, Monetary, and Financial Policies Compare," *Journal of Economic Dynamics and Control* 81 (2017): 50–64.
4 Steve Hanke, "What Do the Great Depression and the Great Recession Have in Common?" *Forbes*, August 16, 2017, https://www.forbes.com/sites/stevehanke/2017/08/16/what-do-the-great-depression-and-the-great-recession-have-in-common/?sh=2b18808375d3.
5 One respondent, Henry, was born in 1945. According to the Pew Research Center, this is one year before the baby boom began. However, as we note in chapter 2, there is a lack of consensus around the years bounding the baby boom generation.
6 Elizabeth D. Hutchison, "Middle Adulthood," in *Dimensions of Human Behavior, The Changing Life Course*, 4th ed., ed. Elizabeth D. Hutchison (Thousand Oaks, CA: Sage Publications, 2011), 313.

7 Elder, "The Life Course as Developmental Theory."
8 Phyllis Moen, *Encore Adulthood: Boomers on the Edge of Risk, Renewal, and Purpose* (New York: Oxford University Press, 2016), 6.
9 Increased life expectancies are attributed to several factors, including advances in medical science; public health initiatives; declining fertility rates; declining number of deaths from workplace accidents and injuries; and a large generation of people (i.e., the baby boomers) now entering old age. Deborah Carr, *The Golden Years? Social Inequality in Later Life* (New York: Russell Sage Foundation, 2019), 13–16.
10 Vincent J. Roscigno, "Ageism in the Workplace," *Contexts* 9, no. 1 (February 2010): 16–21.
11 Elizabeth D. Hutchison, "A Life Course Perspective," in *Dimensions of Human Behavior, The Changing Life Course*, 4th ed., ed. Elizabeth D. Hutchison (Thousand Oaks, CA: Sage Publications, 2011), 23.
12 William T. Gallo et al., "The Impact of Late Career Job Loss on Myocardial Infarction and Stroke: A 10 Year Follow-up Using the Health and Retirement Survey," *Occupational and Environmental Medicine* 63, no. 10 (October 2006): 683–687; Lauren L. Schmitz and Dalton Conley, "The Impact of Late-Career Job Loss and Genotype on Body Mass Index," NBER Working Paper No. 22348, National Bureau of Economic Research, Cambridge, MA, June 2016, http://doi:10.3386/w22348; Tracy Falba et al., "The Effect of Involuntary Job Loss on Smoking Intensity and Relapse," *Addiction* 100, no. 9 (September 2005): 1330–1339; Jennie E. Brand, Becca R. Levy, and William T. Gallo, "Effects of Layoffs and Plant Closings on Subsequent Depression among Older Workers," *Research on Aging* 30, no. 6 (November 2008), 701–721; William T. Gallo et al., "Health Effects of Involuntary Job Loss among Older Workers: Findings from the Health and Retirement Survey," *Journal of Gerontology: Social Sciences* 55B, no. 3 (May 2000): S131–S140.
13 Lora A. Phillips Lassus, Steven Lopez, and Vincent J. Roscigno, "Aging Workers and the Experience of Job Loss," *Research in Social Stratification and Mobility* 41 (September 2015): 87.
14 Anne Case and Angus Deaton, "Rising Morbidity and Mortality in Midlife among White Non-Hispanic Americans in the 21st Century," *PNAS* 112, no. 49 (2015): 15078–15083.
15 Katherine A. Hempstead and Julie A. Phillips, "Rising Suicide among Adults Aged 40–64 Years: The Role of Job and Financial Circumstances," *American Journal of Preventive Medicine* 48, no. 5 (February 2015): 491–500.
16 V. Lee Hamilton et al., "Hard Times and Vulnerable People: Initial Effects of Plant Closing on Autoworkers' Mental Health," *Journal of Health and Social Behavior* 31, no. 2 (June 1990): 123–140; Carrie R. Leana and Daniel C. Feldman, *Coping with Job Loss: How Individuals, Organizations, and Communities Respond to Layoffs* (New York: Lexington Books, 1992); Barbara K. Shelton, "The Social and Psychological Impact of Unemployment," *Journal of Employment Counseling* 22, no. 1 (March 1985): 18–22.
17 Janina C. Latack, Angelo J. Kinicki, and Gregory E. Prussia, "An Integrative Process Model of Coping with Job Loss," *Academy of Management Review* 20, no. 2 (April 1995): 327; Harold G. Kaufman, *Professionals in Search of Work: Coping with the Stress of Job Loss and Underemployment* (New York: Wiley, 1982); Michael Podgursky and Paul Swaim, "Job Displacement and Earnings

Loss—Evidence from the Displaced Worker Survey," *Industrial and Labor Relations Review* 41, no. 1 (October 1987): 17–29.

18 Stephen Fineman, *White Collar Unemployment: Impact and Stress* (Chichester, UK: Wiley, 1983).

19 Katherine S. Newman, *Falling from Grace: Downward Mobility in the Age of Affluence* (Berkeley, CA: University of California Press, 1999); Paul Letkemann, "Unemployed Professionals, Stigma Management and Derivative Stigmata," *Work, Employment and Society* 16, no. 3 (September 2002): 511–522.

20 Ofer Sharone, *Flawed System/Flawed Self: Job Searching and Unemployment Experiences* (Chicago: University of Chicago Press, 2014); Dawn R. Norris, *Job Loss, Identity, and Mental Health* (New Brunswick, NJ: Rutgers University Press, 2016).

21 Yiannis Gabriel, David E. Gray, and Harshita Goregaokar, "Job Loss and Its Aftermath among Managers and Professionals: Wounded, Fragmented and Flexible," *Work, Employment and Society* 27, no. 1 (2013): 56–72.

22 Sewin Chan and Ann Huff Stevens, "Job Loss and Employment Patterns of Older Workers," *Journal of Labor Economics* 19, no. 2 (April 2001): 484–521, https://doi.org/10.1086/319568.

23 Ann Huff Stevens, "Persistent Effects of Job Displacement: The Importance of Multiple Job Losses," *Journal of Labor Economics* 15, no. 1 (January 1997): 165–188; Ariel Gelrud Shiro and Kristin Butcher, "Job Displacement in the United States by Race, Education, and Parental Income," Brookings, Future of the Middle Class Initiative, July 2022, https://www.brookings.edu/wp-content/uploads/2022/07/20220719_FMCI_ShiroButcher_JobDisplacement_FINAL.pdf.

24 Sewin Chan and Ann Huff Stevens, "How Does Job Loss Affect the Timing of Retirement?" NBER Working Paper No. 8780, National Bureau of Economic Research, Cambridge, MA, February 2002, http://www.nber.org/papers/w8780.

25 Gulgun Bayaz Ozturk and William T. Gallo, *Effect of Job Loss on Wealth Accumulation of Older Workers*, report prepared for the U.S. Department of Labor, January 2013, https://www.dol.gov/sites/dolgov/files/OASP/legacy/files/FINAL_REPORT_wealth_effects_job_loss_older_workers.pdf.

26 Karen Sternheimer, "Downward Mobility," *Everyday Sociology* (blog), April 22, 2010, https://www.everydaysociologyblog.com/2010/04/downward-mobility.html.

27 As Damaske notes, existing gender inequalities in the labor market are reproduced among unemployed women and men. Damaske, *The Tolls of Uncertainty*. See also Jeff Hayes and Heidi Hartmann, *Women and Men Living on the Edge: Economic Insecurity after the Great Recession*, Institute for Women's Policy Research, C386, September 2011, https://iwpr.org/women-and-men-living-on-the-edge-economic-insecurity-after-the-great-recession/.

28 Cassandra was one of two self-employed respondents in our sample; both respondents worked in industries that declined during the Great Recession.

29 Adam Hadi, "Construction Employment Peaks before the Recession and Falls Sharply throughout It," *Monthly Labor Review*, April 2011, https://www.bls.gov/opub/mlr/2011/04/art4full.pdf.

30 At the federal level, unemployed workers at this time became eligible for up to seventy-three weeks of unemployment benefits. Ross Eisenbrey, "The Obama Administration Pushes for a Better Response to Unemployment," *Working Economics* (blog), Economic Policy Institute, January 28, 2016, https://www.epi.org/blog/the-obama-administration-pushes-for-better-response-to-unemployment/#.

31. As Cassandra noted, "It's easier to go through McDonald's than it is to go to the food shelf. And then you go to the food shelf, and then there's all this stuff that you have to cook and put together and that's hard."
32. Individuals born in 1954 or earlier receive their full Social Security benefits at age sixty-six. Individuals born in 1960 and later receive their full Social Security benefits at age sixty-seven. Social Security Administration, "Retirement Benefits," Publication No. 05-10035, 2023, https://www.ssa.gov/pubs/EN-05-10035.pdf.
33. Population Reference Bureau, "Unmarried Baby Boomers Face Disadvantages as They Grow Older," March 6, 2014, https://www.prb.org/resources/unmarried-baby-boomers-face-disadvantages-as-they-grow-older/#:~:text=And%20given%20that%2033%20percent,because%20they%20aren't%20married.
34. Sociologist Phyllis Moen attributes this gender discrepancy to the fact that women of the baby boom generation are less likely to remarry after divorce or widowhood. See Moen, *Encore Adulthood*.
35. Respondents whose multiple job losses contributed to a hard fall include Wendy (lost two jobs), Dawn (lost two jobs), Nadine (lost two jobs), and Charles (lost four jobs).
36. Ariel Gelrud Shiro and Kristin F. Butcher, "The Long-Term Economic Scars of Job Displacements," Brookings, July 21, 2022, https://www.brookings.edu/articles/the-long-term-economic-scars-of-job-displacements/.
37. Huff Stevens, "Persistent Effects of Job Displacement."
38. The Investopedia Team, "Short Sales vs. Foreclosures: What's the Difference?" Investopedia, August 22, 2022, https://www.investopedia.com/ask/answers/100314/whats-difference-between-short-sales-and-foreclosures.asp#.
39. We used a variety of sampling methods, including snowball sampling. With this approach, we invited interviewees to share recruitment flyers with family, friends, neighbors, and former colleagues who were similarly experiencing late-career job loss. One individual advertised the study on a LISTSERV created for co-workers who were downsized alongside him. His efforts resulted in seven of his co-workers joining our study.
40. Brigitte Yuille, "Severance Package Explained: The Layoff Payoff," Investopedia, updated June 6, 2024, https://www.investopedia.com/articles/pf/08/negotiating-severance-agreements.asp.
41. With a defined-benefit pension plan, an employer guarantees a specified monthly benefit at retirement. These types of pension plans were common in the post–World War II economy. Today workers are more likely to have a defined contribution plan. With this plan, an individual or the employer or both contribute a percentage of earnings to the individual's retirement account. U.S. Department of Labor, "Types of Retirement Plans," accessed November 2, 2023, https://www.dol.gov/general/topic/retirement/typesofplans.
42. See Damaske, *The Tolls of Uncertainty*.
43. Many U.S. homeowners refinanced their homes in the wake of the Great Recession. Mortgage interest rates dropped below 5 percent in 2010 and remained low for more than a decade. Peter Miller, "Mortgage Rates Chart: Historical and Current Rate Trends," The Mortgage Reports, June 27, 2023, https://themortgagereports.com/61853/30-year-mortgage-rates-chart#loan-purpose.
44. Recall that Heather and Cassandra, two respondents with hard falls, had worked in fields that declined precipitously with the mortgage crisis associated with the Great Recession.

45. U.S. Bureau of Labor Statistics, "The Recession of 2007–2009," *BLS Spotlight on Statistics*, February 2012, https://www.bls.gov/spotlight/2012/recession/pdf/recession_bls_spotlight.pdf.
46. For individuals born before 1954, like Benjamin, Martin, and Cat were, full benefits begin at age sixty-six. An individual can start receiving Social Security as early as age sixty-two, but, as Meg experienced, this early withdrawal is associated with a 30 percent reduction in the benefit amount.
47. Financial consultants advise having a minimum of three to six months of savings to cover living expenses. In a recession, when unemployment is more likely and fewer jobs are available, more savings are necessary. Vanguard, "What's the Right Emergency Fund Amount?" accessed September 6, 2023, https://investor.vanguard.com/investor-resources-education/emergency-fund/whats-the-right-emergency-fund-amount#.
48. As research shows, women of the baby boom generation were systematically excluded from occupations and industrial sectors that rewarded their workers with high wages, pensions, and other benefits that can ease the transition to unemployment. Angela M. O'Rand, "The Precious and the Precocious: Understanding Cumulative Disadvantage and Cumulative Advantage over the Life Course," *Gerontologist* 36, no. 2 (April 1996): 233.
49. Gordon B. Dahl and Matthew M. Knepper, "Age Discrimination across the Business Cycle," NBER Working Paper No. 27581, National Bureau of Economic Research, Cambridge, MA, July 2020, http://www.nber.org/papers/w27581.
50. Robert N. Butler, "Age-ism: Another Form of Bigotry," pt. 1, *Gerontologist* 9 no. 4, (1969): 243–246.
51. Robert N. Butler, "The Effects of the Medical and Health Progress on the Social and Economic Aspects of the Life Cycle" (paper delivered at the National Institute of Industrial Gerontology, Washington, D.C., March 13, 1969), as cited in Robert N. Butler, "Dispelling Ageism: The Cross-Cutting Intervention," *Annals of the American Academy of Political and Social Science* 503 (1989): 138–147.
52. Kristen Weir, "Ageism Is One of the Last Socially Acceptable Prejudices. Psychologists Are Working to Change That," American Psychological Association, March 1, 2023, https://www.apa.org/monitor/2023/03/cover-new-concept-of-aging.
53. Butler, "Dispelling Ageism."
54. Becca R. Levy et al., "Ageism Amplifies Cost and Prevalence of Health Conditions," *Gerontologist* 60, no. 1 (2018): 174–181. See also Sibila Marques et al., "'Being Old and Ill' across Different Countries: Social Status, Age Identification and Older People's Subjective Health," *Psychology and Health* 30, no. 6 (2015): 699–714.
55. U.S. Equal Employment Opportunity Commission, Age Discrimination Employment Act of 1967, SEC. 623 [Section 4], accessed July 19, 2021, https://www.eeoc.gov/statutes/age-discrimination-employment-act-1967.
56. Lassus, Lopez, and Roscigno, "Aging Workers and the Experience of Job Loss."
57. The full list of prohibited grounds are "race, creed, color, sex, national origin, ancestry, religion, age, disability, sexual orientation or marital status." Minnesota Department of Labor and Industry, "Employment Termination," accessed September 4, 2023, https://www.dli.mn.gov/business/employment-practices/employment-termination#.
58. Stephen Fineman, *Organizing Age* (New York: Oxford University Press, 2011), 62.
59. Fineman, *Organizing Age*; see also Vincent J. Roscigno et al., "Age Discrimination, Social Closure and Employment," *Social Forces* 86, no. 1 (September 2007):

313–334; Ellie D. Berger, *Ageism at Work: Deconstructing Age and Gender in the Discriminating Labour Market* (Toronto: University of Toronto Press, 2021).

60 David Neumark, "The Age Discrimination in Employment Act and the Challenge of Population Aging," *Research on Aging* 31, no. 1 (2009): 41–68; David Neumark and Patrick Button, "Did Age Discrimination Protections Help Older Workers Weather the Great Recession?" *Journal of Policy Analysis and Management* 33, no. 3 (2014): 566–601.

61 Annie Lennox, "Keep Young and Beautiful," track 11 on *Diva*, RCA Records, 1992. Cassandra began singing this version, which was a cover of a 1930s song.

62 Laura Hurd Clarke and Alexandra Korotchenko, "Aging and the Body: A Review," *Canadian Journal on Aging* 20, no. 3 (2011): 495–510.

63 Rebecca L. Pearl and Ivona Percec, "Ageism and Health in Patients Undergoing Cosmetic Procedures," *Aesthetic Surgery Journal* 39, no. 7 (2018): NP288–NP292.

Chapter 3 Generations at Work

1 Matthew Twombly and Kendrick McDonald, "A Timeline of 1968: The Year That Shattered America," *Smithsonian Magazine*, January 2018, https://www.smithsonianmag.com/history/timeline-seismic-180967503/.

2 Douglas Coupland, *Generation X: Tales for an Accelerated Culture* (New York: St. Martin's Press, 1991).

3 Karl Mannheim, "The Problem of Generations," in *Karl Mannheim: Essays on the Sociology of Knowledge*, ed. Paul Kecskemeti (London: Routledge & Kegan Paul, 1928 [republished in 1972]), 276–320.

4 Specifically, individuals between the ages of seventeen and twenty-five.

5 Cort Rudolph and Hannes Zacher, "'The COVID-19 Generation': A Cautionary Note," *Work, Aging and Retirement* 6, no. 3 (2020): 139–145; William Strauss and Neil Howe, *Generations: The History of America's Future, 1584 to 2069* (New York: Quill William Morrow, 1991).

6 Pew Research Center, "The Whys and Hows of Generations Research," September 3, 2015, https://www.pewresearch.org/politics/2015/09/03/the-whys-and-hows-of-generations-research/.

7 Jennie Bristow, *Stop Mugging Grandma: The 'Generation Wars' and Why Boomer Blaming Won't Solve Anything* (New Haven, CT: Yale University Press, 2019); Margaret Morganroth Gullette, "Boomers: From Adorable Baby Bulge to #BoomerRemover," *Age, Culture, Humanities: An Interdisciplinary Journal* 6 (September 2022): 1–6, https://doi.org/10.7146/ageculturehumanities.v6i.133335.

8 Lynne C. Lancaster and David Stillman, *When Generations Collide: Who They Are. Why They Clash. How to Solve the Generational Puzzle at Work* (New York: Harper Business, 2003).

9 Strauss and Howe, *Generations*.

10 Michael Dimock, "Defining Generations: Where Millennials End and Generation Z Begins," January 17, 2019, https://www.pewresearch.org/short-reads/2019/01/17/where-millennials-end-and-generation-z-begins/; Pew Research Center, "The Whys and Hows."

11 Eddy S. Ng, Sean T. Lyons, and Linda Schweitzer, *Generational Career Shifts: How Matures, Boomers, Gen Xers, and Millennials View Work* (Bingley, UK: Emerald Publishing, 2018): 6.

12. Jonathan White, "Thinking Generations," *British Journal of Sociology* 64, no. 2 (2013): 216–247.
13. White, "Thinking Generations," 216.
14. Gianluca Mezzofiore, "A 25-Year-Old Politician Got Heckled during a Climate Crisis Speech. Her Deadpan Retort: 'OK, Boomer,'" CNN.com, November 7, 2019, https://www.cnn.com/2019/11/06/asia/new-zealand-ok-boomer-trnd/index.html.
15. Brad Meisner, "Are You OK, Boomer? Intensification of Ageism and Intergenerational Tensions on Social Media amid COVID-19," *Leisure Sciences* 43, no. 1–2 (2020): 56–61; Rudolf and Zacher, "'The COVID-19 Generation.'"
16. Gullette, "Boomers."
17. Greg Martin and Steven Roberts, "Exploring Legacies of the Baby Boomers in the Twenty-First Century," *Sociological Review* 69, no. 4 (2021): 727–742; White, "Thinking Generations."
18. Meagan Johnson and Larry Johnson, *From Boomers to Linksters—Managing the Friction between Generations at Work* (New York: AMACOM, 2010).
19. Lancaster and Stillman, *When Generations Collide*.
20. Valerie Grubb, *Clash of the Generations: Managing the New Workplace Reality* (Hoboken, NJ: Wiley, 2017); Ron Zemke, Claire Raines, and Bob Filipczak, *Generations at Work: Managing the Clash of Veterans, Boomers, Xers, and Nexters in Your Workplace* (New York: AMACOM, 1999).
21. Amanda Lisetti, *Generations Reimagined: The Complete Guide Uncovering the Real Differences between Generation Z, Millennials, Generation X, Boomers, Silents, and Generation Alpha* (independently pub., 2023), Kindle; Haydn Shaw, *Sticking Points: How to Get 5 Generations Working Together in the 12 Places They Come Apart* (Carol Stream, IL: Tyndale Momentum, 2020).
22. Ng, Lyons, and Schweitzer, *Generational Career Shifts*; Emma Parry and Peter Urwin, "Generational Differences in Work Values: A Review of Theory and Evidence," *International Journal of Management Reviews* 13, no. 1 (2011): 79–96, https://doi.org/10.1111/j.1468-2370.2010.00285.x; Lucy Cennamo and Dianne Gardner, "Generational Differences in Work Values, Outcomes and Person-Organisation Values Fit," *Journal of Managerial Psychology* 23, no. 8 (2008): 891–906, https://doi.org/10.1108/02683940810904385.
23. Fineman, *Organizing Age*, 50–53.
24. Philip N. Cohen, "Opinion: Generation Labels Mean Nothing. It's Time to Retire Them," *Washington Post*, July 7, 2021, https://www.washingtonpost.com/opinions/2021/07/07/generation-labels-mean-nothing-retire-them/.
25. Cohen, "Opinion."
26. For example, Fineman, *Organizing Age*; Gullette, "Boomers"; Martin and Roberts, "Exploring Legacies."
27. Cohen's letter had the support of over 300 cosignatories. Philip N. Cohen, "Open Letter to the Pew Research Center on Generation Labels," accessed June 20, 2023, https://docs.google.com/forms/d/e/1FAIpQLSecsM1JavYMlNI-XlKDYngFKsEFBGFs_imv7R5KO8e15NYeCg/viewform.
28. Michael Dimock, "5 Things to Keep in Mind When You Hear about Gen Z, Millennials, Boomers and Other Generations," Pew Research Center, May 22, 2023, https://www.pewresearch.org/short-reads/2023/05/22/5-things-to-keep-in-mind-when-you-hear-about-gen-z-millennials-boomers-and-other-generations/.
29. Kim Parker, "How Pew Research Center Will Report on Generations Moving Forward," Pew Research Center, May 22, 2023, https://www.pewresearch.org

/short-reads/2023/05/22/how-pew-research-center-will-report-on-generations-moving-forward/.
30 Cf. Sean T. Lyons and Linda Schweitzer, "A Qualitative Exploration of Generational Identity: Making Sense of Young and Old in the Context of Today's Workplace," *Work, Aging and Retirement* 3, no. 2 (2017): 220.
31 "If men define situations as real, they are real in their consequences." William I. Thomas and Dorothy Swaine Thomas, *The Child in America: Behavior Problems and Programs* (New York: Knopf, 1928), 572.
32 White, "Thinking Generations."
33 Lyons and Schweitzer, "Generational Identity,"; Katrina Pritchard and Rebecca Whiting, "Baby Boomers and the Lost Generation: On the Discursive Construction of Generations at Work," *Organization Studies* 35, no. 11 (2014): 1605–1626.
34 Glen Elder, Monica Kirkpatrick Johnson, and Robert Crosnoe, "The Emergence and Development of Life Course Theory," in *Handbook of the Life Course*, ed. Jeylan Mortimer and Michael Shanahan (New York: Springer Publishing, 2003), 3–19.
35 Elder, *Children of the Great Depression*; Rudolf and Zacher, "'The COVID-19 Generation.'"
36 Elder, Kirkpatrick, and Crosnoe, "Emergence and Development."
37 DEED Labor Market Information Office, "Generations in the Twin Cities Metro Area," April 2019, https://mn.gov/deed/assets/Generations-TwinCities_tcm1045-384981.pdf.
38 Kelvin Pollard and Paola Scommegna, "Just How Many Baby Boomers Are There?" Population Reference Bureau, April 16, 2014, https://www.prb.org/resources/just-how-many-baby-boomers-are-there/.
39 Cohen, "Opinion."
40 Landon Y. Jones, *Great Expectations: America and the Baby Boom Generation* (New York: Coward, McCann & Geoghegan, 1980).
41 Claudia Deane, Maeve Duggan, and Rich Morin, "Americans Name the 10 Most Significant Historic Events of Their Lifetimes," December 15, 2016, https://www.pewresearch.org/politics/2016/12/15/americans-name-the-10-most-significant-historic-events-of-their-lifetimes/; Howard Schuman and Jacqueline Scott, "Generations and Collective Memories," *American Sociological Review* 54, no. 3 (1989): 359–381.
42 Moen, *Encore Adulthood*.
43 Moen, *Encore Adulthood*, 45.
44 Pew Research Center, "Generations 2010: What Different Generations Do Online," December 16, 2010, https://www.pewresearch.org/internet/2010/12/16/generations-2010-what-different-generations-do-online/.
45 Pew Research Center, "Baby Boomers: From the Age of Aquarius to the Age of Responsibility," December 8, 2005, https://www.pewresearch.org/social-trends/2005/12/08/baby-boomers-from-the-age-of-aquarius-to-the-age-of-responsibility/; Kim Parker and Eileen Patten, "The Sandwich Generation: Rising Financial Burdens for Middle-Aged Americans," Pew Research Center, January 30, 2013, https://www.pewresearch.org/social-trends/2013/01/30/the-sandwich-generation/.
46 D'vera Cohn and Paul Taylor, "Baby Boomers Approach 65—Glumly," Pew Research Center, December 20, 2010, https://www.pewresearch.org/social-trends/2010/12/20/baby-boomers-approach-65-glumly/.
47 Pew Research Center, "Baby Boomers: The Gloomiest Generation," June 25, 2008, https://www.pewresearch.org/social-trends/2008/06/25/baby-boomers-the-gloomiest-generation/.

48 Pew Research Center, "The Whys and Hows."
49 Isabel Wilkerson, *The Warmth of Other Suns: The Epic Story of America's Great Migration* (New York: Random House, 2010).
50 Pew Research Center, "The Whys and Hows."
51 Carol C. McDonough, "The Effect of Ageism on the Digital Divide among Older Adults," *Journal of Gerontology & Geriatric Medicine* 2, no. 1 (2016): 1–7, https://doi:10.24966/ggm-8662/100008.
52 Aisha Gani, "Millennials at Work: Five Stereotypes—and Why They Are (Mostly) Wrong," *Guardian*, March 15, 2016, https://www.theguardian.com/world/2016/mar/15/millennials-work-five-stereotypes-generation-y-jobs.
53 Cf. Andrew Dawson, "Youthquake: Neoliberalism and the Ethnicization of Generation," *Advances in Anthropology* 8 (2018): 13, https://doi.org/10.4236/aa.2018.81002.
54 Allison J. Pugh, "What Good Are Interviews for Thinking about Culture? Demystifying Interpretive Analysis," *American Journal of Cultural Sociology* 1, no. 1 (February 2013): 42–68; Lisa M. B. Sølvberg and Vegard Jarness, "Assessing Contradictions: Methodological Challenges When Mapping Symbolic Boundaries," *Cultural Sociology* 13, no. 2 (June 2019): 178–197.
55 Harvey, *A Brief History of Neoliberalism*.
56 Brown, *Undoing the Demos*.
57 Monbiot, "Neoliberalism."
58 John Buschman, "COVID-19 Doesn't Change Anything: Neoliberalism, Generation-ism, Academic Library Buildings, and Lazy Rivers," *Journal of Academic Librarianship* 48, no. 4 (2022), https://doi.org/10.1016/j.acalib.2022.102558.
59 Robert H. Binstock, "From Compassionate Ageism to Intergenerational Conflict?" *Gerontologist* 50, no. 5 (2010): 574–585; John Macnicol, *Neoliberalising Old Age* (Cambridge: Cambridge University Press, 2015); White, "Thinking Generations," 231–232.
60 William Davies, *The Limits of Neoliberalism: Authority, Sovereignty and the Logic of Competition* (London: Sage, 2014); Monbiot, "Neoliberalism."

Chapter 4 In God We Trust

This chapter is a modified version of a previously published article: Annette Nierobisz and Dana Sawchuk, "Religious Coping and Older, Unemployed Workers: Narratives of the Job Loss Experience," *Journal of Religion, Spirituality & Aging* 30, no. 4 (2018): 325–353, https://doi: 10.1080/15528030.2018.1461729. See also the journal's website: https://www.tandfonline.com/journals/wrsa20.

1 We did not ask about religious affiliation during the interviews, though almost all the interviewees who offered this information were Christian. Among the others, one individual identified as Jewish and two reported being influenced by both Buddhism and Christianity.
2 Kenneth I. Pargament and Crystal L. Park, "In Times of Stress: The Religion-Coping Connection," in *The Psychology of Religion: Theoretical Approaches*, ed. Bernard Spilka and Daniel N. McIntosh (Boulder, CO: Westview Press, 1997), 43.
3 U.S. Department of Labor, "American Job Centers," Employee and Training Administration, accessed August 17, 2022, https://www.dol.gov/agencies/eta/american-job-centers; U.S. Department of Labor, "American Job Centers," U.S.

Department of Labor, accessed August 17, 2022, https://www.dol.gov/general/topic/training/onestop.
4 Stephen A. Wandner, "Reemploying America: The Public Workforce System and the Great Recession," *Urban Wire* (blog), Urban Institute, October 16, 2012, https://www.urban.org/urban-wire/reemploying-america-public-workforce-system-and-great-recession.
5 Stephen A. Wandner, "One-Time Funding Increase Not Enough to Shrink High Unemployment," *Urban Wire* (blog), Urban Institute, October 19, 2012, https://www.urban.org/urban-wire/one-time-funding-increase-not-enough-shrink-high-unemployment.
6 Ram A. Cnaan, Robert J. Wineburg, and Stephanie C. Boddie, *The Newer Deal: Social Work and Religion in Partnership* (New York: Columbia University Press, 1999); Mark Chaves and William Tsitsos, "Congregations and Social Services: What They Do, How They Do It, and with Whom," *Nonprofit and Voluntary Sector Quarterly* 30, no. 4 (2001): 660–683; Mark Chaves and Alison J. Eagle, "Congregations and Social Services: An Update from the Third Wave of the National Congregations Study," *Religions* 7, no. 5 (2016): 55, https://doaj.org/article/2bf57ae226b245b7a77ff6245fcad84d?frbrVersion=3.
7 David A. Reingold, Maureen Pirog, and David Brady, "Empirical Evidence on Faith-Based Organizations in an Era of Welfare Reform," *Social Service Review* 81, no. 2 (2007): 246; Robert Wineburg et al., "Leveling the Playing Field: Epitomizing Devolution through Faith-Based Organizations," *Journal of Sociology & Social Welfare* 35, no. 1 (2008): 17–42. Funds, however, cannot be directly used for worship or proselytizing, and belief cannot be used as a rationale to deny services to those with differing beliefs.
8 Marianne Cooper, *Cut Adrift: Families in Insecure Times* (Berkeley, CA: University of California Press, 2014); Wineburg et al., "Leveling the Playing Field"; Forrest Stuart, *Down, Out, and Under Arrest: Policing and Everyday Life in Skid Row* (Chicago: University of Chicago Press, 2016); Robert P. Weiss, "Charitable Choice as Neoliberal Social Welfare Strategy," *Social Justice* 28, no. 1 (83) (2001): 35–53.
9 Jason Hackworth, *Faith-Based: Religious Neoliberalism and the Politics of Welfare in the United States* (Athens: University of Georgia Press, 2012); Jason Hackworth, "Faith, Welfare, and the Formation of the Modern American Right," in *Religion in the Neoliberal Age: Political Economy and Modes of Governance*, ed. Tuomas Martikainen and François Gauthier (London: Ashgate, 2013), 91–106; Jason Hackworth, "Religious Neoliberalism," in *The Sage Handbook on Neoliberalism*, ed. Damien Cahill, Melinda Cooper, Martijn Konings, and David Primrose (Thousand Oaks, CA: Sage, 2018), 323–334.
10 John Trutko et al., *Formative Evaluation of Job Clubs Operated by Faith- and Community-Based Organizations: Findings from Site Visits and Options for Future Evaluation: Final Report* (submitted to the Chief Evaluation Office, U.S. Department of Labor by Capital Research Corporation and George Washington University, May 2014).
11 Michael R. Wear, *Reclaiming Hope: Lessons Learned in the Obama White House about the Future of Faith in America* (Nashville, TN: Thomas Nelson, 2017), 64; Olivera Perkins, "Job Clubs Help the Unemployed Weather Joblessness (Gallery)," *Cleveland Plain Dealer*, December 30, 2014, https://www.cleveland.com/business/2014/12/job_clubs_help_the_unemployed.html.
12 Trutko et al., "Formative Evaluation of Job Clubs."

13 Trutko et al., "Formative Evaluation of Job Clubs."
14 We are unaware of any non-Christian faith-based clubs in operation during the time of our study.
15 Trutko et al., "Formative Evaluation of Job Clubs"; Madison Van Oort, "Making the Neoliberal Precariat: Two Faces of Job Searching in Minneapolis," *Ethnography* 16, no. 1 (2015): 74–94; Lane, *A Company of One*.
16 Trutko et al., "Formative Evaluation of Job Clubs."
17 Rose French, "Losing Job Just May Be a 'Blessing' in Disguise," *Minneapolis Star Tribune*, November 19, 2011, 3B. The type of club most frequented by our urban and suburban study interviewees; rural interviewees more often attended public WorkForce center programs.
18 Trutko et al., "Formative Evaluation of Job Clubs."
19 Trutko et al., "Formative Evaluation of Job Clubs"; see also Raymond Garrett-Peters, "'If I Don't Have to Work Anymore, Who Am I?': Job Loss and Collaborative Self-Concept Repair," *Journal of Contemporary Ethnography* 38, no. 5 (2009): 547–583.
20 One of our interviewees passed along a list, with brief descriptions and contact information, of all the area clubs in operation at the time: Bruce Hanson, "Metro Area Job Clubs," Holy Name of Jesus, June 18, 2013, https://www.hnoj.org/sites/hnojparish/files/master_networking_list_1-23-17.pdf.
21 Pew Research Center, *Religious Landscape Study: Adults in the Minneapolis Metro Area*, 2014, https://www.pewforum.org/religious-landscape-study/metro-area/minneapolisst-paul-metro-area/.
22 Hanson, "Metro Area Job Clubs."
23 To preserve our interviewees' anonymity, we are not linking any attendees to specific clubs.
24 Garrett-Peters, "'If I Don't Have to Work Anymore, Who Am I?'"; Lane, *A Company of One*; Norris, *Job Loss, Identity, and Mental Health*; Sharone, *Flawed System/Flawed Self*.
25 Cf. Lane, *A Company of One* and Gershon's "self as business" in Gershon, *Down and Out*.
26 Norris, *Job Loss, Identity, and Mental Health*.
27 Nathan H. Azrin, T. Flores, and S. J. Kaplan, "Job-Finding Club: A Group-Assisted Program for Obtaining Employment," *Behaviour Research and Therapy* 13, no. 1 (1975): 17–27; Denis Gray, "A Job Club for Older Job Seekers: An Experimental Evaluation," *Journal of Gerontology* 38, no. 3 (March 1983): 363–368; Songqi Liu, Jason L. Huang, and Mo Wang, "Effectiveness of Job Search Interventions: A Meta-Analytic Review," *Psychological Bulletin* 140, no. 4 (2014): 1009–1041.
28 Norris, *Job Loss, Identity, and Mental Health*; Sharone, *Flawed System/Flawed Self*.
29 Lane, *A Company of One*.
30 Van Oort, "Making the Neoliberal Precariat," 77.
31 Sharone, *Flawed System/Flawed Self*; Garrett-Peters, "'If I Don't Have to Work Anymore, Who Am I?'"
32 Barbara Ehrenreich, *Bait and Switch: The (Futile) Pursuit of the American Dream* (New York: Holt Paperbacks, 2006).
33 Van Oort, "Making the Neoliberal Precariat," 77.
34 Ofer Sharone, "Constructing Unemployed Job Seekers as Professional Workers: The Depoliticizing Work-Game of Job Searching," *Qualitative Sociology* 30, no. 4 (2007): 412, drawing on Michael Burawoy, *Manufacturing Consent: Changes in*

35 Sharone, *Flawed System/Flawed Self*.
36 Norris, *Job Loss, Identity, and Mental Health*, 68–73.
37 Tom Lauricella, "How Old Are You? As Old as Your Skills," Personal Journal, *Wall Street Journal*, September 16, 2007, https://www.wsj.com/articles/SB118989485712728792.
38 Sharone, *Flawed System/Flawed Self*.
39 Kenneth I. Pargament, "Religion and Coping: The Current State of Knowledge," in *The Oxford Handbook of Stress, Health, and Coping*, ed. Susan Folkman (New York: Oxford University Press, 2011), 269–288.
40 Terry Lynn Gall et al., "The Trajectory of Religious Coping across Time in Response to the Diagnosis of Breast Cancer," *Psycho-Oncology* 18, no. 11 (2009): 1165–1178; Ingela C. Thuné-Boyle et al., "Do Religious/Spiritual Coping Strategies Affect Illness Adjustment in Patients with Cancer? A Systematic Review of the Literature," *Social Science & Medicine* 63, no. 1 (2006): 151–164; Nalini Tarakeshwar and Kenneth I. Pargament, "Religious Coping in Families of Children with Autism," *Focus on Autism and Other Developmental Disabilities* 16, no. 4 (2001): 247–260; Ileana Ungureanu and Jonathan G. Sandberg, "'Broken Together': Spirituality and Religion as Coping Strategies for Couples Dealing with the Death of a Child: A Literature Review with Clinical Implications," *Contemporary Family Therapy* 32, no. 3 (2010): 302–319; Amy P. Webb et al., "Divorce, Religious Coping, and Depressive Symptoms in a Conservative Protestant Religious Group," *Family Relations* 58, no. 5 (2010): 544–557; Kelly M. Trevino and Kenneth I. Pargament, "Religious Coping with Terrorism and Natural Disaster," *Southern Medical Journal* 100, no. 9 (2007): 946–947.
41 Crystal L. Park, "Religion as a Meaning-Making Framework in Coping with Life Stress," *Journal of Social Issues* 61, no. 4 (2005): 707–729; Crystal L. Park and Susan Folkman, "Meaning in the Context of Stress and Coping," *Review of General Psychology* 1, no. 2 (1997): 115–144; Kenneth I. Pargament, *The Psychology of Religion and Coping: Theory, Research, Practice* (New York: The Guilford Press, 1997).
42 Kenneth I. Pargament et al., "Patterns of Positive and Negative Religious Coping with Major Life Stressors," *Journal for the Scientific Study of Religion* 37, no. 4 (1998): 710–724; Kenneth I. Pargament, Harold G. Koenig, and Lisa M. Perez, "The Many Methods of Religious Coping: Development and Initial Validation of the RCOPE," *Journal of Clinical Psychology* 56, no. 4 (2000): 519–543; Kenneth I. Pargament, Margaret Feuille, and Donna Burdzy, "The Brief RCOPE: Current Psychometric Status of a Short Measure of Religious Coping," *Religions* 2, no. 1 (2011): 51–76.
43 Pargament et al., "Patterns of Positive and Negative Religious Coping"; Pargament, Feuille, and Burdzy, "The Brief RCOPE."
44 Julie J. Exline et al., "Anger toward God: Social-Cognitive Predictors, Prevalence, and Links with Adjustment to Bereavement and Cancer," *Journal of Personality and Social Psychology* 100, no. 1 (2011): 129–148.
45 Julie J. Exline and Eric D. Rose, "Religious and Spiritual Struggles," in *Handbook of the Psychology of Religion and Spirituality*, 2nd ed., ed. Raymond F. Paloutzian and Crystal L. Park (New York: Guilford Press, 2013), 380–398; Julie J. Exline et al., "The Religious and Spiritual Struggles Scale: Development and Initial Validation," *Psychology of Religion and Spirituality* 6, no. 3 (2014): 208–222.

46 Jeffrey P. Bjorck and John W. Thurman, "Negative Life Events, Patterns of Positive and Negative Religious Coping, and Psychological Functioning," *Journal for the Scientific Study of Religion* 46, no. 2 (2007): 159–167; Julie J. Exline, "Religious and Spiritual Struggles," in *APA Handbook of Psychology, Religion, and Spirituality*, vol. 1, *Context, Theory, and Research*, ed. Kenneth I. Pargament, Julie J. Exline, and James W. Jones (Washington, DC: American Psychological Association, 2013), 459–475; Kelly M. McConnell et al., "Examining the Links between Spiritual Struggles and Symptoms of Psychopathology in a National Sample," *Journal of Clinical Psychology* 62, no. 12 (2006): 1469–1484; Pargament et al., "Patterns of Positive and Negative Religious Coping."

47 Pew Research Center, "The Age Gap in Religion around the World," Pew Research Center's Religion & Public Life Project, Pew Research Center, June 13, 2018, https://www.pewresearch.org/religion/2018/06/13/the-age-gap-in-religion-around-the-world/.

48 Pargament, Koenig, and Perez, "The Many Methods of Religious Coping."

49 Clemens M. Lechner and Thomas Leopold, "Religious Attendance Buffers the Impact of Unemployment on Life Satisfaction: Longitudinal Evidence from Germany," *Journal for the Scientific Study of Religion* 54, no. 1 (2015): 166–174; Manfusa Shams and Paul R. Jackson, "Religiosity as a Predictor of Well-Being and Moderator of the Psychological Impact of Unemployment," *British Journal of Medical Psychology* 66, no. 4 (1993): 341–352.

50 Cooper, *Cut Adrift*.

51 Cooper, *Cut Adrift*, 3.

52 Cooper, "When Religion Fills the Gap," in *Cut Adrift*, 158–188.

53 Cooper, *Cut Adrift*.

54 Cooper, *Cut Adrift*, 22–23.

55 Berit Ingersoll-Dayton, Neal Krause, and David Morgan, "Religious Trajectories and Transitions over the Life Course," *International Journal of Aging and Human Development* 55, no. 1 (2002): 51–70.

56 Pargament, Feuille, and Burdzy, "The Brief RCOPE," 56; Pargament et al., "Patterns of Positive and Negative Religious Coping," 711.

57 Nancy Branton, "Bringing Christ into Career Decisions," Wooddale Church Job Transition Support Group, June 2017, http://jobtransition.net/wp-content/uploads/2013/07/Job-Seeker-Scripture-Updated.pdf.

58 Cf. "Religious Methods of Coping to Gain Control," in Pargament, Feuille, and Burdzy, "The Brief RCOPE," 56; Pargament et al., "Patterns of Positive and Negative Religious Coping," 711.

59 Cooper, *Cut Adrift*; see also Scott Schieman et al., "The Sense of Divine Control and Psychological Distress: Variations across Race and Socioeconomic Status," *Journal for the Scientific Study of Religion* 45, no. 4 (2006): 529–549.

60 Approximately one-third of interviewees with a soft landing employed religious coping compared with more than two-thirds of the remaining interviewees (including both those with hard falls and others we classified as "in between").

61 Joy L. Berrenberg, "The Belief in Personal Control Scale: A Measure of God-Mediated and Exaggerated Control," *Journal of Personality Assessment* 51 (1987): 194–206; Neal Krause, "God-Mediated Control and Psychological Well-Being in Late Life," *Research on Aging* 27, no. 2 (2005): 136–164; Deane H. Shapiro et al., "Aging and Sense of Control," *Psychological Reports* 77, no. 2 (1995): 616–618.

62 Ehrenreich, *Bait and Switch*, 142.
63 Barbara Ehrenreich, *Bright-Sided: How Positive Thinking Is Undermining America* (New York: Picador, 2009); Claudia Strauss, "Positive Thinking about Being Out of Work in Southern California after the Great Recession," in *Anthropologies of Unemployment: New Perspectives on Work and Its Absence*, ed. Jong Bum Kwon and Carrie M. Lane (Ithaca, NY: Cornell University Press, 2016), 171–190.
64 Norris, *Job Loss, Identity, and Mental Health*.
65 Cooper, *Cut Adrift*.
66 Pargament, Feuille, and Burdzy, "The Brief RCOPE," 56; Pargament et al., "Patterns of Positive and Negative Religious Coping," 711.
67 Christopher G. Ellison and Linda K. George, "Religious Involvement, Social Ties, and Social Support in a Southeastern Community," *Journal for the Scientific Study of Religion* 33, no. 1 (1994): 46–61.
68 Pargament et al., "Patterns of Positive and Negative Religious Coping"; Pargament, Feuille, and Burdzy, "The Brief RCOPE"; Exline and Rose, "Religious and Spiritual Struggles"; Exline et al., "The Religious and Spiritual Struggles Scale."
69 Cooper had similar findings in her interview sample. Cooper, *Cut Adrift*.
70 Myleme O. Harrison et al., "The Epidemiology of Religious Coping: A Review of Recent Literature," *International Review of Psychiatry* 13, no. 2 (2001), 86–93; Pargament et al., "Patterns of Positive and Negative Religious Coping."
71 Ehrenreich, *Bait and Switch*, 221.
72 See also Ehrenreich, "Aiming Higher," in *Bait and Switch*.
73 Pargament, "Religion and Coping."
74 Job Transition Support Group, "The 6 Steps," Job Transition Support Group: A Ministry of Wooddale Church, n.d., https://jobtransition.net/the-six-steps/.
75 Pew Research Center, "America's Changing Religious Landscape," May 12, 2015, https://www.pewresearch.org/religion/2015/05/12/americas-changing-religious-landscape/; Gregory A. Smith, *About Three-in-Ten U.S. Adults Are Now Religiously Unaffiliated* (Pew Research Center Report, Pew Research Center, December 14, 2021), https://www.pewresearch.org/religion/2021/12/14/about-three-in-ten-u-s-adults-are-now-religiously-unaffiliated/.
76 Rebecca Leppert and Dalia Fahmy, "10 Facts about Religion and Government in the United States," Pew Research Center, updated July 5, 2022, https://www.pewresearch.org/fact-tank/2022/07/05/10-facts-about-religion-and-government-in-the-united-states/; Nomi Stolzenberg, "Religious Identity and Supreme Court Justices—A Brief History," *The Conversation*, October 19, 2020, https://theconversation.com/religious-identity-and-supreme-court-justices-a-brief-history-146999; Kenneth D. Wald and David C. Leege, "Culture, Religion and American Political Life," in *The Oxford Handbook of Religion and American Politics*, ed. Corwin E. Smidt, Lyman A. Kellstedt, and James L. Guth (New York: Oxford University Press, 2009), 129–163.

Chapter 5   "Here's Where I Am, Here's Where I'll Stay"

This chapter is a modified version of a chapter appearing as Annette Nierobisz, "Flexible Workers and Other Fantastical Myths of the Neoliberal Era," in *The Handbook on Unemployment and Society*, ed. Ofer Sharone, Victor Chen, and Sabina Pultz (Northampton, MA: Edward Elgar Publishing, 2025).

1. William T. Bielby and Denise D. Bielby, "I Will Follow Him: Family Ties, Gender-Role Beliefs, and Reluctance to Relocate for a Better Job," *American Journal of Sociology* 97, no. 5 (1992): 1241–1267.
2. Martin Abraham, Sebastian Bähr, and Mark Trappmann, "Gender Differences in Willingness to Move for Interregional Job Offers," *Demographic Research* 40 (2019): 1537–1602.
3. Elizabeth Ann Whitaker, "Moving On to Stay Put: Employee Relocation in the Face of Employment Insecurity," in *Beyond the Cubicle: Job Insecurity, Intimacy, and the Flexible Self*, ed. Allison J. Pugh (New York: Oxford University Press, 2017), 203–228.
4. David C. Baldridge, Kimberly A. Eddleston, and John F. Veiga, "Saying 'No' to Being Uprooted: The Impact of Family and Gender on Willingness to Relocate," *Journal of Occupational and Organizational Psychology* 79, no. 1 (2010): 131–149; Janet M. Rives and Janet M. West, "Wife's Employment and Worker Relocation Behavior," *Journal of Socio-Economics* 22, no. 1 (1993): 13–22.
5. Baldridge, Eddleston, and Veiga, "Saying 'No' to Being Uprooted"; Lillian T. Eby and Joyce E. A. Russell, "Predictors of Employee Willingness to Relocate for the Firm," *Journal of Vocational Behavior* 57, no. 1 (2000): 42–61; Kimberlee A. Shauman and Yu Xie, "Geographic Mobility: Sex Differences and Family Constraints," *Demography* 33, no. 4 (1996): 455–468; Abraham, Bähr, and Trappmann, "Gender Differences in Willingness to Move"; Janne M. Brett, Linda K. Stroh, and Anne H. Reilly, "Pulling Up Roots in the 1990s: Who's More Willing to Relocate?" *Journal of Organizational Behavior* 14, no. 1 (1993): 49–60; Daniel C. Feldman and Mark C. Bolino, "Moving On Out: When Are Employees Willing to Follow Their Organizations during Corporate Relocations?" *Journal of Organizational Behavior* 19, no. 3 (1998): 275–288; Cynthia D. Fisher and James B. Shaw, "Relocation Attitudes and Adjustment: A Longitudinal Study," *Journal of Organizational Behavior* 15, no. 3 (1994): 209–224.
6. John Hagan, Ross Macmillan, and Blair Wheaton, "New Kid in Town: Social Capital and the Life Course Effects of Family Migration on Children," *American Sociological Review* 61, no. 3 (1996): 368–385.
7. Rives and West, "Wife's Employment and Worker Relocation Behavior."
8. Eby and Russell, "Predictors of Employee Willingness to Relocate"; Feldman and Bolino, "Moving On Out"; Sam Gould and Larry E. Penley, "A Study of the Correlates of the Willingness to Relocate," *Academy of Management Journal* 28, no. 2 (1985): 472–478; Abraham Sagie, Moshe Krausz, and Yehuda Weinstain, "To Move or Not to Move: Factors Affecting Employees' Actual Relocation When an Entire Plant Moves," *Journal of Occupational and Organizational Psychology* 74, no. 3 (2001): 343–358; Shauman and Xie, "Geographic Mobility."
9. Joan R. Rodgers and John L. Rodgers, "The Effect of Geographic Mobility on Male Labor-Force Participants in the United States," *Journal of Labor Research* 21, no. 1 (2000): 117–132.
10. Louis Swanson, A. E. Luloff, and Rex H. Warland, "Factors Influencing Willingness to Move: An Examination of Nonmetropolitan Residents," *Rural Sociology* 44, no. 4 (1979): 719–735.
11. Raymond A. Noe and Alison E. Barber, "Willingness to Accept Mobility Opportunities: Destination Makes a Difference," *Journal of Organizational Behavior* 14, no. 2 (1993): 159–175.
12. Gould and Penley, "A Study of the Correlates of the Willingness to Relocate"; Feldman and Bolino, "Moving On Out."

13 Feldman and Bolino, "Moving On Out."
14 Baldridge, Eddleston, and Veiga, "Saying 'No' to Being Uprooted."
15 Jorge Gonzalez et al., "Friends and Family: The Role of Relationships in Community and Workplace Attachment," *Journal of Business Psychology* 33, no. 1 (2018): 89–104.
16 Christopher Ingraham, "This Is How Much Time Americans Spend Commuting to Work," *World Economic Forum*, March 3, 2016, https://www.weforum.org/agenda/2016/03/average-american-commute-time-to-work/.
17 Phillip H. Mirvis and Douglas T. Hall, "Psychological Success and the Boundaryless Career," in *The Boundaryless Career: A New Employment Principle for a New Organizational Era*, ed. Michael B. Arthur and Denise M. Rousseau (New York: Oxford University Press, 1996), 237–255.
18 Whitaker, "Moving On to Stay Put."
19 Michael B. Arthur and Denise M. Rousseau, "Introduction: The Boundaryless Career as a New Employment Principle," in *The Boundaryless Career*, ed. Arthur and Rousseau.
20 Art Budros, "The Mean and Lean Firm and Downsizing: Causes of Involuntary and Voluntary Downsizing Strategies," *Sociological Forum* 17, no. 2 (2002): 307–342; Arthur and Rousseau, "Introduction: The Boundaryless Career."
21 Carrie M. Lane, *A Company of One*; Gershon, *Down and Out*. As we discussed in the previous chapter, such notions of the self as business were also promoted in the Wooddale job club, which several of our interviewees attended.
22 Whitaker, "Moving On to Stay Put."
23 Norris, *Job Loss, Identity, and Mental Health*, 146.
24 Elder, "Time, Human Agency, and Social Change."
25 Scott Cohn, "America's Best States to Live in 2012," CNBC, June 7, 2012, https://www.cnbc.com/2012/07/10/Americas-Best-States-to-Live-in-2012.html; Elliot Davis, "U.S. News Ranks Best States for 2021," *US News & World Report*, March 9, 2021, https://www.usnews.com/news/best-states/articles/us-news-releases-best-states-rankings; Derek Robertson, "The States of Our Union ... Are Still Not All Strong. Our Fourth Quasi-Annual Ranking," *Politico Magazine*, January 30, 2018, https://www.politico.com/magazine/story/2018/01/30/fourth-states-of-union-ranking-216547/.
26 Katherine Ellsworth-Krebs, Louise Reid, and Colin J. Hunter, "Integrated Framework of Home Comfort: Relaxation, Companionship and Control," *Building Research & Information* 47, no. 2 (2019): 202–218.
27 Anthony Giddens, *Modernity and Self-Identity: Self and Society in the Late Modern Age* (Stanford, CA: Stanford University Press, 1991).
28 David Cooper, "As Wisconsin's and Minnesota's Lawmakers Took Divergent Paths, So Did Their Economies," *Economic Policy Institute*, May 8, 2018, https://www.epi.org/publication/as-wisconsins-and-minnesotas-lawmakers-took-divergent-paths-so-did-their-economies-since-2010-minnesotas-economy-has-performed-far-better-for-working-families-than-wisconsin/.
29 Monique Morrisey, "Women Over 65 Are More Likely to Be Poor Than Men, Regardless of Race, Educational Background, and Marital Status," *Economic Policy Institute*, March 8, 2016, https://www.epi.org/publication/women-over-65-are-more-likely-to-in-poverty-than-men/.
30 Astra Taylor, *The Age of Insecurity: Coming Together as Things Fall Apart* (Toronto: House of Anansi Press, 2023).

31 For example, Baldridge, Eddleston, and Veiga, "Saying 'No' to Being Uprooted."
32 Representing the last decades of a person's life, late adulthood is considered to begin at age sixty-five and continue through age eighty-five and older. Individuals in this life course stage can experience physiological, neurodegenerative, and/or psychological challenges that may result in spouses, children, and extended family members engaging in caregiving activities. See Elizabeth D. Hutchison, "Middle Adulthood," in *Dimensions of Human Behavior*, ed. Hutchison, 304–348.
33 Aliya Hamid Rao, *Crunch Time: How Married Couples Confront Unemployment* (Oakland, CA: University of California Press, 2020). See also Judith Bom et al., "The Impact of Informal Caregiving for Older Adults on the Health of Various Types of Caregivers: A Systematic Review," *Gerontologist* 59, no. 5 (2019): e629–e642, https://doi.org/10.1093/geront/gny137; Elizabeth D. Hutchison, "A Life Course Perspective," in *Dimensions of Human Behavior*, ed. Hutchison, 1–38; and Allison Williams et al., "Gender and Sex Differences in Carers' Health, Burden and Work Outcomes: Canadian Carers of Community-Dwelling Older People with Multiple Chronic Conditions," *International Journal of Care and Caring* 1, no. 3 (2017): 331–349, https://bristoluniversitypressdigital.com/view/journals/ijcc/1/3/article-p331.xml.
34 Dorothy A. Miller, "The 'Sandwich' Generation: Adult Children of the Aging," *Social Work* 26, no. 5 (1981): 419–423.
35 Hutchison, "A Life Course Perspective"; Rao, *Crunch Time*. Rao notes that adult children in White families are more likely to receive financial assistance from their parents. In Black families, by comparison, monetary assistance is more likely to come from adult children to their parents. Rao attributes this directional difference to the racialization of wealth in the United States.
36 Viktor Gecas, "Self-Agency and the Life Course," in *Handbook of the Life Course*, ed. Jeylan T. Mortimer and Michael J. Shanahan (New York: Springer Publishing, 2003), 370.
37 Jeylan T. Mortimer and Jon Lorence, "Occupational Experience and the Self-Concept: A Longitudinal Study," *Social Psychology Quarterly* 42, no. 4 (1979): 309.
38 Mortimer and Lorence, "Occupational Experience and the Self-Concept."
39 Minnesota offers twenty-six weeks of unemployment insurance. This is more than double the twelve weeks Floridians receive. See the Center on Budget and Policy Priorities, "Policy Basics: How Many Weeks of Unemployment Compensation Are Available?" November 6, 2023, https://www.cbpp.org/research/economy/how-many-weeks-of-unemployment-compensation-are-available. Additionally, the average weekly benefit in Minnesota, $410 in 2023, is higher than the average weekly benefit residents of forty-four other states receive. See Rowan, "The States with the Best and Worst Unemployment Benefits."
40 Allison J. Pugh, *The Tumbleweed Society: Working and Caring in an Age of Insecurity* (New York: Oxford University Press, 2015).
41 Edgar Cabanas and Eva Illouz, *Manufacturing Happy Citizens: How the Science and Industry of Happiness Control Our Lives* (Medford, MA: Polity Press, 2019).

Chapter 6   Silver Linings and Positive Thinking

1 Suran Ahn and Na Kyoung Song, "Unemployment, Recurrent Unemployment, and Material Hardships among Older Workers Since the Great Recession," *Social Work Research* 41, no. 4 (2017): 249–262; Jennie E. Brand, "The Far-Reaching

Impact of Job Loss and Unemployment," *Annual Review of Sociology* 41 (2015): 359–375; Kenneth A. Couch, "Late Life Job Displacement," *Gerontologist* 38, no. 1 (1998): 7–17; Frances McKee-Ryan et al., "Psychological and Physical Well-Being during Unemployment: A Meta-Analytic Study," *Journal of Applied Psychology* 90, no. 1 (2005): 53–76; Karsten I. Paul and Klaus Moser, "Unemployment Impairs Mental Health: Meta-Analyses," *Journal of Vocational Behavior* 74, no. 3 (2009): 264–282; Richard Montanaro, "After the Fall: An Exploration of the Coping Behavior of Positive Appraisal in Midcareer Adults' Responses to Involuntary Job Loss" (PhD dissertation, Fielding Graduate University, 2011), ProQuest, 3453410; Jelena Zikic and Ute-Christine Klehe, "Job Loss as a Blessing in Disguise: The Role of Career Exploration and Career Planning in Predicting Reemployment Quality," *Journal of Vocational Behavior* 69, no. 3 (2006): 391–409; Jelena Zikic and Julia Richardson, "Unlocking the Careers of Business Professionals following Job Loss: Sensemaking and Career Exploration of Older Workers," *Canadian Journal of Administrative Sciences/Revue canadienne des sciences de l'administration* 24, no. 1 (2007): 58–73.

2. Brand, "The Far-Reaching Impact"; McKee-Ryan et al., "Psychological and Physical Well-Being"; Frances McKee-Ryan and Robyn Maitoza, "Job Loss, Unemployment, and Families," in *The Oxford Handbook of Job Loss and Job Search*, ed. Ute-Christine Klehe and Edwin Van Hooft (New York: Oxford University Press, 2018), 87–97; Paul and Moser, "Unemployment Impairs Mental Health."

3. Yaohua Helen He, A. Colantonio, and Victor W. Marshall, "Later-Life Career Disruption and Self-Rated Health: An Analysis of General Social Survey Data," *Canadian Journal on Aging* 22, no. 1 (2010): 45–57.

4. Hamilton et al., "Hard Times and Vulnerable People"; Leana and Feldman, *Coping with Job Loss*; Barbara K. Shelton, "The Social and Psychological Impact of Unemployment"; Kaufman, *Professionals in Search of Work*; Latack, Kinicki, and Prussia, "An Integrative Process Model"; Podgursky and Swaim, "Job Displacement and Earnings Loss"; Fineman, *White Collar Unemployment*; Newman, *Falling from Grace*; Norris, *Job Loss, Identity, and Mental Health*; Sharone, *Flawed System/Flawed Self*.

5. Chan and Huff Stevens, "Job Loss and Employment Patterns"; Ute-Christine Klehe et al., "Too Old to Tango? Job Loss and Job Search among Older Workers," in Klehe and Van Hooft, *The Oxford Handbook of Job Loss and Job Search*, 433–464; Roscigno et al., "Age Discrimination, Social Closure and Employment."

6. Richard W. Johnson and Barbara A. Butrica, *Age Disparities in Unemployment and Reemployment during the Great Recession and Recovery*, Urban Institute Unemployment and Recovery Project Brief 3 (Washington, DC: May 2012); Ahn and Song, "Unemployment, Recurrent Unemployment, and Material Hardships."

7. Loring P. Jones, "A Typology of Adaptations to Unemployment," *Journal of Employment Counseling* 26, no. 2 (1989): 50–59; Craig B. Little, "Technical-Professional Unemployment: Middle-Class Adaptability to Personal Crisis," *Sociological Quarterly* 17 (1976): 262–274.

8. Fineman, *White Collar Unemployment*, 36; Janina C. Latack and Janelle B. Dozier, "After the Ax Falls: Job Loss as a Career Transition," *Academy of Management Review* 11, no. 2 (1986): 375–392.

9. Zikic and Richardson, "Unlocking the Careers of Business Professionals"; Montanaro, "After the Fall"; Zikic and Klehe, "Job Loss as a Blessing in Disguise"; Yiannis Gabriel, David E. Gray, and Harshita Goregaokar, "Temporary

Derailment or the End of the Line? Managers Coping with Unemployment at 50," *Organization Studies* 31, no. 12 (2010): 1687–1712.
10. Gabriel, Gray, and Goregaokar, "Job Loss and Its Aftermath," 68.
11. Benjamin H. Snyder, *The Disrupted Workplace: Time and the Moral Order of Flexible Capitalism* (New York: Oxford University Press, 2016), 191.
12. Strauss, "Positive Thinking about Being Out of Work."
13. Allison J. Pugh, "Introduction: The Broader Impacts of Precariousness," in *Beyond the Cubicle: Job Insecurity, Intimacy, and the Flexible Self*, ed. Allison J. Pugh (New York: Oxford University Press, 2017), 5.
14. Douglas Ezzy, *Narrating Unemployment* (New York: Routledge, 2017).
15. Ofer Sharone, *The Stigma Trap: College-Educated, Experienced, and Long-Term Unemployed* (New York: Oxford University Press, 2024), 78.
16. Strauss, "Positive Thinking about Being Out of Work"; Cabanas and Illouz, *Manufacturing Happy Citizens*; Ehrenreich, *Bright-Sided*; Pugh, "The Broader Impacts of Precariousness."
17. Hollister, "Employment Stability in the U.S. Labor Market."
18. Kalleberg, *Good Jobs, Bad Jobs*.
19. Peter Cappelli et al., *Change at Work: How American Industry and Workers Are Coping with Corporate Restructuring and What Workers Must Do to Take Charge of Their Own Careers* (New York: Oxford University Press, 1997).
20. Gershon, *Down and Out*; Richard Sennett, *The Culture of the New Capitalism* (New Haven, CT: Yale University Press, 2006).
21. Carrie M. Lane, *A Company of One*; Ruby Mendenhall et al., "Job Loss at Mid-Life: Managers and Executives Face the 'New Risk Economy,'" *Social Forces* 87, no. 1 (2008): 185–209; Sharone, *Flawed System/Flawed Self*; Snyder, *The Disrupted Workplace*.
22. Martha Crowley et al., "Neo-Taylorism at Work: Occupational Change in the Post-Fordist Era," *Social Problems* 57, no. 3 (2010): 421–447; Erin Kelly and Phyllis Moen, *Overload: How Good Jobs Went Bad and What We Can Do about It* (Princeton, NJ: Princeton University Press, 2020).
23. Joel Goh, Jeffrey Pfeffer, and Stefanos A. Zenios, "Workplace Stressors & Health Outcomes: Health Policy for the Workplace," *Behavioral Science and Policy* 1, no. 1 (2015): 43–52; Jeffrey Pfeffer, *Dying for a Paycheck: How Modern Management Harms Employee Health and Company Performance—and What We Can Do about It* (New York: Harper Business, 2018).
24. Gershon, *Down and Out*.
25. Kalleberg, *Good Jobs, Bad Jobs*.
26. Wolff, Owens, and Burak, "How Much Wealth Was Destroyed?"
27. Cabanas and Illouz, *Manufacturing Happy Citizens*.
28. Kalleberg, *Good Jobs, Bad Jobs*, 31.
29. Cabanas and Illouz, *Manufacturing Happy Citizens*; Ehrenreich, *Bright-Sided*.
30. Edgar Cabanas and Eva Illouz, "The Making of a 'Happy Worker': Positive Psychology in Neoliberal Organizations," in Pugh, *Beyond the Cubicle*, 25–49.
31. Abraham Maslow, "A Theory of Human Motivation," *Psychological Review* 50, no. 4 (1943): 370–396.
32. Cabanas and Illouz, *Manufacturing Happy Citizens*, 102.
33. Stephanie Gilbert and E. Kevin Kelloway, "Positive Psychology and the Healthy Workplace," in *Workplace Well-Being: How to Build Psychologically Healthy Workplaces*, 1st ed., ed. Arla Day, E. Kevin Kelloway, and Joseph J. Hurrell

(Hoboken, NJ: John Wiley & Sons, 2014), 50–70. See also Larry Froman, "Positive Psychology in the Workplace," *Journal of Adult Development* 17 (2010): 59–69.
34 Ehrenreich, *Bright-Sided*; Norman Vincent Peale, *The Power of Positive Thinking* (Ada, MI: Spire Books, an imprint of Fleming H. Revell Company, 1959).
35 Cabanas and Illouz, *Manufacturing Happy Citizens*.
36 Cabanas and Illouz, *Manufacturing Happy Citizens*.
37 Strauss, "Positive Thinking about Being Out of Work."
38 Ehrenreich, *Bright-Sided*.
39 Pugh, *The Tumbleweed Society*; Pugh, "The Broader Impacts of Precariousness."
40 Ethel L. Mickey, "'Eat, Pray, Love Bullshit': Women's Empowerment through Wellness at an Elite Professional Conference," *Journal of Contemporary Ethnography* 48, no. 1 (2019): 103–127.
41 Maslow, "A Theory of Human Motivation," 382.
42 Norris, *Job Loss, Identity, and Mental Health*.
43 Strauss, "Positive Thinking about Being Out of Work."
44 Strauss, "Positive Thinking about Being Out of Work."
45 Kelly and Moen, *Overload*.
46 Sarah Damaske, *The Tolls of Uncertainty*.
47 Rao, *Crunch Time*.
48 Ezzy, *Narrating Unemployment*; Letkemann, "Unemployed Professionals"; Norris, *Job Loss, Identity, and Mental Health*.
49 Sharone, *Flawed System/Flawed Self*; Sharone, *The Stigma Trap*.
50 Cabanas and Illouz, *Manufacturing Happy Citizens*; Ehrenreich, *Bright-Sided*.
51 Ann Swidler, "Culture in Action: Symbols and Strategies," *American Sociological Review* 51, no. 2 (1986): 273–286.
52 Cabanas and Illouz, *Manufacturing Happy Citizens*.
53 Whitney Goodman, *Toxic Positivity: Keeping It Real in a World Obsessed with Being Happy* (New York: TarcherPerigee, 2022).
54 Lizzie Ward, "Caring for Ourselves? Self-Care and Neoliberalism," in *Ethics of Care: Critical Advances in International Perspective*, eds. Marian Barnes, T. Brannelly, Lizzie Ward, and N. Ward (Bristol, UK: Policy Press, an imprint of Bristol University Press, 2016), 45–56.

Chapter 7   Where Are They Now? And What Can We Do?

1 David Harvey, "Neoliberalism as Creative Destruction," *Annals of the American Academy of Political and Social Science* 610, no. 1 (2007): 22.
2 Antonio Gramsci, *Selections from the Prison Notebooks of Antonio Gramsci*, ed. and trans. Quintin Hoare and Geoffrey Nowell Smith (New York: International Publishers, 1971).
3 Ben S. Bernanke and Olivier Blanchard, "What Caused the U.S. Pandemic-Era Inflation?" Brookings Institution, June 13, 2023, https://www.brookings.edu/articles/what-caused-the-u-s-pandemic-era-inflation/.
4 Center for Microeconomic Data, *Quarterly Report on Household Debt and Credit: 2023: Q3* (Federal Reserve Bank of New York, November 2023), https://www.newyorkfed.org/medialibrary/Interactives/householdcredit/data/pdf/HHDC_2023Q3.pdf?sc_lang=en.
5 Roxanna Edwards, Lawrence S. Essien, and Michael Daniel Levinstein, "U.S. Labor Market Shows Improvement in 2021, but the COVID-19 Pandemic

Continues to Weigh on the Economy," *Monthly Labor Review*, U.S. Bureau of Labor Statistics, June 2022, https://doi.org/10.21916/mlr.2022.16.

6. Kim Parker and Juliana Menasce Horowitz, "Majority of Workers Who Quit a Job in 2021 Cite Low Pay, No Opportunities for Advancement, Feeling Disrespected," Pew Research Center, March 9, 2022, https://www.pewresearch.org/short-reads/2022/03/09/majority-of-workers-who-quit-a-job-in-2021-cite-low-pay-no-opportunities-for-advancement-feeling-disrespected/.

7. J. Richard Johnson, "What's New about Quiet Quitting (and What's Not)," *Transdisciplinary Journal of Management* (2023): 1–14, https://tjm.scholasticahq.com/article/72079-what-s-new-about-quiet-quitting-and-what-s-not.

8. Lauren Kaori Gurley, "Record Hot Labor Market Has Minnesota Scrambling for Workers," *Washington Post*, September 4, 2022, https://www.washingtonpost.com/business/2022/09/04/minnesota-jobs-unemployment-rate/.

9. U.S. Bureau of Labor Statistics, "Minnesota Had the Lowest Jobless Rate in August 2022," *TED: The Economics Daily*, September 26, 2022, https://www.bls.gov/opub/ted/2022/minnesota-had-the-lowest-jobless-rate-in-august-2022.htm.

10. Neil Irwin, "Workers Are Gaining Leverage over Employers Right before Our Eyes," *New York Times*, June 5, 2021, https://www.nytimes.com/2021/06/05/upshot/jobs-rising-wages.html.

11. As we note in appendix A, five interviewees died since we last met them, and another six did not provide an email address at their first interview.

12. Survey response rates have been dropping sharply in recent decades. In a 2012 report, the Pew Research Center acknowledges that response rates to their public opinion surveys were as low as 9 percent. Pew Research Center, "Assessing the Representativeness of Public Opinion Surveys," May 15, 2012, https://www.pewresearch.org/politics/2012/05/15/assessing-the-representativeness-of-public-opinion-surveys/. Our higher than typical response rate might be due to our contacting people who had already participated in a first interview with us.

13. Individuals fifty-five years of age and over incurred the highest rates of joblessness lasting one year or longer at this time. Pew Charitable Trusts, *A Year or More*. See also Henry S. Farber, "Employment, Hours, and Earnings Consequences of Job Loss: US Evidence from the Displaced Workers Survey," *Journal of Labor Economics* 35, no. S1 (July 2017): S235–S272.

14. The experience of unretiring is common. In her book, *Work, Retire, Repeat*, economist Teresa Ghilarducci examines the reasons why "retirement insecurity" is so common in the United States. See Teresa Ghilarducci, *Work, Retire, Repeat: The Uncertainty of Retirement in the New Economy* (Chicago: The University of Chicago Press, 2024).

15. Farber, "Employment, Hours, and Earnings Consequences of Job Loss."

16. Because we offered the option of checking as many of the response categories as applicable, these numbers do not add up to twenty-five.

17. Sidney A. Rothstein, *Recoding Power: Tactics for Mobilizing Tech Workers* (New York: Oxford University Press, 2022).

18. Rothstein also examined two additional sites, one in Germany and one in the United States, where tech workers acquiesced to their layoffs. This contrast and comparison allowed him to determine which factors lead workers to contest a layoff. Rothstein, *Recoding Power*.

19 Aaliyah Demry, "Allina Health Doctors Vote to Unionize," Minnesota Public Radio News, October 14, 2023, https://www.mprnews.org/story/2023/10/14/allina-health-doctors-vote-to-unionize.
20 Sharone, *The Stigma Trap*.
21 Mills, *The Sociological Imagination*, 8.
22 The foundational tome of this movement is widely considered to be Gustavo Gutiérrez, *A Theology of Liberation: History, Politics, and Salvation*, ed. and trans. Sister Caridad Inda and John Eagleson (Maryknoll, NY: Orbis Books, 1973). See also José Larrea Gayarre, "The Challenges of Liberation Theology to Neoliberal Economic Policies," *Social Justice* 21, no. 4 (1994): 34–45.
23 The teachings associated with the Second Vatican Council ("Vatican II") play a role here, as do the documents from a 1968 meeting of Latin American bishops in Medellín, Colombia. See II Conferencia General del Episcopado Latinoamericano, *Medellín conclusiones: La Iglesia en la actual transformación de América Latina a la luz del concilio* (Bogotá, Colombia: Secretariado General del Consejo Episcopal Latinoamericano, 1990); Second Vatican Council, *Vatican Council II: The Conciliar and Post Conciliar Documents*, ed. Austin Flannery (Northport, NY: Costello Publishing, 1987).
24 Madeleine Cousineau Adriance, *Promised Land: Base Christian Communities and the Struggle for the Amazon* (Albany, NY: State University of New York Press, 1995); Dana Sawchuk, "The Catholic Church in the Nicaraguan Revolution: A Gramscian Analysis," *Sociology of Religion* 58, no. 1 (1997): 39–51.
25 Taylor, *Age of Insecurity*.
26 Astra Taylor, "Why Does Everyone Feel So Insecure All the Time?" *New York Times*, August 18, 2023, https://www.nytimes.com/2023/08/18/opinion/inequality-insecurity-economic-wealth.html.
27 Taylor, *Age of Insecurity*, 12.
28 Taylor, *Age of Insecurity*, 25.
29 Center on Budget and Policy Priorities, "Tracking the COVID-19 Economy's Effects on Food, Housing, and Employment Hardships," Special Series: COVID Hardship Watch, accessed on October 3, 2023, https://www.cbpp.org/research/poverty-and-inequality/tracking-the-covid-19-recessions-effects-on-food-housing-and.
30 Taylor, *Age of Insecurity*, 93.
31 Taylor, *Age of Insecurity*, 291.
32 See Roger Sanjek, *Gray Panthers* (Philadelphia: University of Pennsylvania Press, 2009); Dana Sawchuk, "The Raging Grannies: Defying Stereotypes and Embracing Aging through Activism," *Journal of Women & Aging* 21, no. 3 (2009): 171–185. In addition, there is ample evidence of current collective action that shakes neoliberal assumptions. The mobilization of ordinary people to provide mutual support and material aid to one another during the early days of the pandemic, for example, was a genuine challenge to the neoliberal order. See George Monbiot, "The Horror Films Got It Wrong. This Virus Has Turned Us into Caring Neighbours," *Guardian*, March 31, 2020, https://www.theguardian.com/commentisfree/2020/mar/31/virus-neighbours-covid-19. We can also see the important role ordinary people, rather than experts and state actors, have played in challenging and dismantling the U.S. system of mass incarceration. See Jocelyn Simonson, *Radical Acts of Justice: How Ordinary People Are Dismantling Mass Incarceration* (New York: The New Press, 2023).

Appendix A

1. Cohn, "America's Best States to Live"; Robertson, "The States of Our Union."
2. Hine et al., "State of the Economy."
3. Karen Kosanovich and Eleni Theodossiou Sherman, *Trends in Long-Term Unemployment* (Washington, DC: Bureau of Labor Statistics, 2015), https://www.bls.gov/spotlight/2015/long-term-unemployment/pdf/long-term-unemployment.pdf.
4. William E. Lass, "The Story behind Minnesota's Weirdly Shaped Northern Border," *MinnPost*, February 4, 2014, https://www.minnpost.com/mnopedia/2014/02/story-behind-minnesotas-weirdly-shaped-northern-border/.
5. Robert S. Weiss, *Learning from Strangers: The Art and Method of Qualitative Interview Studies* (New York: The Free Press, 1995).
6. Pew defines the baby boom generation as those Americans born from 1946 to 1964. Pew Research Center, "The Whys and Hows." We accepted one interviewee who was born in 1945 with the understanding that the U.S. population began growing in the early 1940s. Deborah Carr, "The Psychological Consequences of Work-Family Trade-Offs for Three Cohorts of Men and Women," *Social Psychology Quarterly* 65, no. 2 (2002): 103–124, https://doi.org/10.2307/3090096.
7. Respondents' length of employment varied from a few months to thirty-plus years. The individuals who had the shortest years of service to the employer typically had two or more back-to-back job losses.
8. Of the two non-white-collar workers who participated in this study, one was a jeweler and the other a shipping and receiving clerk.
9. United States Census Bureau, "QuickFacts: Minnesota," accessed June 7, 2021, https://www.census.gov/quickfacts/MN#qf-headnote-a; Minnesota Department of Health, "Minnesota Employment Demographics," Minnesota Department of Health, updated October 3, 2022, https://www.health.state.mn.us/communities/occhealth/data/employdemographics.html. In 2014, approximately 5 percent of Minnesota's working population identified as Black, and another 6 percent identified as another race/ethnicity.
10. American Immigration Council, *Immigrants in Minnesota* (Washington DC: August 6, 2020), https://www.americanimmigrationcouncil.org/sites/default/files/research/immigrants_in_minnesota.pdf.
11. Weiss, *Learning from Strangers*.
12. Barney Glaser and Anselm L. Strauss, *The Discovery of Grounded Theory: Strategies for Qualitative Research* (New Brunswick, NJ: Aldine Publishing Co., 1967).
13. Weiss, *Learning from Strangers*.
14. Michael Q. Patton, *Qualitative Research & Evaluation Methods*, 3rd ed. (Thousand Oaks, CA: Sage Publications, 2002).
15. We chose to use Qualtrics because of its robust data security features. Additionally, we assumed that the popularity of this platform would mean that our interviewees were familiar with completing these types of surveys.
16. We obviously did not contact the five individuals who died in the years since their first interview: Caroline, Kenneth, Lars, Meg, and Seymour. Also excluded from the recontact were six individuals who did not provide an email address at their first interview, and an additional three who had previously opted out of taking Qualtrics surveys and therefore did not receive our three email requests. Of the remaining forty-eight interviewees, seven outreach emails bounced back to us.

After locating four of these individuals on Facebook and LinkedIn, we invited them to get back in touch, and three responded with their new email address. Of the forty-three interviewees who we assume received an email invitation from us, twenty-five completed the questionnaire. Finally, as we note in our concluding chapter, although our questionnaire email reached an inbox, we do not actually know if the intended recipient received this email.

17 Each questionnaire respondent received a $25 Amazon gift card.
18 When we conducted the first round of interviews, in 2013 and 2014, it was not common practice to ask people their gender identity. For this reason, we asked respondents if their gender identity had changed since their initial *American Idle* interview.
19 This question and its corresponding response categories were adopted from a follow-up survey of workers laid off in a 1998 downsizing at United Defense in Fridley, Minnesota. See Kenneth A. Root and Rosemarie J. Park, *Forced Out: Older Workers Confront Job Loss* (Boulder, CO: First Forum Press, 2009), 239.
20 Some of our response categories were adopted from a follow-up survey of laid-off workers in Root and Park, *Forced Out*, 247.
21 These interviews took place in restaurants and coffee shops. One interview was conducted in Annette's office at Carleton College.
22 The digital recordings were erased from our recording equipment as soon as we verified that the primary audio was successfully transferred.

Bibliography

II Conferencia General del Episcopado Latinoamericano. *Medellín conclusiones: La Iglesia en la actual transformación de América Latina a la luz del concilio.* Bogotá, Colombia: Secretariado General del Consejo Episcopal Latinoamericano, 1990.

Abraham, Martin, Sebastian Bähr, and Mark Trappmann. "Gender Differences in Willingness to Move for Interregional Job Offers." *Demographic Research* 40 (June 2019): 1537–1602.

Adriance, Madeleine Cousineau. *Promised Land: Base Christian Communities and the Struggle for the Amazon.* Albany, NY: State University of New York Press, 1995.

Ahn, Suran, and Na Kyoung Song. "Unemployment, Recurrent Unemployment, and Material Hardships among Older Workers Since the Great Recession." *Social Work Research* 41, no. 4 (December 2017): 249–262.

American Immigration Council. *Immigrants in Minnesota.* Washington, DC: August 6, 2020. https://www.americanimmigrationcouncil.org/sites/default/files/research/immigrants_in_minnesota.pdf.

Arthur, Michael B., and Denise M. Rousseau. "Introduction: The Boundaryless Career as a New Employment Principle." In *The Boundaryless Career: A New Employment Principle for a New Organizational Era.* Edited by Michael B. Arthur and Denise M. Rousseau, 3–20. New York: Oxford University Press, 1996.

Azrin, Nathan H., T. Flores, and S. J. Kaplan. "Job-Finding Club: A Group-Assisted Program for Obtaining Employment." *Behaviour Research and Therapy* 13, no. 1 (February 1975): 17–27.

Baldridge, David C., Kimberly A. Eddleston, and John F. Veiga. "Saying 'No' to Being Uprooted: The Impact of Family and Gender on Willingness to Relocate." *Journal of Occupational and Organizational Psychology* 79, no. 1 (December 2010): 131–149.

Berger, Ellie D. *Ageism at Work: Deconstructing Age and Gender in the Discriminating Labour Market.* Toronto: University of Toronto Press, 2021.

Bernanke, Ben S., and Olivier Blanchard. "What Caused the U.S. Pandemic-Era Inflation?" Brookings Institution. June 13, 2023. https://www.brookings.edu/articles/what-caused-the-u-s-pandemic-era-inflation/.

Berrenberg, Joy L. "The Belief in Personal Control Scale: A Measure of God-Mediated and Exaggerated Control." *Journal of Personality Assessment* 51 (March 1987): 194–206.

Bertrand, Marianne, and Sendhil Mullainathan. "Are Emily and Greg More Employable Than Lakisha and Jamal? A Field Experiment on Labor Market Discrimination." *American Economic Review* 94, no. 4 (2004): 991–1013.

Bielby, William T., and Denise D. Bielby. "I Will Follow Him: Family Ties, Gender-Role Beliefs, and Reluctance to Relocate for a Better Job." *American Journal of Sociology* 97, no. 5 (March 1992): 1241–1267.

Binstock, Robert H. "From Compassionate Ageism to Intergenerational Conflict?" *Gerontologist* 50, no. 5 (2010): 574–585.

Bjorck, Jeffrey P., and John W. Thurman. "Negative Life Events, Patterns of Positive and Negative Religious Coping, and Psychological Functioning." *Journal for the Scientific Study of Religion* 46, no. 2 (May 2007): 159–167.

Bom, Judith, Pieter Bakx, Frederik Schut, and Eddy van Doorslaer. "The Impact of Informal Caregiving for Older Adults on the Health of Various Types of Caregivers: A Systematic Review." *Gerontologist* 59, no. 5 (September 2019): e629–e642. https://doi.org/10.1093/geront/gny137.

Brand, Jennie E. "The Far-Reaching Impact of Job Loss and Unemployment." *Annual Review of Sociology* 41 (August 2015): 359–375.

Brand, Jennie E., Becca R. Levy, and William T. Gallo. "Effects of Layoffs and Plant Closings on Subsequent Depression among Older Workers." *Research on Aging* 30, no. 6 (November 2008): 701–721.

Branton, Nancy. "Bringing Christ into Career Decisions." Wooddale Church Job Transition Support Group. June 2017. http://jobtransition.net/wp-content/uploads/2013/07/Job-Seeker-Scripture-Updated.pdf.

Brett, Janne M., Linda K. Stroh, and Anne H. Reilly. "Pulling Up Roots in the 1990s: Who's More Willing to Relocate?" *Journal of Organizational Behavior* 14, no. 1 (January 1993): 49–60.

Bristow, Jennie. *Stop Mugging Grandma: The 'Generation Wars' and Why Boomer Blaming Won't Solve Anything*. New Haven, CT: Yale University Press, 2019.

Brown, Wendy. *Undoing the Demos: Neoliberalism's Stealth Revolution*. Cambridge, MA; London: Zone Books, 2015.

Budros, Art. "The Mean and Lean Firm and Downsizing: Causes of Involuntary and Voluntary Downsizing Strategies." *Sociological Forum* 17, no. 2 (June 2002): 307–342.

Burawoy, Michael. *Manufacturing Consent: Changes in the Labor Process under Monopoly Capitalism*. Chicago: University of Chicago Press, 1979.

Buschman, John. "COVID-19 Doesn't Change Anything: Neoliberalism, Generationism, Academic Library Buildings, and Lazy Rivers." *Journal of Academic Librarianship* 48, no. 4 (2022). https://doi.org/10.1016/j.acalib.2022.102558.

Butler, Robert N. "Age-ism: Another Form of Bigotry." *Gerontologist* 9, no. 4, pt. 1 (1969): 243–246.

———. "Dispelling Ageism: The Cross-Cutting Intervention." *Annals of the American Academy of Political and Social Science* 503 (May 1989): 138–147.

———. "The Effects of the Medical and Health Progress on the Social and Economic Aspects of the Life Cycle." Paper delivered at the National Institute of Industrial Gerontology, Washington, DC. March 13, 1969.

Cabanas, Edgar, and Eva Illouz. "The Making of a 'Happy Worker': Positive Psychology in Neoliberal Organizations." In *Beyond the Cubicle: Job Insecurity, Intimacy, and the Flexible Self*. Edited by Allison J. Pugh, 25–49. New York: Oxford University Press, 2017.

———. *Manufacturing Happy Citizens: How the Science and Industry of Happiness Control Our Lives*. Medford, MA: Polity Press, 2019.

Cappelli, Peter, Laurie Bassi, Harry Katz, David Knoke, Paul Osterman, and Michael Useem. *Change at Work: How American Industry and Workers Are Coping with Corporate Restructuring and What Workers Must Do to Take Charge of Their Own Careers*. New York: Oxford University Press, 1997.

Carr, Deborah. *The Golden Years? Social Inequality in Later Life*. New York: Russell Sage Foundation, 2019.

———. "The Psychological Consequences of Work-Family Trade-Offs for Three Cohorts of Men and Women." *Social Psychology Quarterly* 65, no. 2 (2002): 103–124. https://doi.org/10.2307/3090096.

Case, Anne, and Angus Deaton. "Rising Morbidity and Mortality in Midlife among White Non-Hispanic Americans in the 21st Century." *PNAS* 112, no. 49 (2015): 15078–15083. https://doi.org/10.1073/pnas.1518393112.

Cennamo, Lucy, and Dianne Gardner. "Generational Differences in Work Values, Outcomes and Person-Organisation Values Fit." *Journal of Managerial Psychology* 23, no. 8 (2008): 891–906. https://doi.org/10.1108/02683940810904385.

Center for Microeconomic Data. *Quarterly Report on Household Debt and Credit: 2023: Q3*. Federal Reserve Bank of New York. November 2023. https://www.newyorkfed.org/microeconomics/hhdc.

Center on Budget and Policy Priorities. "Policy Basics: How Many Weeks of Unemployment Compensation Are Available?" Accessed November 6, 2023. https://www.cbpp.org/research/economy/how-many-weeks-of-unemployment-compensation-are-available.

———. "Tracking the COVID-19 Economy's Effects on Food, Housing, and Employment Hardships." Special Series: COVID Hardship Watch. Accessed October 30, 2023. https://www.cbpp.org/research/poverty-and-inequality/tracking-the-covid-19-recessions-effects-on-food-housing-and.

Chan, Sewin, and Ann Huff Stevens. "How Does Job Loss Affect the Timing of Retirement?" NBER Working Paper No. 8780. National Bureau of Economic Research, Cambridge, MA. February 2002. http://www.nber.org/papers/w8780.

———. "Job Loss and Employment Patterns of Older Workers." *Journal of Labour Economics* 19, no. 2 (April 2001): 484–521.

Chaves, Mark, and Alison J. Eagle. "Congregations and Social Services: An Update from the Third Wave of the National Congregations Study." *Religions* 7, no. 5 (2016): 55. https://doaj.org/article/2bf57ae226b245b7a77ff6245fcad84d?frbrVersion=3.

Chaves, Mark, and William Tsitsos. "Congregations and Social Services: What They Do, How They Do It, and with Whom." *Nonprofit and Voluntary Sector Quarterly* 30, no. 4 (2001): 660–683.

Clarke, Laura Hurd, and Alexandra Korotchenko. "Aging and the Body: A Review." *Canadian Journal on Aging* 20, no. 3 (2011): 495–510.

Cnaan, Ram A., Robert J. Wineburg, and Stephanie C. Boddie. *The Newer Deal: Social Work and Religion in Partnership*. New York: Columbia University Press, 1999.

Cohen, Philip N. "Generation Labels Mean Nothing. It's Time to Retire Them." *Washington Post*, July 7, 2021. https://www.washingtonpost.com/opinions/2021/07/07/generation-labels-mean-nothing-retire-them/.

———. "Open Letter to the Pew Research Center on Generation Labels." Accessed June 20, 2023. https://docs.google.com/forms/d/e/1FAIpQLSecsM1JavYMlNI-XlKDYngFKsEFBGFs_imv7R5KO8e15NYeCg/viewform.

Cohn, D'vera, and Paul Taylor. "Baby Boomers Approach 65—Glumly." Pew Research Center. December 20, 2010. https://www.pewresearch.org/social-trends/2010/12/20/baby-boomers-approach-65-glumly/.

Cohn, Scott. "America's Best States to Live in 2012." CNBC, June 7, 2012. https://www.cnbc.com/2012/07/10/Americas-Best-States-to-Live-in-2012.html.

Cooper, David. "As Wisconsin's and Minnesota's Lawmakers Took Divergent Paths, So Did Their Economies." *Economic Policy Institute*. May 8, 2018. https://www.epi.org/publication/as-wisconsins-and-minnesotas-lawmakers-took-divergent-paths-so-did-their-economies-since-2010-minnesotas-economy-has-performed-far-better-for-working-families-than-wisconsin/.

Cooper, Marianne. *Cut Adrift: Families in Insecure Times*. Berkeley, CA: University of California Press, 2014.

Couch, Kenneth A. "Late Life Job Displacement." *Gerontologist* 38, no. 1 (February 1998): 7–17.

Coupland, Douglas. *Generation X: Tales for an Accelerated Culture*. New York: St. Martin's Press, 1991.

Crowley, Martha, Daniel Tope, Lindsey Joyce Chamberlain, and Randy Hodson. "Neo-Taylorism at Work: Occupational Change in the Post-Fordist Era." *Social Problems* 57, no. 3 (August 2010): 421–447.

Dahl, Gordon B., and Matthew M. Knepper. "Age Discrimination Across the Business Cycle." NBER Working Paper No. 27581. National Bureau of Economic Research, Cambridge, MA. July 2020. http://www.nber.org/papers/w27581.

Damaske, Sarah. *The Tolls of Uncertainty: How Privilege and the Guilt Gap Shape Unemployment in America*. Princeton, NJ: Princeton University Press, 2021.

Davies, William. *The Limits of Neoliberalism: Authority, Sovereignty and the Logic of Competition*. London: Sage, 2014.

Davis, Elliot. "U.S. News Ranks Best States for 2021." *US News & World Report*. March 9, 2021. https://www.usnews.com/news/best-states/articles/us-news-releases-best-states-rankings.

Dawson, Andrew. "Youthquake: Neoliberalism and the Ethnicization of Generation." *Advances in Anthropology* 8 (2018): 10–17. https://doi.org/10.4236/aa.2018.81002.

Deane, Claudia, Maeve Duggan, and Rich Morin. "Americans Name the 10 Most Significant Historic Events of Their Lifetimes." Pew Research Center. December 15, 2016. https://www.pewresearch.org/politics/2016/12/15/americans-name-the-10-most-significant-historic-events-of-their-lifetimes/.

DEED Labor Market Information Office. "Generations in the Twin Cities Metro Area." April 2019. https://mn.gov/deed/assets/Generations-TwinCities_tcm1045-384981.pdf.

Demry, Aaliyah. "Allina Health Doctors Vote to Unionize." Minnesota Public Radio News, October 14, 2023. https://www.mprnews.org/story/2023/10/14/allina-health-doctors-vote-to-unionize.

Dimock, Michael. "5 Things to Keep in Mind When You Hear about Gen Z, Millennials, Boomers and Other Generations." Pew Research Center. May 22, 2023. https://www.pewresearch.org/short-reads/2023/05/22/5-things-to-keep-in-mind-when-you-hear-about-gen-z-millennials-boomers-and-other-generations/.

———. "Defining Generations: Where Millennials End and Generation Z Begins." Pew Research Center. January 17, 2019. https://www.pewresearch.org/short-reads/2019/01/17/where-millennials-end-and-generation-z-begins/.

Duca, John V. "The Great Depression versus the Great Recession in the U.S.: How Fiscal, Monetary, and Financial Policies Compare." *Journal of Economic Dynamics and Control* 81 (2017): 50–64.

Dudley, Susan. "Jimmy Carter: The Great Deregulator." *The Regulatory Review*, March 6, 2023. https://www.theregreview.org/2023/03/06/dudley-jimmy-carter-the-great-deregulator/.

Eby, Lillian T., and Joyce E. A. Russell. "Predictors of Employee Willingness to Relocate for the Firm." *Journal of Vocational Behavior* 57, no. 1 (August 2000): 42–61.

Edwards, Roxanna, Lawrence S. Essien, and Michael Daniel Levinstein. "U.S. Labor Market Shows Improvement in 2021, but the COVID-19 Pandemic Continues to Weigh on the Economy." *Monthly Labor Review.*, U.S. Bureau of Labor Statistics. June 2022. https://doi.org/10.21916/mlr.2022.16.

Ehrenreich, Barbara. *Bait and Switch: The (Futile) Pursuit of the American Dream*. New York: Holt Paperbacks, 2006.

———. *Bright-Sided: How Positive Thinking Is Undermining America*. New York: Picador, 2009.

Eisenbrey, Ross. "The Obama Administration Pushes for a Better Response to Unemployment." *Working Economics* (blog). Economic Policy Institute. January 28, 2016. https://www.epi.org/blog/the-obama-administration-pushes-for-better-response-to-unemployment/#.

Elder, Glen. *Children of the Great Depression: Social Change in Life Experiences*. Chicago: University of Chicago Press, 1974.

———. "The Life Course as Developmental Theory." *Child Development* 69, no. 1 (1998): 1–12.

———. "Time, Human Agency, and Social Change: Perspectives on the Life Course." *Social Psychology Quarterly* 57, no. 1 (March 1994): 4–15.

Elder, Glen H., Monica Kirkpatrick Johnson, and Robert Crosnoe. "The Emergence and Development of Life Course Theory." In *Handbook of the Life Course*. Edited by Jeylan T. Mortimer and Michael J. Shanahan, 3–19. New York: Springer Publishing, 2003.

Ellison, Christopher G., and Linda K. George. "Religious Involvement, Social Ties, and Social Support in a Southeastern Community." *Journal for the Scientific Study of Religion* 33, no. 1 (March 1994): 46–61.

Ellsworth-Krebs, Katherine, Louise Reid, and Colin J. Hunter. "Integrated Framework of Home Comfort: Relaxation, Companionship and Control." *Building Research & Information* 47, no. 2 (February 2019): 202–218.

Exline, Julie J. "Religious and Spiritual Struggles." In *APA Handbook of Psychology, Religion, and Spirituality*. Vol. 1, *Context, Theory, and Research*. Edited by Kenneth I. Pargament, Julie J. Exline, and James W. Jones, 459–475. Washington, DC: American Psychological Association, 2013.

Exline, Julie J., Kenneth I. Pargament, Joshua B. Grubbs, and Ann Mari Yali. "The Religious and Spiritual Struggles Scale: Development and Initial Validation." *Psychology of Religion and Spirituality* 6, no. 3 (August 2014): 208–222.

Exline, Julie J., Crystal L. Park, Joshua M. Smyth, and Michael P. Carey. "Anger toward God: Social-Cognitive Predictors, Prevalence, and Links with Adjustment to Bereavement and Cancer." *Journal of Personality and Social Psychology* 100, no. 1 (January 2011): 129–148.

Exline, Julie J., and Eric D. Rose. "Religious and Spiritual Struggles." In *Handbook of the Psychology of Religion and Spirituality*. 2nd ed. Edited by Raymond F. Paloutzian and Crystal L. Park, 380–398. New York: Guilford Press, 2013.

Ezzy, Douglas. *Narrating Unemployment*. New York: Routledge, 2017.

Falba, Tracy, Hsun-Mei Teng, Jody L. Sindelar, and William T. Gallo. "The Effect of Involuntary Job Loss on Smoking Intensity and Relapse." *Addiction* 100, no. 9 (September 2005): 1330–1339.

Farber, Henry S. "Employment, Hours, and Earnings Consequences of Job Loss: US Evidence from the Displaced Workers Survey." *Journal of Labor Economics* 35, no. S1 (July 2017): S235–S272.

Feldman, Daniel C., and Mark C. Bolino. "Moving On Out: When Are Employees Willing to Follow Their Organizations during Corporate Relocations?" *Journal of Organizational Behavior* 19, no. 3 (May 1998): 275–288.

Fineman, Stephen. *Organizing Age*. New York: Oxford University Press, 2011.

———. *White Collar Unemployment: Impact and Stress*. Chichester, UK: Wiley, 1983.

Fisher, Cynthia D., and James B. Shaw. "Relocation Attitudes and Adjustment: A Longitudinal Study." *Journal of Organizational Behavior* 15, no. 3 (May 1994): 209–224.

French, Rose. "Losing Job Just May Be a 'Blessing' in Disguise." *Minneapolis Star Tribune*, November 19, 2011, 3B.

Froman, Larry. "Positive Psychology in the Workplace." *Journal of Adult Development* 17 (2010): 59–69.

Gabriel, Yiannis, David E. Gray, and Harshita Goregaokar. "Job Loss and Its Aftermath among Managers and Professionals: Wounded, Fragmented and Flexible." *Work, Employment and Society* 27, no. 1 (2013): 56–72.

———. "Temporary Derailment or the End of the Line? Managers Coping with Unemployment at 50." *Organization Studies* 31, no. 12 (December 2010): 1687–1712.

Gall, Terry L., Manal Guirguis-Younger, Claire C. Charbonneau, and Peggy Florack. "The Trajectory of Religious Coping across Time in Response to the Diagnosis of Breast Cancer." *Psycho-Oncology* 18, no. 11 (November 2009): 1165–1178.

Gallo, William T., Elizabeth H. Bradley, Michele Siegel, and Stanislav V. Kasl. "Health Effects of Involuntary Job Loss among Older Workers: Findings from the Health and Retirement Survey." *Journal of Gerontology: Social Sciences* 55B, no. 3 (May 2000): S131–S140.

Gallo, William T., Hsun-Mei Teng, Tracy A. Falba, Stanislav V. Kasl, Harlan M. Krumholz, and Elizabeth H. Bradley. "The Impact of Late Career Job Loss on Myocardial Infarction and Stroke: A 10 Year Follow up Using the Health and Retirement Survey." *Occupational and Environmental Medicine* 63, no. 10 (October 2006): 683–687.

Gani, Aisha. "Millennials at Work: Five Stereotypes—and Why They Are (Mostly) Wrong." *Guardian*, March 15, 2016. https://www.theguardian.com/world/2016/mar/15/millennials-work-five-stereotypes-generation-y-jobs.

Garrett-Peters, Raymond. "'If I Don't Have to Work Anymore, Who Am I?': Job Loss and Collaborative Self-Concept Repair." *Journal of Contemporary Ethnography* 38, no. 5 (October 2009): 547–583.

Gayarre, José Larrea. "The Challenges of Liberation Theology to Neoliberal Economic Policies." *Social Justice* 21, no. 4 (1994): 34–45.

Gecas, Viktor. "Self-Agency and the Life Course." In *Handbook of the Life Course*. Edited by Jeylan T. Mortimer and Michael J. Shanahan, 369–388. New York: Springer Publishing, 2003.

Gershon, Ilana. *Down and Out in the New Economy*. Chicago: University of Chicago Press, 2017.

Ghilarducci, Teresa. *Work, Retire, Repeat: The Uncertainty of Retirement in the New Economy*. Chicago: The University of Chicago Press, 2024.

Giddens, Anthony. *Modernity and Self-Identity: Self and Society in the Late Modern Age*. Stanford, CA: Stanford University Press, 1991.

Gilbert, Stephanie, and E. Kevin Kelloway. "Positive Psychology and the Healthy Workplace." In *Workplace Well-Being: How to Build Psychologically Healthy Workplaces*. Edited by Arla Day, E. Kevin Kelloway, and Joseph J. Hurrell, 50–70. Hoboken, NJ: John Wiley & Sons, 2014.

Glaser, Barney, and Anselm L. Strauss. *The Discovery of Grounded Theory: Strategies for Qualitative Research*. New Brunswick, NJ: Aldine Publishing Co., 1967.

Goh, Joel, Jeffrey Pfeffer, and Stefanos A. Zenios. "Workplace Stressors & Health Outcomes: Health Policy for the Workplace." *Behavioral Science and Policy* 1, no. 1 (January 2015): 43–52.

Gonzalez, Jorge, Belle Rose Ragins, Kyle Ehrhardt, and Romila Singh. "Friends and Family: The Role of Relationships in Community and Workplace Attachment." *Journal of Business Psychology* 33, no. 1 (February 2018): 89–104.

Goodman, Whitney. *Toxic Positivity: Keeping It Real in a World Obsessed with Being Happy*. New York: TarcherPerigee, 2022.

Gould, Elise. "Older Workers Were Devastated by the Pandemic Downturn and Continue to Face Adverse Employment Outcomes: EPI Testimony for the Senate Special Committee on Aging." Economic Policy Institute. April 29, 2021. https://www.epi.org/publication/older-workers-were-devastated-by-the-pandemic-downturn-and-continue-to-face-adverse-employment-outcomes-epi-testimony-for-the-senate-special-committee-on-aging/.

Gould, Sam, and Larry E. Penley. "A Study of the Correlates of the Willingness to Relocate." *Academy of Management Journal* 28, no. 2 (June 1985): 472–478.

Gramsci, Antonio. *Selections from the Prison Notebooks of Antonio Gramsci*. Edited and translated by Quintin Hoare and Geoffrey Nowell Smith. New York: International Publishers, 1971.

Gray, Denis. "A Job Club for Older Job Seekers: An Experimental Evaluation." *Journal of Gerontology* 38, no. 3 (March 1983): 363–368.

Grubb, Valerie. *Clash of the Generations: Managing the New Workplace Reality*. Hoboken, NJ: Wiley, 2017.

Grusky, David B., Bruce Western, and Christopher Wimer. "The Consequences of the Great Recession." In *The Great Recession*. Edited by David B. Grusky, Bruce Western, and Christopher Wimer, 3–20. New York: Russell Sage Foundation, 2011.

Gullette, Margaret Morganroth. "Boomers: From Adorable Baby Bulge to #Boomer-Remover." *Age, Culture, Humanities: An Interdisciplinary Journal* 6 (September 2022): 1–6. https://doi.org/10.7146/ageculturehumanities.v6i.133335.

Gurley, Lauren Kaori. "Record Hot Labor Market Has Minnesota Scrambling for Workers." *Washington Post*, September 4, 2022. https://www.washingtonpost.com/business/2022/09/04/minnesota-jobs-unemployment-rate/.

Gutiérrez, Gustavo. *A Theology of Liberation: History, Politics, and Salvation.* Edited and translated by Sister Caridad Inda and John Eagleson. Maryknoll, NY: Orbis Books, 1973.

Hackworth, Jason. "Compassionate Neoliberalism? Evangelical Christianity, the Welfare State, and the Politics of the Right." *Studies in Political Economy* 86, no. 1 (March 2016): 83–108.

———. *Faith-Based: Religious Neoliberalism and the Politics of Welfare in the United States.* Athens: University of Georgia Press, 2012.

———. "Faith, Welfare, and the Formation of the Modern American Right." In *Religion in the Neoliberal Age: Political Economy and Modes of Governance.* Edited by Tuomas Martikainen and François Gauthier, 91–106. London: Ashgate, 2013.

———. "Religious Neoliberalism." In *The Sage Handbook on Neoliberalism.* Edited by Damien Cahill, Melinda Cooper, Martijn Konings, and David Primrose, 323–334. Thousand Oaks, CA: Sage, 2018.

Hadi, Adam. "Construction Employment Peaks before the Recession and Falls Sharply throughout It." *Monthly Labor Review*, April 2011. https://www.bls.gov/opub/mlr/2011/04/art4full.pdf.

Hagan, John, Ross Macmillan, and Blair Wheaton. "New Kid in Town: Social Capital and the Life Course Effects of Family Migration on Children." *American Sociological Review* 61, no. 3 (June 1996): 368–385.

Hamilton, V. Lee, Clifford L. Broman, William S. Hoffman, and Deborah S. Renner. "Hard Times and Vulnerable People: Initial Effects of Plant Closing on Autoworkers' Mental Health." *Journal of Health and Social Behavior* 31, no. 2 (June 1990): 123–140.

Hanke, Steve. "What Do the Great Depression and the Great Recession Have in Common?" *Forbes*, August 16, 2017. https://www.forbes.com/sites/stevehanke/2017/08/16/what-do-the-great-depression-and-the-great-recession-have-in-common/?sh=2b18808375d3.

Hanson, Bruce. "Metro Area Job Clubs." Holy Name of Jesus. June 18, 2013. https://www.hnoj.org/sites/hnojparish/files/master_networking_list_1-23-17.pdf.

Harrison, Myleme O., Harold Koenig, Judith Hays, and Anedi G. Eme-Akwari. "The Epidemiology of Religious Coping: A Review of Recent Literature." *International Review of Psychiatry* 13, no. 2 (May 2001): 86–93.

Harvey, David. *A Brief History of Neoliberalism.* New York: Oxford University Press, 2007.

———. "Neoliberalism as Creative Destruction." *Annals of the American Academy of Political and Social Science* 610, no. 1 (2007): 22–44.

Hayes, Jeff, and Heidi Hartmann. *Women and Men Living on the Edge: Economic Insecurity after the Great Recession.* Institute for Women's Policy Research, C386. September 2011. https://iwpr.org/wp-content/uploads/2020/09/C386.pdf.

He, Yaohua Helen, A. Colantonio, and Victor W. Marshall. "Later-Life Career Disruption and Self-Rated Health: An Analysis of General Social Survey Data." *Canadian Journal on Aging* 22, no. 1 (March 2010): 45–57.

Hempstead, Katherine A., and Julie A. Phillips. "Rising Suicide among Adults Aged 40–64 Years: The Role of Job and Financial Circumstances." *American Journal of Preventive Medicine* 48, no. 5 (February 2015): 491–500.

Hine, Steve, Oriane Casale, Amanda Rohrer, Mustapha Hammida, and David Senf. "State of the Economy." *Minnesota Economic Trends.* Minnesota Department of Employment and Economic Development. June 2014. https://mn.gov/deed/newscenter/publications/trends/june-2014/state-economy.jsp.

Hochschild, Arlie. *Strangers in Their Own Land*. New York: The New Press, 2016.
Hollister, Matissa. "Employment Stability in the U.S. Labor Market: Rhetoric versus Reality." *Annual Review of Sociology* 37 (August 2011): 305–324.
Hout, Michael, Asaf Levanon, and Erin Cumberworth. "Job Loss and Unemployment." In *The Great Recession*. Edited by David B. Grusky, Bruce Western, and Christopher Wimer, 59–81. New York: Russell Sage Foundation, 2011.
Hutchison, Elizabeth D. "A Life Course Perspective." In *Dimensions of Human Behavior: The Changing Life Course*, 4th ed. Edited by Elizabeth D. Hutchison, 1–38. Thousand Oaks, CA: Sage, 2011.
———. "Middle Adulthood." In *Dimensions of Human Behavior: The Changing Life Course*, 4th ed. Edited by Elizabeth D. Hutchison, 304–348. Thousand Oaks, CA: Sage, 2011.
Ingersoll-Dayton, Berit, Neal Krause, and David Morgan. "Religious Trajectories and Transitions over the Life Course." *International Journal of Aging and Human Development* 55, no. 1 (2002): 51–70.
Ingraham, Christopher. "This Is How Much Time Americans Spend Commuting to Work." *World Economic Forum*. March 3, 2016. https://www.weforum.org/stories/2016/03/average-american-commute-time-to-work/.
The Investopedia Team. "Short Sales vs. Foreclosures: What's the Difference?" Investopedia. August 22, 2022. https://www.investopedia.com/ask/answers/100314/whats-difference-between-short-sales-and-foreclosures.asp#.
Irwin, Neil. "Workers Are Gaining Leverage over Employers Right before Our Eyes." *New York Times*, June 5, 2021. https://www.nytimes.com/2021/06/05/upshot/jobs-rising-wages.html.
Job Transition Support Group. "The 6 Steps." Job Transition Support Group: A Ministry of Wooddale Church. n.d. https://jobtransition.net/the-six-steps/.
Johnson, Meagan, and Larry Johnson. *From Boomers to Linksters—Managing the Friction between Generations at Work*. New York: AMACOM, 2010.
Johnson, Richard J. "What's New about Quiet Quitting (and What's Not)." *Transdisciplinary Journal of Management* (2023): 1–14. https://tjm.scholasticahq.com/article/72079-what-s-new-about-quiet-quitting-and-what-s-not.
Johnson, Richard W., and Barbara A. Butrica. *Age Disparities in Unemployment and Reemployment during the Great Recession and Recovery*. Urban Institute Unemployment and Recovery Project Brief 3. Washington, DC: May 2012.
Jones, Landon Y. *Great Expectations: America and the Baby Boom Generation*. New York: Coward, McCann & Geoghegan, 1980.
Jones, Loring P. "A Typology of Adaptations to Unemployment." *Journal of Employment Counseling* 26, no. 2 (2011): 50–59.
Kalleberg, Arne L. *Good Jobs, Bad Jobs: The Rise of Polarized and Precarious Employment Systems in the United States, 1970s to 2000s*. New York: Russell Sage Foundation, 2011.
———. *Precarious Lives: Job Insecurity and Well-Being in Rich Democracies*. Medford, MA: Polity, 2018.
Kaufman, Harold G. *Professionals in Search of Work: Coping with the Stress of Job Loss and Underemployment*. New York: Wiley, 1982.
Kelly, Erin L., and Phyllis Moen. *Overload: How Good Jobs Went Bad and What We Can Do about It*. Princeton, NJ: Princeton University Press, 2020.
Keren, Hila. "Divided and Conquered: The Neoliberal Roots and Emotional Consequences of the Arbitration Revolution." *Florida Law Review* 72 (May 2020): 575–638.

Klehe, Ute-Christine, Irene E. de Pater, Jessie Koen, and Mari Kira. "Too Old to Tango? Job Loss and Job Search among Older Workers." In *The Oxford Handbook of Job Loss and Job Search*. Edited by Ute-Christine Klehe and Edwin Van Hooft, 433–464. New York: Oxford University Press, 2018.

Kopcke, Richard W., and Anthony Webb. "How Has the Financial Crisis Affected the Finances of Older Households?" Working paper, Center for Retirement Research at Boston College. Accessed September 25, 2021. http://web.stanford.edu/group/scspi/_media/working_papers/Kopcke_Webb_older-households.pdf.

Kosanovich, Karen, and Eleni Theodossiou Sherman. *Trends in Long-Term Unemployment*. Washington, DC: Bureau of Labor Statistics, 2015. https://www.bls.gov/spotlight/2015/long-term-unemployment/pdf/long-term-unemployment.pdf.

Krause, Neal. "God-Mediated Control and Psychological Well-Being in Late Life." *Research on Aging* 27, no. 2 (March 2005): 136–164.

Lamont, Michèle. "From Having to Being: Self-Worth and the Current Crisis of American Society." *British Journal of Sociology* 70, no. 3 (June 2019): 660–707.

Lancaster, Lynne C., and David Stillman. *When Generations Collide: Who They Are. Why They Clash. How to Solve the Generational Puzzle at Work*. New York: Harper Business, 2003.

Lane, Carrie M. *A Company of One: Insecurity, Independence, and the New World of White-Collar Unemployment*. Ithaca, NY: Cornell University Press, 2011.

Lass, William E. "The Story behind Minnesota's Weirdly Shaped Northern Border." *MinnPost*, February 4, 2014. https://www.minnpost.com/mnopedia/2014/02/story-behind-minnesotas-weirdly-shaped-northern-border/.

Lassus, Lora A. Phillips, Steven Lopez, and Vincent J. Roscigno. "Aging Workers and the Experience of Job Loss." *Research in Social Stratification and Mobility* 41 (September 2015): 81–91.

Latack, Janina C., and Janelle B. Dozier. "After the Ax Falls: Job Loss as a Career Transition." *Academy of Management Review* 11, no. 2 (April 1986): 375–392.

Latack, Janina C., Angelo J. Kinicki, and Gregory E. Prussia. "An Integrative Process Model of Coping with Job Loss." *Academy of Management Review* 20, no. 2 (April 1995): 311–342.

Lauricella, Tom. "How Old Are You? As Old as Your Skills." *Wall Street Journal*, Personal Journal, September 16, 2007. https://www.wsj.com/articles/SB118989485712728792.

Leana, Carrie R., and Daniel C. Feldman. *Coping with Job Loss: How Individuals, Organizations, and Communities Respond to Layoffs*. New York: Lexington Books, 1992.

Lechner, Clemens M., and Thomas Leopold. "Religious Attendance Buffers the Impact of Unemployment on Life Satisfaction: Longitudinal Evidence from Germany." *Journal for the Scientific Study of Religion* 54, no. 1 (March 2015): 166–174.

Lennox, Annie. "Keep Young and Beautiful." Track 11 on *Diva*. RCA Records. 1992.

Leppert, Rebecca, and Dalia Fahmy. "10 Facts about Religion and Government in the United States." Pew Research Center. Updated July 5, 2022. https://www.pewresearch.org/fact-tank/2022/07/05/10-facts-about-religion-and-government-in-the-united-states/.

Letkemann, Paul. "Unemployed Professionals, Stigma Management and Derivative Stigmata." *Work, Employment and Society* 16, no. 3 (September 2002): 511–522.

Levinson, Marc. *An Extraordinary Time: The End of the Postwar Boom and the Return of the Ordinary Economy*. New York: Basic Books, 2016.

Levy, Becca R., Martin D. Slade, E-Shien Chang, Sneha Kannoth, and Shi-Yi Wang. "Ageism Amplifies Cost and Prevalence of Health Conditions." *Gerontologist* 60, no. 1 (2018): 174–181.

Lisetti, Amanda. *Generations Reimagined: The Complete Guide Uncovering the Real Differences between Generation Z, Millennials, Generation X, Boomers, Silents, and Generation Alpha*. Independently published, 2023. Kindle.

Little, Craig B. "Technical-Professional Unemployment: Middle-Class Adaptability to Personal Crisis." *Sociological Quarterly* 17 (March 1976): 262–274.

Liu, Songqi, Jason L. Huang, and Mo Wang. "Effectiveness of Job Search Interventions: A Meta-Analytic Review." *Psychological Bulletin* 140, no. 4 (2014): 1009–1041.

Lyons, Sean T., and Linda Schweitzer. "A Qualitative Exploration of Generational Identity: Making Sense of Young and Old in the Context of Today's Workplace." *Work, Aging and Retirement* 3, no. 2 (2017): 209–224.

Macnicol, John. *Neoliberalising Old Age*. Cambridge: Cambridge University Press, 2015.

Mannheim, Karl. "The Problem of Generations." In *Karl Mannheim: Essays on the Sociology of Knowledge*. Edited by Paul Kecskemeti, 276–320. London: Routledge & Kegan Paul, 1928 (republished in 1972).

Marques, Sibila, Hannah J. Swift, Christin-Melanie Vauclair, Maria Luísa Lima, Christopher Bratt, and Dominic Abrams. "'Being Old and Ill' across Different Countries: Social Status, Age Identification and Older People's Subjective Health." *Psychology and Health* 30, no. 6 (2015): 699–714.

Martin, Greg, and Steven Roberts. "Exploring Legacies of the Baby Boomers in the Twenty-First Century." *Sociological Review* 69, no. 4 (2021): 727–742.

Maslow, Abraham H. "A Theory of Human Motivation." *Psychological Review* 50, no. 4 (July 1943): 370–396.

McConnell, Kelly M., Kenneth I. Pargament, Christopher G. Ellison, and Kevin J. Flannelly. "Examining the Links between Spiritual Struggles and Symptoms of Psychopathology in a National Sample." *Journal of Clinical Psychology* 62, no. 2 (December 2006): 1469–1484.

McDonough, Carol C. "The Effect of Ageism on the Digital Divide among Older Adults." *Journal of Gerontology & Geriatric Medicine* 2, no. 1 (2016): 1–7. https://doi:10.24966/ggm-8662/100008.

McKee-Ryan, Frances, and Robyn Maitoza. "Job Loss, Unemployment, and Families." In *The Oxford Handbook of Job Loss and Job Search*. Edited by Ute-Christine Klehe and Edwin Van Hooft, 87–97. New York: Oxford University Press, 2018.

McKee-Ryan, Frances, Zhaoli Song, Connie R. Wanberg, and Angelo J. Kinicki. "Psychological and Physical Well-Being during Unemployment: A Meta-Analytic Study." *Journal of Applied Psychology* 90, no. 1 (January 2005): 53–76.

Meisner, Brad. "Are You OK, Boomer? Intensification of Ageism and Intergenerational Tensions on Social Media amid COVID-19." *Leisure Sciences* 43, no. 1–2 (2020): 56–61. https://doi.org/10.1080/01490400.2020.1773983.

Menand, Louis. "The Price Is Right: The Rise and Fall of Neoliberalism." *New Yorker*, July 17, 2023. https://www.newyorker.com/magazine/2023/07/24/the-rise-and-fall-of-neoliberalism.

Mendenhall, Ruby, Ariel Kalil, Laurel J. Spindel, and Cassandra M. D. Hart. "Job Loss at Mid-Life: Managers and Executives Face the 'New Risk Economy.'" *Social Forces* 87, no. 1 (September 2008): 185–209.

Mezzofiore, Gianluca. "A 25-Year-Old Politician Got Heckled during a Climate Crisis Speech. Her Deadpan Retort: 'OK, Boomer.'" CNN.com, November 7, 2019. https://www.cnn.com/2019/11/06/asia/new-zealand-ok-boomer-trnd/index.html.

Mickey, Ethel L. "'Eat, Pray, Love' Bullshit": Women's Empowerment through Wellness at an Elite Professional Conference. *Journal of Contemporary Ethnography* 48, no. 1 (February 2019): 103–127.

Miller, Dorothy A. "The 'Sandwich' Generation: Adult Children of the Aging." *Social Work* 26, no. 5 (September 1981): 419–423.

Miller, Peter. "Mortgage Rates Chart: Historical and Current Rate Trends." The Mortgage Reports. June 27, 2023. https://themortgagereports.com/61853/30-year-mortgage-rates-chart#loan-purpose.

Mills, C. Wright. *The Sociological Imagination*. London: Oxford University Press, 1959.

Minnesota Department of Health. "Minnesota Employment Demographics." Minnesota Department of Health. Updated October 3, 2022. https://www.health.state.mn.us/communities/occhealth/data/employdemographics.html.

Minnesota Department of Labor and Industry. "Employment Termination." Accessed September 4, 2023. https://www.dli.mn.gov/business/employment-practices/employment-termination#.

Mirvis, Phillip H., and Douglas T. Hall. "Psychological Success and the Boundaryless Career." In *The Boundaryless Career: A New Employment Principle for a New Organizational Era*. Edited by Michael B. Arthur and Denise M. Rousseau, 237–255. New York: Oxford University Press, 1996.

Moen, Phyllis. *Encore Adulthood: Boomers on the Edge of Risk, Renewal, and Purpose*. New York: Oxford University Press, 2016.

Monbiot, George. "The Horror Films Got It Wrong. This Virus Has Turned Us into Caring Neighbours." *Guardian*, March 31, 2020. https://www.theguardian.com/commentisfree/2020/mar/31/virus-neighbours-covid-19.

———. "Neoliberalism—the Ideology at the Root of All Our Problems." *Guardian*, April 15, 2016. https://www.theguardian.com/books/2016/apr/15/neoliberalism-ideology-problem-george-monbiot.

Monge-Naranjo, Alexander, and Faisal Sohail. "The Composition of Long-Term Unemployment Is Changing toward Older Workers." *Regional Economist*. October 2015. https://www.stlouisfed.org/~/media/Publications/Regional-Economist/2015/October/unemployment.pdf.

Montanaro, Richard. "After the Fall: An Exploration of the Coping Behavior of Positive Appraisal in Midcareer Adults' Responses to Involuntary Job Loss." PhD diss., Fielding Graduate University, 2011. ProQuest (3453410).

Morrisey, Monique. "Women Over 65 Are More Likely to Be Poor Than Men, Regardless of Race, Educational Background, and Marital Status." *Economic Policy Institute*. March 8, 2016. https://www.epi.org/publication/women-over-65-are-more-likely-to-in-poverty-than-men/.

Mortimer, Jeylan T., and Jon Lorence. "Occupational Experience and the Self-Concept: A Longitudinal Study." *Social Psychology Quarterly* 42, no. 4 (December 1979): 307–323.

Neumark, David. "The Age Discrimination in Employment Act and the Challenge of Population Aging." *Research on Aging* 31, no. 1 (2009): 41–68.

Neumark, David, and Patrick Button. "Did Age Discrimination Protections Help Older Workers Weather the Great Recession?" *Journal of Policy Analysis and Management* 33, no. 3 (2014): 566–601.

Newman, Katherine S. *Falling from Grace: Downward Mobility in the Age of Affluence.* Berkeley, CA: University of California Press, 1999.

Ng, Eddy S., Sean T. Lyons, and Linda Schweitzer. *Generational Career Shifts: How Matures, Boomers, Gen Xers, and Millennials View Work.* Bingley, UK: Emerald Publishing, 2018.

Nierobisz, Annette. "Flexible Workers and Other Fantastical Myths of the Neoliberal Era." In *The Handbook on Unemployment and Society.* Edited by Ofer Sharone, Victor Chen, and Sabina Pultz. Northampton, MA: Edward Elgar Publishing, 2025.

Nierobisz, Annette, and Dana Sawchuk. "Religious Coping and Older, Unemployed Workers: Narratives of the Job Loss Experience." *Journal of Religion, Spirituality & Aging* 30, no. 4 (2018): 325–353. https://doi: 10.1080/15528030.2018.1461729.

Noe, Raymond A., and Alison E. Barber. "Willingness to Accept Mobility Opportunities: Destination Makes a Difference." *Journal of Organizational Behavior* 14, no. 2 (1993): 159–175.

Norris, Dawn R. *Job Loss, Identity, and Mental Health.* New Brunswick, NJ: Rutgers University Press, 2016.

O'Rand, Angela M. "The Precious and the Precocious: Understanding Cumulative Disadvantage and Cumulative Advantage over the Life Course." *Gerontologist* 36, no. 2 (April 1996): 230–238.

Oster, Emily. *The Family Firm: A Data-Driven Guide to Better Decision Making in the Early School Years.* New York: Penguin Press, 2021.

Ozturk, Gulgun Bayaz, and William T. Gallo. *Effect of Job Loss on Wealth Accumulation of Older Workers.* Report prepared for the U.S. Department of Labor. January 2013. https://www.dol.gov/sites/dolgov/files/OASP/legacy/files/FINAL_REPORT_wealth_effects_job_loss_older_workers.pdf.

Pargament, Kenneth I. *The Psychology of Religion and Coping: Theory, Research, Practice.* New York: The Guilford Press, 1997.

———. "Religion and Coping: The Current State of Knowledge." In *The Oxford Handbook of Stress, Health, and Coping.* Edited by Susan Folkman, 269–288. New York: Oxford University Press, 2011.

Pargament, Kenneth I., Margaret Feuille, and Donna Burdzy. "The Brief RCOPE: Current Psychometric Status of a Short Measure of Religious Coping." *Religions* 2, no. 1 (February 2011): 51–76.

Pargament, Kenneth I., Harold G. Koenig, and Lisa M. Perez. "The Many Methods of Religious Coping: Development and Initial Validation of the RCOPE." *Journal of Clinical Psychology* 56, no. 4 (April 2000): 519–543.

Pargament, Kenneth I., and Crystal L. Park. "In Times of Stress: The Religion-Coping Connection." In *The Psychology of Religion: Theoretical Approaches.* Edited by Bernard Spilka and Daniel N. McIntosh, 43–53. Boulder, CO: Westview Press, 1997.

Pargament, Kenneth I., Bruce W. Smith, Harold G. Koenig, and Lisa Perez. "Patterns of Positive and Negative Religious Coping with Major Life Stressors." *Journal for the Scientific Study of Religion* 37, no. 4 (December 1998), 710–724.

Park, Crystal L. "Religion as a Meaning-Making Framework in Coping with Life Stress." *Journal of Social Issues* 61, no. 4 (November 2005): 707–729.

Park, Crystal L., and Susan Folkman. "Meaning in the Context of Stress and Coping." *Review of General Psychology* 1, no. 2 (June 1997): 115–144.

Parker, Kim. "How Pew Research Center Will Report on Generations Moving Forward." Pew Research Center. May 22, 2023. https://www.pewresearch.org/short

-reads/2023/05/22/how-pew-research-center-will-report-on-generations-moving-forward/.

Parker, Kim, and Juliana Menasce Horowitz. "Majority of Workers Who Quit a Job in 2021 Cite Low Pay, No Opportunities for Advancement, Feeling Disrespected." Pew Research Center. March 9, 2022. https://www.pewresearch.org/short-reads/2022/03/09/majority-of-workers-who-quit-a-job-in-2021-cite-low-pay-no-opportunities-for-advancement-feeling-disrespected/.

Parker, Kim, and Eileen Patten. "The Sandwich Generation: Rising Financial Burdens for Middle-Aged Americans." Pew Research Center. January 30, 2013. https://www.pewresearch.org/social-trends/2013/01/30/the-sandwich-generation/.

Parry, Emma, and Peter Urwin. "Generational Differences in Work Values: A Review of Theory and Evidence." *International Journal of Management Reviews* 13, no. 1 (2011): 79–96. https://doi.org/10.1111/j.1468-2370.2010.00285.x.

Patton, Michael Q. *Qualitative Research & Evaluation Methods*. 3rd ed. Thousand Oaks, CA: Sage Publications, 2002.

Paul, Karsten I., and Klaus Moser. "Unemployment Impairs Mental Health: Meta-Analyses." *Journal of Vocational Behavior* 74, no. 3 (June 2009): 264–282.

Peale, Norman Vincent. *The Power of Positive Thinking*. Ada, MI: Spire Books, 1959.

Pearl, Rebecca L., and Ivona Percec. "Ageism and Health in Patients Undergoing Cosmetic Procedures." *Aesthetic Surgery Journal* 39, no. 7 (2018): NP288–NP292.

Pendenza, Massimo, and Vanessa Lamattina. "Rethinking Self-Responsibility: An Alternative Vision to the Neoliberal Concept of Freedom." *American Behavioral Scientist* 63, no. 1 (January 2019): 100–115.

Perkins, Olivera. "Job Clubs Help the Unemployed Weather Joblessness (Gallery)." *Cleveland Plain Dealer*, December 30, 2014. https://www.cleveland.com/business/2014/12/job_clubs_help_the_unemployed.html.

Peters, Michael. "The Early Origins of Neoliberalism: Colloque Walter Lippman (1938) and the Mt Perelin Society (1947)." *Educational Philosophy and Theory* 55, no. 14 (2021): 1574–1581. https://doi.org/10.1080/00131857.2021.1951704.

Pew Charitable Trusts. *When Do Americans Plan to Retire? A Brief from the Pew Charitable Trusts*. November 19, 2018. https://www.pewtrusts.org/-/media/assets/2018/11/whendoamericansplantoretire_final.pdf.

———. *A Year or More: The High Costs of Long-Term Unemployment*. Addendum to the Pew Fiscal Analysis Initiative. May 2012. http://www.pewtrusts.org/~/media/Assets/2012/05/Long_Term_Unemployment_May2012_Addendum.pdf.

Pew Research Center. "The Age Gap in Religion around the World." Pew Research Center's Religion & Public Life Project. June 13, 2018. https://www.pewresearch.org/religion/2018/06/13/the-age-gap-in-religion-around-the-world/.

———. "America's Changing Religious Landscape." May 12, 2015. https://www.pewresearch.org/religion/2015/05/12/americas-changing-religious-landscape/.

———. "Assessing the Representativeness of Public Opinion Surveys." May 15, 2012. https://www.pewresearch.org/politics/2012/05/15/assessing-the-representativeness-of-public-opinion-surveys/.

———. "Baby Boomers: From the Age of Aquarius to the Age of Responsibility." December 8, 2005. https://www.pewresearch.org/social-trends/2005/12/08/baby-boomers-from-the-age-of-aquarius-to-the-age-of-responsibility/.

———. "Baby Boomers: The Gloomiest Generation." June 25, 2008. https://www.pewresearch.org/social-trends/2008/06/25/baby-boomers-the-gloomiest-generation/.

———. "Generations 2010: What Different Generations Do Online." December 16, 2010. https://www.pewresearch.org/internet/2010/12/16/generations-2010-what-different-generations-do-online/.

———. *Religious Landscape Study, Adults in the Minneapolis Metro Area*. 2014. https://www.pewforum.org/religious-landscape-study/metro-area/minneapolisst-paul-metro-area/.

———. "The Whys and Hows of Generations Research." September 3, 2015. https://www.pewresearch.org/politics/2015/09/03/the-whys-and-hows-of-generations-research/.

Pfeffer, Jeffrey. *Dying for a Paycheck: How Modern Management Harms Employee Health and Company Performance—and What We Can Do about It*. New York: Harper Business, 2018.

Podgursky, Michael, and Paul Swaim. "Job Displacement and Earnings Loss—Evidence from the Displaced Worker Survey." *Industrial and Labor Relations Review* 41, no. 1 (October 1987): 17–29.

Pollard, Kelvin, and Paola Scommegna. "Just How Many Baby Boomers Are There?" Population Reference Bureau. April 16, 2014. https://www.prb.org/resources/just-how-many-baby-boomers-are-there/.

Population Reference Bureau. "Unmarried Baby Boomers Face Disadvantages as They Grow Older." March 6, 2014. https://www.prb.org/resources/unmarried-baby-boomers-face-disadvantages-as-they-grow-older/#.

Pritchard, Katrina, and Rebecca Whiting. "Baby Boomers and the Lost Generation: On the Discursive Construction of Generations at Work." *Organization Studies* 35, no. 11 (2014): 1605–1626.

Pugh, Allison J. "Introduction: The Broader Impacts of Precariousness." In *Beyond the Cubicle: Job Insecurity, Intimacy, and the Flexible Self*. Edited by Allison J. Pugh, 1–21. New York: Oxford University Press, 2017.

———. *The Tumbleweed Society: Working and Caring in an Age of Insecurity*. New York: Oxford University Press, 2015.

———. "What Good Are Interviews for Thinking about Culture? Demystifying Interpretive Analysis." *American Journal of Cultural Sociology* 1, no. 1 (February 2013): 42–68.

Rao, Aliya Hamid. *Crunch Time: How Married Couples Confront Unemployment*. Oakland, CA: University of California Press, 2020.

Reingold, David A., Maureen Pirog, and David Brady. "Empirical Evidence on Faith-Based Organizations in an Era of Welfare Reform." *Social Service Review* 81, no. 2 (June 2007): 245–283.

Ridgway, Shannon. "20+ Examples of Age Privilege." *Everyday Feminism*. January 24, 2013. https://everydayfeminism.com/2013/01/20-examples-of-age-privilege/page/3/.

Rives, Janet M., and Janet M. West. "Wife's Employment and Worker Relocation Behavior." *Journal of Socio-Economics* 22, no. 1 (Spring 1993): 13–22.

Robertson, Derek. "The States of Our Union . . . Are Still Not All Strong. Our Fourth Quasi-Annual Ranking." *Politico Magazine*, January 30, 2018. https://www.politico.com/magazine/story/2018/01/30/fourth-states-of-union-ranking-216547/.

Rodgers, Joan R., and John L. Rodgers. "The Effect of Geographic Mobility on Male Labor-Force Participants in the United States." *Journal of Labor Research* 21, no. 1 (March 2000): 117–132.

Root, Kenneth A., and Rosemarie J. Park. *Forced Out: Older Workers Confront Job Loss*. Boulder, CO: First Forum Press, 2009.

Roscigno, Vincent J. "Ageism in the Workplace." *Contexts* 9, no. 1 (February 2010): 16–21.

Roscigno, Vincent J., Sherry Mong, Reginald Byron, and Griff Tester. "Age Discrimination, Social Closure and Employment." *Social Forces* 86, no. 1 (September 2007): 313–334.

Rothstein, Sidney A. *Recoding Power: Tactics for Mobilizing Tech Workers*. New York: Oxford University Press, 2022.

Rowan, Lisa. "The States with the Best and Worst Unemployment Benefits—and Why They're So Different." *Forbes Advisor*, March 17, 2021. https://www.forbes.com/advisor/personal-finance/best-and-worst-states-for-unemployment/.

Rubin, Beth A. "Employment Insecurity and the Frayed American Dream." *Sociology Compass* 8, no. 9 (September 2014): 1083–1099.

Rudolph, Cort, and Hannes Zacher. "'The COVID-19 Generation': A Cautionary Note." *Work, Aging and Retirement* 6, no. 3 (2020): 139–145.

Sagie, Abraham, Moshe Krausz, and Yehuda Weinstein. "To Move or Not to Move: Factors Affecting Employees' Actual Relocation When an Entire Plant Moves." *Journal of Occupational and Organizational Psychology* 74, no. 3 (September 2001): 343–358.

Sanjek, Roger. *Gray Panthers*. Philadelphia: University of Pennsylvania Press, 2009.

Sawchuk, Dana. "The Catholic Church in the Nicaraguan Revolution: A Gramscian Analysis." *Sociology of Religion* 58, no. 1 (1997): 39–51.

———. "The Raging Grannies: Defying Stereotypes and Embracing Aging through Activism." *Journal of Women & Aging* 21, no. 3 (2009): 171–185.

Schieman, Scott, Tetyana Pudrovska, Leonard I. Pearlin, and Christopher G. Ellison. "The Sense of Divine Control and Psychological Distress: Variations across Race and Socioeconomic Status." *Journal for the Scientific Study of Religion* 45, no. 4 (December 2006): 529–549.

Schmitz, Lauren L., and Dalton Conley. "The Impact of Late-Career Job Loss and Genotype on Body Mass Index." NBER Working Paper No. 22348. National Bureau of Economic Research, Cambridge, MA. June 2016. http://doi:10.3386/w22348.

Schuman, Howard, and Jacqueline Scott. "Generations and Collective Memories." *American Sociological Review* 54, no. 3 (1989): 359–381.

Second Vatican Council. *Vatican Council II: The Conciliar and Post Conciliar Documents*. Edited by Austin Flannery. Northport, NY: Costello Publishing, 1987.

Senate Special Committee on Aging. *America's Aging Workforce: Opportunities and Challenges*. December 2017. https://www.aging.senate.gov/imo/media/doc/Aging%20Workforce%20Report%20FINAL.pdf.

Sennett, Richard. *The Culture of the New Capitalism*. New Haven, CT: Yale University Press, 2006.

Shams, Manfusa, and Paul R. Jackson. "Religiosity as a Predictor of Well-Being and Moderator of the Psychological Impact of Unemployment." *British Journal of Medical Psychology* 66, no. 4 (December 1993): 341–352.

Shapiro, Deane H., Curt A. Sandman, Michael Grossman, and Barbara Grossman. "Aging and Sense of Control." *Psychological Reports* 77, no. 2 (October 1995): 616–618.

Sharone, Ofer. "Constructing Unemployed Job Seekers as Professional Workers: The Depoliticizing Work-Game of Job Searching." *Qualitative Sociology* 30, no. 4 (July 2007): 403–416.

———. *Flawed System/Flawed Self: Job Searching and Unemployment Experiences*. Chicago: University of Chicago Press, 2014.

———. *The Stigma Trap: College-Educated, Experienced, and Long-Term Unemployed.* New York: Oxford University Press, 2024.

Shauman, Kimberlee A., and Yu Xie. "Geographic Mobility: Sex Differences and Family Constraints." *Demography* 33, no. 4 (November 1996): 455–468.

Shaw, Haydn. *Sticking Points: How to Get 5 Generations Working Together in the 12 Places They Come Apart.* Carol Stream, IL: Tyndale Momentum, 2020.

Shelton, Barbara K. "The Social and Psychological Impact of Unemployment." *Journal of Employment Counseling* 22, no. 1 (March 1985): 18–22.

Shiro, Ariel Gelrud, and Kristin Butcher. "Job Displacement in the United States by Race, Education, and Parental Income." Brookings, Future of the Middle Class Initiative. July 2022. https://www.brookings.edu/wp-content/uploads/2022/07/20220719_FMCI_ShiroButcher_JobDisplacement_FINAL.pdf.

———. "The Long-Term Economic Scars of Job Displacements." Brookings. July 21, 2022. https://www.brookings.edu/articles/the-long-term-economic-scars-of-job-displacements/.

Simonson, Jocelyn. *Radical Acts of Justice: How Ordinary People Are Dismantling Mass Incarceration.* New York: The New Press, 2023.

Smith, Gregory A. "About Three-in-Ten U.S. Adults Are Now Religiously Unaffiliated." Pew Research Center Report. Pew Research Center. December 14, 2021. https://www.pewresearch.org/religion/2021/12/14/about-three-in-ten-u-s-adults-are-now-religiously-unaffiliated/.

Snyder, Benjamin H. *The Disrupted Workplace: Time and the Moral Order of Flexible Capitalism.* New York: Oxford University Press, 2016.

Social Security Administration. "Retirement Benefits." Publication No. 05-10035. 2023. https://www.ssa.gov/pubs/EN-05-10035.pdf.

Sølvberg, Lisa M. B., and Vegard Jarness. "Assessing Contradictions: Methodological Challenges When Mapping Symbolic Boundaries." *Cultural Sociology* 13, no. 2 (June 2019): 178–197.

Sternheimer, Karen. 2010. "Downward Mobility." *Everyday Sociology* (blog). April 22, 2010. https://www.everydaysociologyblog.com/2010/04/downward-mobility.html.

Stevens, Ann Huff. "Persistent Effects of Job Displacement: The Importance of Multiple Job Losses." *Journal of Labor Economics* 15, no. 1 (January 1997): 165–188.

Stolzenberg, Nomi. "Religious Identity and Supreme Court Justices—A Brief History." *The Conversation*, October 19, 2020. http://theconversation.com/religious-identity-and-supreme-court-justices-a-brief-history-146999.

Strauss, Claudia. "Positive Thinking about Being Out of Work in Southern California after the Great Recession." In *Anthropologies of Unemployment: New Perspectives on Work and Its Absence.* Edited by Jong Kwon and Carrie Lane, 171–190. Ithaca, NY: Cornell University Press, 2016.

Strauss, William, and Neil Howe. *Generations: The History of America's Future, 1584 to 2069.* New York: Quill William Morrow, 1991.

Stuart, Forrest. *Down, Out, and Under Arrest: Policing and Everyday Life in Skid Row.* Chicago: University of Chicago Press, 2016.

Swanson, Louis E., A. E. Luloff, and Rex H. Warland. "Factors Influencing Willingness to Move: An Examination of Nonmetropolitan Residents." *Rural Sociology* 44, no. 4 (January 1979): 719–735.

Swidler, Ann. "Culture in Action: Symbols and Strategies." *American Sociological Review* 51, no. 2 (April 1986): 273–286.

Tarakeshwar, Nalini, and Kenneth I. Pargament. "Religious Coping in Families of Children with Autism." *Focus on Autism and Other Developmental Disabilities* 16, no. 4 (November 2001): 247–260.

Taylor, Astra. *The Age of Insecurity: Coming Together as Things Fall Apart*. Toronto: House of Anansi Press, 2023.

———. "Why Does Everyone Feel So Insecure All the Time?" *New York Times*, August 18, 2023, https://www.nytimes.com/2023/08/18/opinion/inequality-insecurity-economic-wealth.html.

Thomas, William I., and Dorothy Swaine Thomas. *The Child in America: Behavior Problems and Programs*. New York: Knopf, 1928.

Thuné-Boyle, Ingela C., Jan A. Stygall, Mohammed R. Keshtgar, and Stanton P. Newman. "Do Religious/Spiritual Coping Strategies Affect Illness Adjustment in Patients with Cancer? A Systematic Review of the Literature." *Social Science & Medicine* 63, no. 1 (July 2006): 151–164.

Trawinski, Lori A. *Nightmare on Main Street: Older Americans and the Mortgage Market Crisis*. AARP, #2010–08. Washington, DC: AARP Public Policy Institute, 2012. http://www.aarp.org/content/dam/aarp/research/public_policy_institute/cons_prot/2012/nightmare-on-main-street-AARP-ppi-cons-prot.pdf.

Trevino, Kelly M., and Kenneth I. Pargament. "Religious Coping with Terrorism and Natural Disaster." *Southern Medical Journal* 100, no. 9 (September 2007): 946–947.

Trutko, John, Carolyn O'Brien, Stephen Wandner, and Burt Barnow. *Formative Evaluation of Job Clubs Operated by Faith- and Community-Based Organizations: Findings from Site Visits and Options for Future Evaluation: Final Report*. Submitted to the Chief Evaluation Office, U.S. Department of Labor by Capital Research Corporation and George Washington University. May 2014.

Twombly, Matthew, and Kendrick McDonald. "A Timeline of 1968: The Year That Shattered America." *Smithsonian Magazine*, January 2018. https://www.smithsonianmag.com/history/timeline-seismic-180967503/.

Ungureanu, Ileana, and Jonathan G. Sandberg. "'Broken Together': Spirituality and Religion as Coping Strategies for Couples Dealing with the Death of a Child: A Literature Review with Clinical Implications." *Contemporary Family Therapy* 32, no. 3 (June 2010): 302–319.

U.S. Bureau of Labor Statistics. "Minnesota Had the Lowest Jobless Rate in August 2022." *TED: The Economics Daily*. September 26, 2022. https://www.bls.gov/opub/ted/2022/minnesota-had-the-lowest-jobless-rate-in-august-2022.htm.

———. "The Recession of 2007–2009." *BLS Spotlight on Statistics*. February 2012. https://www.bls.gov/spotlight/2012/recession/pdf/recession_bls_spotlight.pdf.

U.S. Census Bureau. "QuickFacts: Minnesota." Accessed June 7, 2021. https://www.census.gov/quickfacts/MN#qf-headnote-a.

U.S. Department of Labor. "American Job Centers." Employee and Training Administration. Accessed August 17, 2022. https://www.dol.gov/agencies/eta/american-job-centers.

———. "American Job Centers." U.S. Department of Labor. Accessed August 17, 2022. https://www.dol.gov/general/topic/training/onestop.

———. "Types of Retirement Plans." Accessed November 2, 2023. https://www.dol.gov/general/topic/retirement/typesofplans.

U.S. Equal Employment Opportunity Commission. Age Discrimination Employment Act of 1967, SEC. 623 [Section 4]. Accessed July 19, 2021. https://www.eeoc.gov/statutes/age-discrimination-employment-act-1967.

U.S. News and World Report. *Best States 2021: Ranking Performance throughout All 50 States.* Accessed July 5, 2021. https://www.usnews.com/media/best-states/overall-rankings-2021.pdf.

Vanguard. "What's the Right Emergency Fund Amount?" Accessed September 6, 2023. https://investor.vanguard.com/investor-resources-education/emergency-fund/whats-the-right-emergency-fund-amount#.

Van Oort, Madison. "Making the Neoliberal Precariat: Two Faces of Job Searching in Minneapolis." *Ethnography* 16, no. 1 (March 2015): 74–94.

Wald, Kenneth D., and David C. Leege. "Culture, Religion and American Political Life." In *The Oxford Handbook of Religion and American Politics.* Edited by Corwin E. Smidt, Lyman A. Kellstedt, and James L. Guth, 129–163. New York: Oxford University Press, 2009.

Wandner, Stephen A. "One-Time Funding Increase Not Enough to Shrink High Unemployment." *Urban Wire* (blog). Urban Institute. October 19, 2012. https://www.urban.org/urban-wire/one-time-funding-increase-not-enough-shrink-high-unemployment.

———. "Reemploying America: The Public Workforce System and the Great Recession." *Urban Wire* (blog). Urban Institute. October 16, 2012. https://www.urban.org/urban-wire/reemploying-america-public-workforce-system-and-great-recession.

Ward, Lizzie. "Caring for Ourselves? Self-Care and Neoliberalism." In *Ethics of Care: Critical Advances in International Perspective.* Edited by Marian Barnes, T. Brannelly, Lizzie Ward, and N. Ward, 45–56. Bristol, UK: Policy Press, an imprint of Bristol University Press, 2016.

Wear, Michael R. *Reclaiming Hope: Lessons Learned in the Obama White House about the Future of Faith in America.* Nashville, TN: Thomas Nelson, 2017.

Webb, Amy P., Christopher G. Ellison, Michael J. McFarland, Jerry W. Lee, Kelly Morton, and James Walters. "Divorce, Religious Coping, and Depressive Symptoms in a Conservative Protestant Religious Group." *Family Relations* 59, no. 5 (November 2010): 544–557.

Weir, Kristen. "Ageism Is One of the Last Socially Acceptable Prejudices, Psychologists Are Working to Change That." *American Psychological Association.* March 1, 2023. https://www.apa.org/monitor/2023/03/cover-new-concept-of-aging.

Weiss, Robert P. "Charitable Choice as Neoliberal Social Welfare Strategy." *Social Justice* 28, no. 1 (83) (Spring 2001): 35–53.

Weiss, Robert S. *Learning from Strangers: The Art and Method of Qualitative Interview Studies.* New York: The Free Press, 1995.

Whitaker, Elizabeth Ann. "Moving On to Stay Put: Employee Relocation in the Face of Employment Insecurity." In *Beyond the Cubicle: Job Insecurity, Intimacy, and the Flexible Self.* Edited by Allison J. Pugh, 203–228. New York: Oxford University Press, 2017.

White, Jonathan. "Thinking Generations." *British Journal of Sociology* 64, no. 2 (2013): 216–247.

Widner, Daniel, and Stephen Chicoine. "It's All in the Name: Employment Discrimination against Arab Americans." *Sociological Forum* 26, no. 4 (2011): 806–823.

Wilkerson, Isabel. *The Warmth of Other Suns: The Epic Story of America's Great Migration.* New York: Random House, 2010.

Williams, Allison, Li Wang, Wendy Duggleby, Maureen Markle-Reid, and Jenny Ploeg. "Gender and Sex Differences in Carers' Health, Burden and Work

Outcomes: Canadian Carers of Community-Dwelling Older People with Multiple Chronic Conditions." *International Journal of Care and Caring* 1, no. 3 (October 2017): 331–349.

Wineburg, Robert J., Brian L. Coleman, Stephanie C. Boddie, and Ram A. Cnaan. "Leveling the Playing Field: Epitomizing Devolution through Faith-Based Organizations." *Journal of Sociology & Social Welfare* 35, no. 1 (March 2008): 17–42.

Wolff, Edward N., Lindsay A. Owens, and Esra Burak. "How Much Wealth Was Destroyed in the Great Recession?" In *The Great Recession*. Edited by David B. Grusky, Bruce Western, and Christopher Wimer, 127–158. New York: Russell Sage Foundation, 2011.

Yuille, Brigitte. "Severance Package Explained: The Layoff Payoff." Investopedia. Updated June 6, 2024. https://www.investopedia.com/articles/pf/08/negotiating-severance-agreements.asp.

Zemke, Ron, Claire Raines, and Bob Filipczak. *Generations at Work: Managing the Clash of Veterans, Boomers, Xers, and Nexters in Your Workplace*. New York: AMACOM, 1999.

Zikic, Jelena, and Ute-Christine Klehe. "Job Loss as a Blessing in Disguise: The Role of Career Exploration and Career Planning in Predicting Reemployment Quality." *Journal of Vocational Behavior* 69, no. 3 (December 2006): 391–409.

Zikic, Jelena, and Julia Richardson. "Unlocking the Careers of Business Professionals following Job Loss: Sensemaking and Career Exploration of Older Workers." *Canadian Journal of Administrative Sciences/Revue canadienne des sciences de l'administration* 24, no. 1 (May 2007): 58–73.

Index

Note: Page numbers in *italics* indicate a table.

activism, 27, 35, 110, 116
advice and hope, 25, 42, 108–109, 116
Aesthetic Surgery Journal, 26
age: benefits eligibility, 22–23; life stage norms, 14–15, 65; relocation decisions and, 66–67, 71–73; work experience and, 24–25, 39–40. *See also* ageism; generations
age discrimination, 9, 23–24, 25, 83, 101–102, 104, 111. *See also* ageism
Age Discrimination in Employment Act (ADEA) (1967), 9, 24, 25
ageism, 7, 15, 23–26, 30–31, 41, 53, 116. *See also* generationalism
agency, human, 14, 22, 25–26, 62, 77–78
Age of Aquarius, 34–35
age of flexibility, about, 32, 35–39, 42–44, 85–87. *See also* neoliberalism; precarious employment
Age of Insecurity: Coming Together as Things Fall Apart (Taylor), 113–114
age of security, 3–4, 32, 36–38, 42, 99. *See also* employment contract; post–World War II economy
age structuring concept, 14–15
Allina Health (Minnesota) workers, 111
Amazon employees, 111
American Job Centers (AJCs), 48, 49–50
American Psychological Association, 24
anger, 62, 65

artistic creativity, 92, 105–106
attachments, home and place, 71–72, 73, 76, 79–80
attitudes, 40, 41, 51, 52, 87, 96, 97. *See also* job searching; positive thinking
Australian study, 84

baby boomers: defined, 9, 14, 24, 30, 140n5, 162n6; as population group, 3, 9, 31–32, 34, 137n4; socialization experiences, 65, 96–97; unmarried women, 18, 35, 73; women's occupational exclusions, 23, 144n48; on younger workers, 39–43
Bait and Switch (Ehrenreich), 61
Basilica Employment Ministry (Catholic Basilica of St. Mary, Minneapolis), 50
benefits, employment: decline of, 19, 22, 44; Fortune 500 companies and, 104, 105; gender inequalities in, 23, 144n48; unemployment insurance, 8, 17, 19, 23, 142n30. *See also* health insurance; pension plans
"benevolent religious reappraisal," 53
Benjamin (too soon), 22, 23, 34
Beth (soft landing), 21, 25, 88, 91
BIPOC (Black, Indigenous, and People of Color) communities, 9, 36, 118, 138n8
Black Lives Matter era, 30
blaming the individual, 16, 52–53, 83, 112, 114

185

"blessing in disguise" narrative, 83, 84, 94, 95. *See also* silver linings rhetoric
body and beauty work, 25–26. *See also* ageism
#Boomer-Remover, 24, 31
bootstrapping ideology, 5, 83, 84–85, 99. *See also* neoliberalism
bounded career model, 3–4, 69, 79, 85. *See also* employment contract; post-World War II economy
Branton, Nancy, 56
breadwinner model, male, 22, 66, 85, 93
Brian (in between), 55, 74
Brookings Institution, 19
Bruno (in between), 74
Buschman, John, 44
Bush Administration (George W.), 11, 49
business logic, commonsense, 6, 65, 109–110, 111, 115
Butler, Robert, 23–24

Cabanas, Edgar, 81, 86–87
career consultants, Christian, 56
career expectations and trajectories, 21, 32–33, 65, 66–67, 70, 92–93
careeronestop.org, 49
caregiving duties, 34, 66–67, 74–75
Carl (soft landing), 68, 71, 88, 89, 95
Caroline (in between), 42, 56, 115
Carter Administration, 5
Cassandra (hard fall), 17–18, 25, 57, 59, 73, 142n28, 143n31, 143n44
Cat (too soon), 22–23, 39, 59, 68, 89, 107–108, 109, 113, 115
Catholic church, 60–61
Catholic Social Teaching, 1960s, 113, 161n23
Charitable Choice legislation, 48–49
Charles (hard fall), 25, 26, 38, 60, 64–65, 70, 103–104, 105, 106, 109, 111, 115
Charlotte (in between), 57, 59, 76, 90
"Chicago boys" economists, 138n13
children and parenting, 66–67
Children of the Great Depression (Elder), 13
Chilean government, 138n13
Christianity, influence of, 5, 46, 49–50, 60, 61–62, 115. *See also* religious affiliations; religious coping strategies
Christopher (in between), 36
church and state, 11, 48–49, 50–51. *See also* faith-based job clubs

Civil Rights Movement, 34, 35
class action lawsuit, 111
climate change conflict, 31
Clinton Administration, 48–49
coaching, job, 87
Cohen, Philip N., 31, 33, 146n27
Cold War economic policies, 138n13
Colin (soft landing), 21, 77
collective consciousness, 30, 34, 35, 99
collectivity/collective good, 6, 27, 86, 110–111, 114–115
community attachment, 11, 67, 71–72
community-based job clubs, 48, 49–50. *See also* faith-based job clubs
commuting distance, 65, 68, 77, 89, 108
Company of One, A (Lane), 6
competitive ethos, 25–26, 44–45, 115. *See also* ageism; neoliberalism
comunidades eclesiales de base (cebs), 113
congregational support, 54, 58–60
consciousness-raising, 112–113
construction industry, 88
consultancy work, 20, 21, 22, 29–30, 93, 106
consumerism, 4, 93–94, 115
contracting work. *See* consultancy work; self-employment
contract work, short-term, 78, 102
Cooper, Marianne, 54, 58, 59
coping strategies. *See* positive thinking; religious coping strategies
corporate ethos and practices, 4, 86–87, 90, 91, 99, 110, 114
corporate restructuring. *See* downsizing
cosmetic strategies, 26
Coupland, Douglas, 28
COVID-19 pandemic, 24, 30, 31, 100–101, 108
credit card debt, 22, 82, 100
Crunch Time: How Married Couples Confront Unemployment (Rao), 74
Csikszentmihalyi, Mihaly, 87
cultural context, dominant, 84, 96–97
curriculum vitaes and résumés, 17–18, 24, 53
Cut Adrift: Families in Insecure Times (Cooper), 54

Damaske, Sarah, 17, 96, 142n27
Dawn (hard fall), 18, 37, 56, 72, 92
Dayton, Mark, 72–73

Index

death. *See* grief and losses
Debt Collective (union), 114
defined-benefit pension plans, 20, 21, 86, 104, 143n41
defined-contribution pension plans, 86
demographic patterns. *See* generations
Department of Employment and Economic Development (MN), 33
Department of Labor, 49
depression and anxiety, 16, 17, 55, 57–58, 124. *See also* mental health effects; religious coping strategies
Depression-era parents. *See* Silent Generation
deregulation, 4, 5
digital divide, 25, 40
diversity, intragenerational, 23, 31–32, 35
divide and conquer strategies, 11, 44, 113–114
divorce, 2, 53, 56, 58, 75, 104
downsizing, general, 1, 4, 20, 38, 43–45, 65, 82, 114. *See also* outcomes and patterns; silver linings rhetoric
downward mobility: gender differences, 10, 17–19, 20, 23; industry type, 23; as intragenerational, 16–18, 20; lifestyle adjustment with, 93–94; risk reduction factors, 20, 21, 22, 23; underemployment, 17–18, 19, 22, 47
dual-career couples, 74
dual consciousness, 99–100
Dylan (soft landing), 25, 72

earnings gap and loss, 21, 36–37, 89, 102, 108
Eastern Job Transitions Group (Eastern Lutheran Church, Eagan, MN), 50
Economic Policy Institute report (2018), 72–73
economic recessions, 2, 4, 144n47. *See also* Great Recession
educational credentials, 17–18, 37
egalitarianism, 4, 5–6, 48, 114–115
Ehrenreich, Barbara, 61, 87
Elder, Glen, 13–14
eldercare, 11, 74–75
"emotional capitalism," 81, 84, 86–87. *See also* positive thinking
emotional distress. *See* mental health effects
emotional support, 50, 58–60
empathy, 115
employment contract, postwar: age of security to insecurity, 3–6, 43–44, 69–70, 79–80, 85–86; excluded groups, 138n8; generational shift in, 20, 29–30, 32, 37–39, 42; value conflicts, 65, 70. *See also* flexible worker ideal
employment counseling field, 21, 60–61, 87, 96, 112–113
employment gap, 16
Employment Service, national, 48
employment status, 2023, 124
entitlement, 40–41, 42–43. *See also* privilege, socioeconomic
entrepreneurialism, 84, 105
evangelical Christianity, 5, 49, 60, 62, 115
existential reflection, 77–78
Exline, Julie, 53–54

"failure to launch," 14
faith, religious, 46–47, 54–56, 60–61
faith-based job clubs, 11, 48, 49–50, 60–62, 87
FaithWorks! (job club), 59
family status, 64–67
Felix (soft landing), 20, 37, 104–105, 109, 115
feminist movement, 35
financial impacts. *See* outcomes and patterns
financial precarity, measuring, 100
financial services industry, 22, 23, 144n47
Fineman, Stephen, 15, 24, 25, 31
Flawed System/Flawed Self (Sharone), 96
flexibility. *See* neoliberal economy
flexible worker ideal, 11, 69–71, 75–76, 80, 85, 99. *See also* geographic (in)flexibility
follow-up study, 123–125
foreclosures, housing, 7, 14, 18–19, 29, 73, 79, 87. *See also* house sales
Fortune 500 companies (Minnesota), 8, 20, 72, 105, 118
401(k) accounts, 18, 82, 92, 109, 114
framing and reframing job loss: individualist vs collective views, 109–111; market forces view, 65, 109–110, 111, 115. *See also* positive thinking; religious coping strategies; silver linings rhetoric
France, pension protests, 27
Frank (soft landing), 21, 73
free-market ideology, 5, 6, 99
Friedman, Milton, 138n13
friendships and networks, 67, 95
frog, stewing (proverb), 4–5, 6

Gabriel, Yiannis, 16
gender differences: breadwinner norm and, 22, 66; downward mobility, 10, 17–19, 20, 23; personal growth experiences, 91–96; poverty and, 18, 143n34
gender inequalities, 17, 23, 142n27
generationalism: (un)employment experiences and, 35–39; in management discourse, 29–30, 31; neoliberalism and, 43–45, 99; in public sphere, 30–31, 33, 115; self-understandings, 32, 34–35, 40, 41, 99, 104; worker solidarity vs, 41–42, 44; younger worker stereotypes, 39–41. *See also* ageism; intergenerational conflict
generations: categorization of cohorts, 10–11, 30–32, 33–35, 36, 39; as interpretive framework, 28, 29, 30–31, 34–35, 99; problems with labeling, 31–32, 146n27. See also *individual cohorts*
Generation X, 28, 30, 39
Generation Y. *See* millennials
geographic (in)flexibility, 68–69, 79
German tech workers, 110
Gershon, Ilana, 6
Ghilarducci, Teresa, 160n14
Glaser, Barney, 122–123
global socioeconomic impacts, 7, 17, 23, 30, 100–101
God's plan framework, 53, 54, 56–58, 60–62. *See also* religious coping strategies
Golden Age, postwar, 2, 28. *See also* social contract
government, views on role of, 5, 48–49, 115, 138n14
Gramsci, Antonio, 100
grassroots action, 113, 161n32
Gray Panthers, 116
Great Depression, 4, 5–6, 13, 30, 36, 48, 114–115
Great Recession: overview, 2, 7–8, 9, 14, 15, 17, 23, 86; housing crisis, 2, 17, 18–19, 73; life-course framework and, 13–14
"Great Resignation," 100–101
grief and losses, 29, 53, 76, 94, 104, 107–108
grounded theory approach, 122–123
Gullette, Margaret Morganroth, 31

Hackworth, Jason, 49
happiness imperative, 12, 81, 87, 97, 116
Happy Days (television show), 28

"harder-they-fall" effect, 15–16
hard falls, 15–19, 29, 35, 58, 88, 103–104. *See also* downward mobility; religious coping strategies; silver linings rhetoric; *individual outcomes*
Harvey, David, 100
health and well-being, 68, 88–89, 106–107. *See also* mental health effects; physical and mental health
health care expenses, 22, 38, 88, 90
health care industry, 39, 89, 107–108, 111
health condition concerns, 19, 22, 59, 107
health insurance, 18, 19, 20, 21, 47, 72, 86, 88
Heather (hard fall), 18–19, 22, 143n44
hegemonic discourses, 84, 100. *See also* positive thinking
Helen (hard fall), 19, 29–30, 31, 32, 35, 37, 75, 77–78, 91, 94
Henry (soft landing), 90, 94
higher education attainment, 17–18, 29, 37, 46–47, 92–93
hiring panels and practices, 24–25
hobbies and personal interests, 91–92, 105
homeownership, 9, 36, 73, 78
home rootedness, 75, 79–80
hope, 108–109, 116
house sales, 18, 19, 87
housing crisis, 7, 14, 18–19, 79
Howe, Neil, 30
human agency. *See* agency, human
human resources industry, 17, 29

IBM tech workers (Burlington, VT), 110–111
identity: generational self-understandings, 32, 34–35, 40, 41, 99, 104; personal pursuit of, 84; reevaluation of, 109; threats to, 2, 15–16, 29, 83; work-related, 22, 47, 51–52
identity-based expectations, 2, 4–5, 8, 14–15, 16, 65. *See also* employment contract, postwar
illness and injury, 92, 106
Illouz, Eva, 81, 86–87
in-betweeners, 21–23, 105–108. See also *individual outcomes*
individualism, 6, 43–44, 48–49, 52–53, 86–87, 99, 114. *See also* job clubs; neoliberalism; positive thinking; religious coping strategies
individual respondents' characteristics, *129–131*

industry type, 21, 22, 23. See also *individual industries*
inflation rates, 5, 100
inflexible worker, 65–66, 74, 115, 123. *See also* relocation decisions, job
information technology field, 21
inheritance as buffer, 77, 90, 107
Institute for Career Transitions (ICT), 112
interdependence, 14. *See also* linked lives
interest rates, 7, 100
intergenerational conflict, 11, 30–31, 36–38, 40, 41, 43, 115. *See also* generationalism
internalization. *See* ageism
interpersonal relationships, 58–60, 94–96
intragenerational diversity, 23, 31–32, 35
intragenerational downward mobility. *See* downward mobility
Isaac (soft landing), 21, 35, 36, 77
IT support workers, 55, 57

job clubs: aging out of, 106; community-based comparison, 49–50; faith-based, 11, 46, 48–53; instrumental and moral support, 111–112; neoliberal framing and strategies, 49, 51, 52; sociological approaches within, 112–113
Job Clubs Initiative (JCI) (2011), 49
job loss. *See* late-career job loss, general
job-related programs, 17
job satisfaction, 84
job searching: age discrimination, 83, 108; barriers, 17–18, 19, 112; as game, 52–53; medical circumstances, 19; plan "B" as temp work, 47; publicly funded workforce agencies, 48; sense of self-efficacy, 78–79; stress of, 94–95
Jones, Loring, 84

Kaaryn (hard fall), 25–26, 40, 60, 62, 68, 94
Kai (soft landing), 21, 25, 52, 73
Kaleb (in between), 35, 39, 55, 59
Kalleberg, Arne, 138n8
Katherine (in between), 56, 58, 75, 94
Keith (hard fall), 57
Kenneth (soft landing), 57, 58, 62, 72, 95, 115
Kevin (soft landing), 94
Kirk (in between), 25, 39

labor force, aging, 33, 137n5
labor market shifts, 100–101. *See also* relocation decisions, job
Lamont, Michèle, 6
Lancaster, Lynne, 30
Lane, Carrie, 6
Lars (soft landing), 21, 57, 71
Latack, Janina, 15
late-career job loss, general: differences of, 7–8, 9, 15; economic constraints, 37–38; later-life reflections on, 98–99, 101–103; as multiple, 16, 18–19, 22, 29, 64–65, 143n35; and sense-making, 83–85; variability of, 10. *See also* downsizing; *individual outcomes*
Latin America, 5, 113, 138n13
lay offs. *See* downsizing
legal recourse, 24, 25, 104, 111
leisure time, 20, 104, 107
liberation theology, 113
libertarianism, 49
life course perspective: about tenets of, 13–14; age and life stage, 14–15, 71–73; faith trajectories and, 55–56; on generational differences, 32–33; historical context, 32, 69–71; linked lives significance, 73–79
life expectancies, increased, 3, 15, 18, 141n9
life priorities, reevaluation of, 88
life satisfaction, 103, 106, 124
lifestyle adjustments, 77–78, 82, 89, 93–94, 107
LinkedIn and job searching, 34
linked lives, 14, 20, 22, 26, 66, 73, 75–76, 80
Little, Craig, 84
Little House on the Prairie (television show), 71
living arrangements, changed, 18
loneliness, 58–60, 104, 112
long-term unemployment, general: debt and, 22, 82, 100; older workers and, 14, 64–65, 84, 139n29. *See also* relocation decisions, job; retirement savings; *individual outcomes*
Loren (in between), 91
loyalty, 40, 42
Luke (soft landing), 70, 73, 78, 115
Lutheran church, 59
Lutheran Social Service of Minnesota, 50
Lyle (in between), 22, 39–40, 60, 68–69, 70, 82–83, 92–93, 94

management discourse: competition ethos, 44–45; generationalism, 29–30, 31; intergenerational conflict, 43; positivity and, 87
management positions, 20, 21, 22, 46–47, 55
management strategies, 85–86, 110–111. *See also* downsizing
Mannheim, Karl, 30, 32
manual labor transition, 104, 105
Margaret (soft landing), 38, 40–41, 42, 73, 76
Marie (in between), 38, 40, 61, 68, 77, 92
marital status, 34, 66–67, *127, 129–131*
Mark (in between), 37–38, 72, 73, 95, 105–106, 109
market-based priorities, 65, 109–110, 111, 115
marriage benefit, 21, 22
Martie (in between), 40, 61
Martin (too soon), 22, 23, 57
Maslow, Abraham, 86–87, 91
meaning-making, 32, 53–54, 57–58, 83–85, 97. *See also* religious coping strategies; silver linings rhetoric
media accounts, 6, 10, 84
medical costs, 19, 90
Medicare, 10, 23, 35
Meg (hard fall), 18, 35, 76, 144n46
men, (White): postwar social contract, 4, 20; breadwinner model, 22, 66, 85, 93. *See also* employment contract, postwar
Menand, Louis, 138n14
mental health effects: about, 15, 16, 20, 29, 83, 87, 103; ageism and, 24, 53; depression and anxiety, 16, 17, 57–58, 124; emotional support and, 51–52, 58–59. *See also* physical and mental health
methodology: about interview approach, 8–9, 16, 121–122, 125; data analysis, 122–123; population sample, 9–10, 119–120, 143n39; follow-up study, 2023, 98–99, 101–103, 123–125; individual respondents' characteristics, *129–131*; research site, 118; sample characteristics, 120–121, *127–128*; survey representativeness, 103
middle-class status, 2, 9, 28–29, 78. *See also* downward mobility
midlife/middle adulthood, 14, 67
military service, 34
millennials, 29, 30, 39–41, 108, 137n4
Mills, C. Wright, 3, 98, 113
minimum wage work, 68
Minneapolis-Saint Paul. *See* Twin Cities
Minnesota: about, 8, 9, 118, 119; Christian dominance in, 62; rootedness in, 71–72; denominational groups, 51; job clubs, 49, 111–112; post-pandemic labor market, 101; social safety net and health insurance, 72; unemployment benefits, 79, 156n39; workplace culture, 72
Minnesota Dislocated Worker Program, 92
Minnesota WorkForce (now CareerForce) center, 21
Moen, Phyllis, 15, 143n34
Monbiot, George, 5
Mormon family parallels, 59
mortgage delinquencies, 73, 87. *See also* foreclosures, housing
mortgage rates, low, 143n43
multinational corporations, 20
multiple job losses, 16, 18–19, 22, 29, 64–65, 143n35

Nadine (hard fall), 18, 46–47, 68, 73, 143n35
Nathan (soft landing), 43, 44, 112–113
neoliberal economy: birth of, 5; downsizing strategy of, 44–45, 85–86; as flexibility logic, 29, 69–70; generational impact, 32–33, 36, 37; job insecurity and, 37–39, 86–87, 114
neoliberalism: defined, 5; as interpretive framework, 3, 6, 27; competitive ethos, 25–26, 44–45, 115; critiques of, 42–43, 116; cultural pervasiveness of, 6, 37, 49, 81, 99, 100; government retrenchment, 48–49, 114; religion and, 49. *See also* employment contract; faith-based job clubs; flexible worker ideal; personal responsibility discourse; positive thinking
networking, 38, 49, 104, 106, 109
networks, social: aging out of, 106; and care work, 74–76; rootedness in, 65–66; of support, 58–60, 67, 69, 95, 104. *See also* linked lives
New Deal reforms, 4, 5–6, 48, 114–115
newspaper industry, 107
New York Times, 114
New Zealand parliamentarian, 31
Nick (in between), 74, 76

Nicole (soft landing), 68, 77, 89
Norman (in between), 59, 76
Norris, Dawn, 16, 59, 70
Northfield, Minnesota, 119
nostalgia, 10, 30, 35, 37, 43
nurse practitioner, 56–57

Oakland Growth Study, 1931, 13
Obama, Michelle, 31
occupational status, 88–89
occupations and industries, affected, 86, 120, *128–131*. See also *individual industries*
"OK boomer" meme, 30–31
Olivia (in between), 25–26, 68
one percent, the, 43, 113
optimism. *See* silver linings rhetoric
outcomes and patterns, job loss: hard falls, 16–19; in between, 21–23, 105–108; individual respondent characteristics, *129–131*; soft landings, 19–21. See also *individual outcomes*
overqualification, 101, 108

Pamela (in between), 92
parental financial assistance, 21, 23
Pargament, Kenneth, 47, 53, 54, 56, 59, 62
Park, Crystal, 47
part-time employment, 29, 78, 101, 102, 107, 108
Peale, Norman Vincent, 87
pension plans: benefits of, 20, 37–39, 86, 92, 115; defined-benefit, 20, 21, 86, 104, 143n41; employer type and, 143n41; 401(k) accounts, 18, 82, 92, 109, 114; gender inequalities, 23, 144n48; stock market crash and, 86
pension protests, France, 27
personal growth experiences, 12, 88, 91–96, 107, 116
Personal Responsibility and Work Opportunity Reconciliation Act (1996), 48–49
personal responsibility discourse, 5, 11, 48–49, 52–53, 84–85, 86, 97, 99
personal savings, 21, 82, 90, 109
Pew Research Center: on generational cohorts, 30, 32, 34, 39, 120, 140n5, 162n6; on post-pandemic job quitting, 100–101; quality of life rankings, 34; on survey response rates, 160n12

physical and mental health: corporate practices and, 15, 83, 91; improvements, 26, 88–90, 105–106
physical appearance, 25–26
physical exercise, 26
place and life stage, 71–73. *See also* linked lives
plastic surgery, 26
popular culture, generations in, 28, 41, 43
positive psychology, 81, 84, 87, 97
positive thinking: buttressing neoliberalism, 97, 112, 115; as cultural imperative, 83, 84–85, 87, 96–97; dual consciousness and, 99–100; as "emotional capitalism," 81, 86–87; hope and, 108; social solidarity and, 116
post–World War II economy: bounded career model, 3–4, 69, 79, 85; defined-benefit pension plans, 20, 21, 86, 104, 143n41; employment contract, 3–4, 20, 69, 96–97; endpoint defined, 28–29; male breadwinner wages, 36; and prosperity, 33, 34, 85; social and political influences, 30. *See also* baby boomers
poverty gender gap, 18, 73, 143n34
Power of Positive Thinking, The (Peale), 87
prayer, 51, 55, 56, 58, 62
precarious employment, 12, 37–38, 78, 101, 102, 114, 138n8. *See also* flexible worker ideal
priorities, reevaluation of life, 77–78, 88
privatization, 4
privilege, socioeconomic, 9, 14, 20, 35, 66, 69. *See also* Whiteness
productivity expectations, 39–40, 86, 90
psychology, positive, 81, 84, 87, 97
public health shift, 97
public issues and personal troubles, 3, 97, 98, 113. *See also* personal responsibility discourse
public workforce programs, 48–49
publishing industry, 64, 88, 89
Pugh, Allison, 80, 87

quality of life measures, 12, 88–91, 103, 106, 107, 124
Qualtrics (survey platform), 123, 162n15
"quiet quitting" at work, 101

racial homogeneity, 9, 36, 120–121
racialization of wealth, 2, 33, 36, 156n35
Raging Grannies, 116
Rao, Aliya Hamid, 74, 96
Reagan Administration, 5, 138n14
recessions, economic, 2, 4. *See also* Great Recession
Recoding Power: Tactics for Mobilizing Tech Workers (Rothstein), 110
recruiters, job, 84
reemployment: challenges, 19, 47, 62; earnings loss, 84; part-time work status, 78, 101, 102; services, 48–49, 52, 119 (*See also* job clubs); underemployment, 17–18, 19, 22, 47. *See also* ageism; downward mobility
reevaluation of life priorities, 93–94, 115, 116
relationships: negative impacts on, 17, 80, 83, 106; renewed focus on, 88, 94–96, 107
religious affiliations, 46, 48, 54, 55–56, 62, 148n1
religious coping strategies, 53–56, 58–62, 99, 106–107
religious neoliberalism, 49, 60–62
religious right, 5, 49, 60, 62, 115
relocation decisions, job: age and social class, 11, 66, 67, 69, 73, 76–79; linked lives and, 73, 74, 76, 79–80; reasons for move, 102–103; risk burden and costs, 70–71, 80, 82, 99, 106; studies of, 66–67
resentment, 36–37, 40, 60–61. *See also* God's plan framework; intergenerational conflict
resiliency narratives, 81, 87, 91, 94, 97, 107
resistance, 11, 68–69, 109–111. *See also* geographic (in)flexibility
restructuring, corporate. *See* downsizing
résumé hacks and bias, 17–18, 53
retirement: early, 20, 36; financial insecurity, 3, 8, 37, 65, 108, 160n14; premature, 16, 88, 102; preparedness, 124; silver linings rhetoric, 83, 93–94; suspended, 83, 103–104; unretiring phenomenon, 160n14
retirement age conflicts, 27
retirement savings: early withdrawal from, 18, 22, 78, 82, 108; employer-sponsored plans, 18, 82, 92, 109, 114; health conditions and, 19; interest rates and losses, 7–8, 14

Rice County WorkForce Office, 119
Roaring Twenties era, 5–6
Roberta (in between), 42, 43, 74, 90–91
Roosevelt Administration, 4, 5–6, 48, 114–115
rootedness, 71–72
Rothstein, Sidney, 110–111, 113, 160n18

Sally (in between), 22, 39, 40, 42, 43, 70, 72, 74, 75, 78, 90–91, 115
sample characteristics, *127–128*
sandwich generation, 34, 74–75. *See also* baby boomers
Sara (hard fall), 19, 22, 25, 36–37, 41, 42, 43, 70, 74, 78, 90–91, 113
Scandinavian roots, 71
scapegoating, 114–115
Sean (too soon), 22, 23, 26, 55, 76
"security projects," 58. *See also* religious coping strategies
self actualization, 88, 91–93, 116
"self as business," 6
self-blame, 15–16, 53, 83, 112
self-efficacy, 16, 26, 78–79
self-employment, 17, 72–73, 90, 120
self-help approaches, 84, 87, 112–113
Seligman, Martin, 87
sense of belonging, 58–60, 71–72
severance packages, 9, 20, 21, 104
Seymour (in between), 94–95, 162
shareholder focus, 4, 42–43, 85, 110
Sharone, Ofer, 16, 52, 84, 96, 112, 113
Siemens Information and Communication Networks (ICN), 110
Silent Generation, 30, 33, 36, 37–39
Silicon Valley families, 54
silver linings rhetoric: artistic creativity, 92, 105–106; cultural context for, 96–97; improved health, 88–91; life priorities reevaluated, 93–94; paradox of, 12, 83, 87–88; renewed relationships focus, 88, 94–95; self-actualization, 91–93
Skype interview, 70–71, 113
sleep, improved, 88–89
snowbirds, 20
social contract, postwar, 4, 15, 42, 79, 85. *See also* employment contract
social inequality growth, 2, 114
social isolation, 112

socialization experiences, 32–33, 96–97
social media discourse, 24, 30–31
social mobility. *See* downward mobility
social movements, 33–34, 35, 113
Social Security benefits, 93, 115; access, 10; age and eligibility, 22–23, 35, 143n32, 144n46; early application for, 18, 144n46
social service provision, 11, 48–49, 50–51. *See also* faith-based job clubs
social welfare benefits, 114–115. *See also* welfare state
socioeconomic and cultural context, 34, 85–87, 97
socioeconomic status and agency, 66, 69, 76–79, 103–105
Sociological Imagination, The (Mills), 3, 98
soft landings: described, 19–21; early retirement, 88, 104–105, 115; gender gap, 20; religious coping, 58, 152n60; and silver linings rhetoric, 88, 89. *See also* pension plans; *individual outcomes*
sole-income providers, 22
solidarity, worker, 41–42, 43, 110–111, 112, 115–116
Sophia (in between), 56, 93, 96
Special State Committee on Aging report, 137n5
spirituality framing, 57, 93
spousal support, 21, 22, 23, 66
Starbucks unionization drives, 111
Stephanie (hard fall), 35, 38, 42, 59–60
stereotypes, 24–25, 29, 30–32, 39–41, 108. *See also* generationalism
stigma, 15, 17, 23, 81, 84, 95, 96, 112
Stigma Trap: College-Educated, Experienced, and Long-Term Unemployed, The (Sharone), 84, 96, 112
Stillman, David, 30
stock market crashes, 2, 13, 79, 86, 140n3
Strauss, Anselm L., 122
Strauss, Claudia, 84, 87
Strauss, William, 30
strike actions, U.S. worker, 111
student activism, 1960s, 35
subprime mortgage crisis, 17, 143n44. *See also* Great Recession; housing crisis
Swarbrick, Chlöe, 31
Swindoll, Charles "Chuck," 51
systems engineering field, 21

Tad (soft landing), 20, 37, 89, 91, 94, 113
Tammy (in between), 71, 90, 91, 92
Taylor, Astra, 113–115, 116
technology-use stereotypes, 25, 40
technology (tech) workers, 84, 110–111, 160n18
temp jobs: low wages, 19, 22, 36–37, 82; management practices, 47; medical costs, 19; and quality of life, 105–106; to stay in place, 68
Teresa (hard fall), 19, 24, 55, 76
Terrence (in between), 95
Thomas theorem, 32
TikTok, 31
Timothy (in between), 55, 57, 92, 93
title insurance industry, 18–19. *See also* housing crisis
"toxic positivity," 97
"toxic" work environments, 83, 90–91
transactional relationships, 38
traumatic events and meaning-making, 53, 55–57, 97. *See also* religious coping strategies
Trump, Donald, 31
Tumbleweed Society, The (Pugh), 80
Twin Cities: Fortune 500 companies, 118; home asset and, 18; job clubs, 46, 48, 50–51, 60–61; workforce centers, 48, 119
"two body problem," 74

underemployment, 17–18, 19, 22, 47. *See also* downward mobility
unemployment: gender gap, 144n48; public workforce programs, 48–49; rates, 2, 9, 100–101, 137n1; statistics and growth, 2. *See also* ageism; faith-based job clubs; long-term unemployment
unemployment benefits, 8, 19, 23, 142n30
unionization, 111
United Defense (Minnesota), worker survey, 163n19
United States: Bureau of Labor Statistics, 17, 120; Christian dominance, 62; happiness imperative, 97; Panel Study of Income Dynamics, 67

Vanessa (in between), 39, 72, 78, 89, 90, 105, 107, 108, 109
Van Oort, Madison, 52

Vermont tech workers, 110–111
Victor (in between), 22, 25, 26, 50, 72, 74, 93, 106–107, 108, 111
Vietnam War generation, 30, 34, 35
volunteerism, 50, 59, 104

wage gap, systemic, 36, 144n48
Wagner-Peyser Act (1933), 48
Wall Street Journal, 53
Washington Post, 31–32
wealth transfer/redistribution, 43, 113
weight loss and bias, 25–26
welfare state: Depression-era expansion, 4, 5–6, 48, 114–115; shrinking of, 44, 48–49, 84–85, 97, 99, 114
Welfare-to-Work program, 49
Wendy (hard fall), 1, 2, 3, 70, 143n35
White, Jonathan, 30–31
White House Office of Faith-Based and Community Initiatives, 11, 49
Whiteness, 2, 4, 9, 33, 36, 120–121, 156n35
Will (soft landing), 93, 95
women: eldercare work, 74–75; employment discrimination, 23, 144n48; as primary breadwinners, 18–19, 46–47; unmarried baby boomers, 18, 35, 73
Wooddale Job Transition Support Group (job club), 50–52, 53, 62, 87
Work, Retire, Repeat (Ghilarducci), 160n14
workers' rights, 4–6, 111
work ethic ideal, 11, 40, 42, 104. *See also* generationalism
work experience, age and, 24–25, 39–40
workforce centers, 48, 119
Workforce Innovation and Opportunity Act (2014), 48
working-class families, 54
work-life balance, 94–95
workplace environments: religious values, 47, 50; stress, 81, 84, 87, 88, 90–91, 99. *See also* positive thinking; silver linings rhetoric
workplace injury, 92
work trajectories, 34, 74–75

younger workers. *See* millennials
youth ideal, 25–26

About the Authors

ANNETTE NIEROBISZ is a professor of sociology and the Ada M. Harrison Distinguished Teaching Professor of the Social Sciences at Carleton College in Northfield, Minnesota. She also has directed the Carleton College summer program, Reimagining Society: Capitalism, Socialism, and the Environment. In addition to a long-standing focus on the sociology of unemployment, her research spans a broad range of topics within the fields of work and occupations, public policy, and criminology. Her articles have appeared in a variety of journals, including *Teaching Sociology*, *Law and Social Inquiry*, *Social Problems*, and the *Canadian Journal of Sociology*. She enjoys helping students discover their sociological imagination, refine their methodological thinking, and construct their own unique investigations of the social world.

DANA SAWCHUK is a professor and chair of the Department of Sociology at Wilfrid Laurier University in Waterloo, Ontario, Canada. In addition to studying job loss and older workers, her research focuses on how older adults think about, use, and are represented in magazines and newspapers, and on the relationship between aging and activism. Her first book, *The Costa Rican Catholic Church, Social Justice, and the Rights of Workers, 1979–1996*, also dealt with workers and neoliberalism. More recently, she has published in journals such as *Leisure Studies*, *Ageing & Society*, the *Journal of Aging Studies*, and *Gerontology & Geriatrics Education*. She enjoys teaching Introduction to Sociology as well as courses on aging, social movements, and religion.